THE GOTHAM LIBRARY
OF THE NEW YORK UNIVERSITY PRESS

The Gotham Library is a series of original works and critical studies. Devoted to significant works and major authors and to literary topics of enduring importance, Gotham Library texts offer the best in literature and criticism.

Comparative and Foreign Language Literature:
Robert J. Clements, Editor

Comparative and English Language Literature:
James W. Tuttleton, Editor

On the Poetry of Matthew Arnold

Essays in Critical Reconstruction

William E. Buckler

New York University Press • New York *and* London

Copyright © 1982 by New York University

Library of Congress Cataloging in Publication Data

Buckler, William Earl
   On the poetry of Matthew Arnold.
   (The Gotham Library of the New York University
Press)
   Bibliography: p.
   Includes Index.
   1. Arnold, Matthew, 1822–1888—Criticism and
interpretation.   I. Title.
PR4024.B78   821'.8   82-3398
ISBN 0-8147-1039-5   AACR2

Manufactured in the United States of America

For
Nancy, Susan, and Joyce

Contents

Acknowledgments

The texts of Arnold used throughout this book are, for the poetry, *The Poems of Matthew Arnold*, 2nd ed., Miriam Allott, ed. (London and New York: Longman, 1979) and, for the prose, *The Complete Prose Works of Matthew Arnold*, R.H. Super, ed. (Ann Arbor: University of Michigan Press, 1960–1977). I wish to thank the publishers for their courteous permission to quote from them. Versions or portions of two chapters in the book have appeared in periodicals, and I am grateful to the editors for permission to reprint them: *The Arnoldian*, Spring 1981 (sections on the *The New Sirens, Resignation,* and *Dover Beach* in Chapter 2) and *Browning Institute Studies*, 1981 (a small portion of Chapter 5).

1.

Introduction: Myths, Misgivings, and Measurings

I

The poetry of Matthew Arnold has for a very long time been imprisoned in a cluster of more or less benign interpretive myths; this has led to a highly repetitive critical Parnassianism that, even at its best, persistently asserts a truth about Arnold's poetry that is less than the truth actually there. The result has been to make Arnold a much duller poet than he in fact is and to deny him both the cohering poetic center that his canon gradually and consistently establishes and the quite distinctive space in mid-century poetry which that canon occupies. Further, it has deprived him of that broad-based but quintessentially *literary* or *poetic* critical consciousness that has found so many echoes and analogues in modern poetry, both British and American. In England, the Arnoldian critical consciousness became subtextual—with all the modifications a distinguished poet brings to his literary inheritances—in Thomas Hardy; in America, T.S. Eliot was a more reluctant but less modifying channel of transference.

The chief interpretive myths that any student of the critical commentary on Arnold will immediately recognize as dominant are three. First, there is the myth that Arnold's poetry, in its general outlines as well as in its details, can be adequately apprehended as autobiographically replicative, the product of a personal matrix endlessly evolving verse structures out of the incidents of his own life, the voice of his poetry being his own voice mediated only by the need to give it formal structure and a respectable degree of prosodic sophistication. Thus Marguerite must be a *real* person who precipitated a *real* identity crisis in the *real* Matthew Arnold; *Dover Beach* must be an incident that took place at Dover while Arnold was on his honeymoon; the action at the center of *Sohrab and Rustum* must not be allowed to go free of large implications for Arnold's failed struggle for self-mastery against the threatening figure of his own father; *Empedocles on Etna* must embody the lightly disguising parable of Arnold's own intensest spiritual struggle. In addition, we are told: "That the whole story [of *Tristram and Iseult*] developed a shadowy autobiographical significance for A. (with Marguerite and Frances Lucy Wightman as the 'two Iseults who did sway/Each her hour of Tristram's day') *can hardly be doubted*."[1]

Second, there is the myth that Arnold's is basically a poetry of statement—that when one has extracted a prose meaning from an Arnold poem, a thematic paraphrase, one's critical task has been essentially accomplished. In this view of things, thought is the *de facto* master of imagination, and Arnold's critical dictum about poetry's being the "application of ideas to life" functions, insofar as his own poetry is concerned, at a very dissociated and mechanical level—poetry as a finished intellectual product rather than an imaginative process, illustrative rather than exploratory. "Application" is not assumed, as in Arnold's critical touchstone theory, to imply a testing of the adequacy of ideas by an empirical measuring of those ideas against an informed and critically enlightened understanding of life, of "those elementary feelings which subsist permanently in the race, and which are independent of time."[2] And since, according to the autobiographical matrix, Arnold is not allowed to emerge as an authentic dramatic or personative poet, he is likewise denied such rich poetic resources as verbal gesturing and tonal irony that, in a poetry of character, customarily root ideas in personality and involve the reader in the creative process of discovering a poem's latent significance in its manifest verbal and structural maneuvers. To those who view Arnold as a poet of statement, what a poem says directly to the mind is the important object of interest; since Arnold is assumed to be the speaker of these versified statements, what they have as an almost total result is a substantial accumulation of ideas that Arnold himself is thought to have held at various points in his career as a practicing poet. Speaker-protagonists in poems like *Resignation, Self-Dependence, Dover Beach, The Buried Life*, and *Philomela*, for example, are not subjected to the sort of psychological scrutiny that is inevitably brought to bear on the personative poems of Tennyson, Browning, Swinburne, and, more recently, Hardy. An overwhelming interest in the summary intellectual positions of the speaker-protagonists in such poems as *Stanzas in Memory of the Author of 'Obermann', Stanzas from the Grande Chartreuse, The Scholar-Gipsy*, and *Obermann Once More* has diverted critical attention from their metaphoric textures and from the distinctive dramatic perspectives inherent in their formal structures and in the precarious fallibility with which their speaker-protagonists attempt to plot their personal curves.

The third myth, implicit but pervasive, is that Arnold, though persistent and conspicuously relevant in very large cultural proportions, lacks that qualifying imaginative center that encloses at some significant level all the various elements in a poet's endeavors and gives us a satisfactory basis for perceiving him as occupying a unique space in a necessarily relative field of endeavor. Arnold is perceived to be derivative in poetic idiom, dependent in ideas, mechanical rather than organic in bringing idiom and ideas into meaningful relationships. He is the propagandist of other people's insights—Goethe's or Carlyle's or Senancour's or those of the Greek philosophers and men of letters. The poetic compositions which he designed in a distinctive and positive way and upon which he expended great imaginative energy have been somewhat indulgently faulted (e.g., *Sohrab and Rustum*) or generally ignored (e.g.,

Balder Dead) or assumed to be wholly misguided and rejected out of hand (e.g., *Merope*), while the complex dramatic poem about which he expressed the severest literary reservations (*Empedocles on Etna*) has been awarded the place of *chef d'oeuvre* in his canon. Inherent in this interpretive situation is the unspoken implication that Arnold was a graceful rhetorician rather than a legitimate poet and that, for the most part, he either did not know exactly what he was talking about or builded best when the poetic craftsman in him simply undermined and contradicted the poetic theorist.

But while one should be willing to entertain the possibility that in a particular case the contemporary critic is more aesthetically astute than the dead poet, one should be willing to yield to the opposite possibility, too. This requires that we make a deliberative effort to see the object at hand, in both its substance and its proportions, as it in fact is, that we avoid critical peremptoriness even when the weight of cumulative authority seems to be overwhelmingly on our side, and that we recognize that in such subtle matters as a significant poet's unique imaginative center, an apparently minor shift in perspective can result in a major alteration in our perception of the poet's distinctive contribution to the tradition.

In the following essay, an attempt will be made to establish the bases for freeing Arnold's poetry from these critical myths. To put the matter more specifically and constructively, an effort is here made to show that, though there are persistent autobiographical analogues detectable in Arnold's poetry, these have been converted to metaphors and function poetically in a way quite comparable to the function of the incidents and historical or mythic personages around which the poems as total or complete actions are shaped. This leads to the conclusion, suggestive at a fundamental level if not actually probative, that Arnold was converting the massive autobiographical tradition of the earlier part of the century into a new poetic mode, creating thereby a "modern expression of a modern outlook"[3] through an idiom that reinstated the centrality of action or plot while retaining formalistically or illusively the persuasive immediacy of the intensest private experience.

Consistent with the foregoing, the argument will be made

that Arnold was a dramatic or personative poet in a manner much more comparable to that of Hardy than to that of Browning or even of Tennyson. Like Hardy, Arnold recognized that, in rendering certain kinds of human experience, whether illusively historical or illusively contemporaneous, no merely formal structure or device could wholly strip the imaginative experience of acute personal relevance, however willing *the poet or his reader* might be to suspend disbelief. Hence, with Arnold as with Hardy, the real challenge to the modern poet lay, not in absolute distinctions between the poet and his *personae*, but in degrees of distinction. Hardy's statement in the Preface to *Wessex Poems and Other Verses* (1898), "The pieces are *in a large degree* dramatic or personative in conception; and this even where they are not obviously so,"[4] has the keenest relevance to Arnold as well as to Hardy. For a long time, Hardy's poetry suffered from the same kind of interpretive hypothesis that still enshrouds Arnold's, namely, that he was a poet of statement, of nakedly expressed thoughts personally held. The basic result was to make him appear to be a much duller poet than almost everyone now recognizes him to be. A comparable hypothesis, despite all the resistance to it inherent in the poems themselves, still weights Arnold's poetry down to the same general effect: it makes him aesthetically interesting at only a very low-grade level.

Finally, it will be argued that it is in his acutely conscious literariness itself that we find Arnold's unique imaginative center, the distinctive, cohering, almost all-encompassing concern that shaped his mission as a poet, providing the center of creative gravity, so to speak, that holds his language, forms, and fictions, with all their repetitions and variety, in a mutually reinforcing pattern. Conscious literariness—the literary practitioner's re-examination of the character and relevance of his craft—has apparently always been an identifiable concern of men of letters, in primitive as well as in highly developed civilizations; certainly, as students of the period know, it has had so large an attraction for poets during the last two hundred years as to border on the obsessive. The Romantics both reflected and created so intense and keen an aesthetic sensibility that, throughout the nineteenth century, it invaded and conditioned the way the mind worked on all of its problems—scientific, religious, social, psychological, and ethical, as well as aesthetic. The function of poetry at the present time has, since the eighteenth century, held a dominant place in the work of poets, either as an explicit subject or as a parable in the distance. "The growth of a poet," "the growth of a poet's mind," "*Dichtung und Wahrheit*," "portrait of the artist," "the modern expression of a modern outlook," are typical metaphors of how poets during the last two hundred years have thought about themselves and of how criticism has come to think about them. So Arnold's acutely conscious literariness is not, broadly considered, unique. Indeed, the inevitable conclusion cuts the other way: not only was there nothing esoteric about Arnold's primary concern in his poetry with poetry itself, but he had chosen a subject of perennial concern to civilized man, one that has fundamental implications for modern men with any sincere curiosity about the resources for guidance still applicable within their strangely altered culture. In other words, an apparently specialized subject assumes a general character of the very broadest cultural relevance for those who have the capacity and the conscientiousness to enter into the genuine questions involved. This, in turn, removes from Arnold's poetry another onus sometimes imposed by readers who demand of the poet that he focus on the rawer aspects of contemporary life for an unrestricted audience. If, as Carlyle had maintained, there is some dimension of the poet in everyone, the honing and refining of the poetic art has, at least conceptually, a universal relevance. On the other hand, the practicing poet's most immediate audience, especially when he is dealing with the health or sickness of poetry itself, is inevitably other practicing poets or prospective poets or readers for whom poetry constitutes a particular enthusiasm. By addressing this audience at the first level, the poet dedicated to redressing the poetic art can keep his subject intact, his metaphors as refined as his motive and goal demand, without feeling cut off from that very much larger audience which those whom he does affect will in turn touch. Though he must assume, if he would be effective, a somewhat Olympian role—that of the figure at the top of the pyramid—his ultimate purpose is to release perceptions that, if the perceptions are compelling and the strategy well designed, will pervade the whole society.[5]

The uniqueness of Arnold's poetic contribution to this very generalized, perhaps universal, concern of modern poets is the relentless programmatic concern that he brought to it: he made a just view of poetry the overwhelming concern of his own poetry because he believed that if poetry was lost, hope was lost and that a misguided poetry must have a fundamentally deleterious effect upon those crucial persons, especially young writers and other aliens from the conventional wisdom of their age, who could look only to a healthy poetry for healthy spiritual guidance. The unique intensity with which Arnold held this modernist/anti-modernist belief is the driving, shaping force of his poetic imagination. It provides not only the energy and control with which he created the artifacts at the center of his poetic canon but also the motive for those extended emblems of poetic architecture (*Balder Dead, Merope*) which have commanded so little critical assent and for the special emphases of the prose documents (prefaces, headnotes) with which he sought to rationalize them. Moreover, it essentially depletes the myth, widely held, of the "two Arnolds"—the self-conflicted Romantic poet versus the supremely confident Classical critic—and reveals a continuity of critical consciousness that makes, for example, *On Translating Homer* relevant to *Empedocles on Etna* and *Essays in Criticism, First Series* both a climax and a new beginning.[6]

II

Fortunately, there is a critical literature, both informal and formal, from Arnold's own pen for the crucial years 1845–1858 that enables us to see how he himself defined the issues and narrowed the focus of what otherwise might have become a runaway subject too soft and impressionistic for genuinely profitable discussion. This critical literature consists chiefly of Arnold's letters to Arthur Hugh Clough for the period 1845–1853[7] and the prose documents that, at various times, he attached to his poems: Preface to First Edition of *Poems*

(1853), Preface to Second Edition of *Poems* (1854), and Preface to *Merope* (1858). This critical literature, which encompasses the dozen or so years when Arnold was most productive as a poet, is crucial as a basis for establishing the parameters in which his aesthetic consciousness worked and for showing that his whole spiritual self is reflected in the stages of anxiety, resolution, and serenity that can be traced in these documents.[8]

In all of the significant references to poetry in general, and to his own poems in particular, contained in the letters to Clough, Arnold concentrates exclusively on the principles by which poetry accomplishes its unique purposes: sound aesthetic "doctrine" regarding form, function, and appropriateness. Thus, in his first such reference (1845),[9] he sets "Passion" against "the growing Popularity of a strong minded writer"— by which he means a writer whose mind is strongly coded to "Reform" purposes—while at the same time he recognizes the imbalance that an overplus of passion brings to poetry: "while we believe in the Universality of Passion as Passion, [we] will keep pure our Aesthetics by remembering its one-sidedness as doctrine" (p. 59). Two fundamental principles of Arnold's aesthetics are thus early put in place: the role of the poet as witness rather than as advocate and the indispensability of passion to poetry, but the equally indispensable consideration that force not overwhelm understanding. In addition, there is the recognition that a sense of contemporary urgency is tending to subordinate poetry as aesthetic experience to utilitarian propaganda.

In his last such reference (1853), Arnold clearly states, though in the self-reflexive language of personal conviction rather than in that of public doctrine, the fundamental function of poetry:

> I am glad you like the Gipsy Scholar—but what does it *do* for you? Homer *animates*—Shakespeare *animates*—in its poor way I think Sohrab and Rustum *animates*—the Gipsy Scholar at best awakens a pleasing melancholy. But this is not what we want.
>
> > The complaining millions of men
> > Darken in labour and pain—

what they want is something to *animate* and *ennoble* them—
not merely to add zest to their melancholy or grace to their
dreams.—I believe a feeling of this kind is the basis of my
nature—and of my poetics. (P. 146)

This brief passage contains one of the basic critical doctrines
upon which Arnold's ensuing career as a critic will be built.
That its language gives it such an experiential autobiographical
rooting is a matter of very considerable importance. Arnold
had been through a prolonged period of anxious uncertainty,
by temperamental disposition and talent forced to write poetry,
but having no very clear notion of just what his "nature" was
or what his "poetics" should be. At the level of analytical or
theoretical discourse, he could say many apt things that would
stand the test of critical maturity, but at the personal level, he
was isolated and unsure, high-minded but irresolute. His
personality had begun inevitably to absorb some of the doubts
and discouragements, even some of the aesthetic disorienta-
tions, of his age, but something in his "nature"—perhaps an
innate seriousness, the structure of his mind or consciousness,
his increased pursuit of learning—made him acutely uncomfortable with the drift of the age and his degree of complicity
in it. His very attachment to Clough appears as a real-life but
nonetheless dramatically ritualized externalization of his distress. Clough was his foil, an exaggerated image of some of his
own tendencies, leading to depression, paralysis, and "death."
While Clough seems to have been a necessary ingredient in the
process through which he had to pass, in those years leading
up to 1853, Arnold sometimes found the processive ritual itself
so painful that he seriously considered throwing Clough over
and retreating more deeply into self-isolation, where he might
or might not have found a more cleansing alternative ritual.
But the presence of Clough, to whom he ultimately clung, and
the peculiarities of their relationship—the older Clough playing
the double role of soul-mate and whipping-boy—provided
Arnold with the opportunity to carry on a dialogue with an
alternative self, a dialogue that assumes something of the
character of a fragmented and extended dramatic monologue.
Clough is a modern type, and so is Arnold. There is a startling

if accidental analogy between Arnold's letters to Clough thus perceived and the dialogue-like monologues by which many of Arnold's most crucial poems are structured.

The climactic recognition toward which Arnold was striving in the five or so years preceding 1853 did not come until he saw his face in another mirror—that of *Empedocles on Etna*[10]— and hence the conversion was both long delayed and commensurately exciting when it did come. In the meantime, the curious discrepancy between Arnold's irreproachable principles and the personal incoherence which, in the letters, he only occasionally allowed to flash out constitutes one of the muted developmental dramas characteristic of the growth of modern poets. He would duly experience some of the joy of poetic creativity: "A thousand things make one compose or not compose: composition seems to keep alive in me a *cheerfulness*— a sort of Tuchtigkeit, or natural soundness and valiancy, which I think the present age is fast losing—this is why I like it" (p. 146). But such eventual satisfaction was made possible only by a relentless search, often under very painful circumstances, for his "nature" and his true "poetics." Seeing it in the detached perspective of historical retrospect, we can say that it was an archetypal Romantic quest (the search for identity) pursued unconsciously under the guidance of an archetypal Classical rubric ("Know thyself"). One can easily believe that it maintained its steadiness for Arnold for the rest of his life, as Newman's conversion held steady for him, because he did not relax his pursuit until his nature and his poetics had become organically one. Arnold's persistent critical empiricism is deeply rooted in personal experience and in his memory of the model by which his own life had been transformed.

Though the chief source of Arnold's discontent was deep within himself and he had to work his way through it by a process such as that described above, it sometimes surfaced in more external metaphors. It was the age rather than the man that was unpoetical: "how deeply *unpoetical* the age and all one's surroundings are. Not unprofound, not ungrand, not unmoving:—but *unpoetical*" (p. 99). This seemingly temperate condemnation of the age on aesthetic grounds becomes much more intense as we remember that, above all else, Arnold wished to be poetical. Within a few months (the time lapse is between early February and late September 1849), he was lashing out against the age with considerably more fury:

> My dearest Clough these are damned times everything is against one—the height to which knowledge is come, the spread of luxury, our philosophical enervation, the absence of great *natures*, the unavoidable contact with millions of small ones, newspapers, cities, light profligate friends, moral desperadoes like Carlyle, our own selves, and the sickening consciousness of our own difficulties: but for God's sake let us be neither fanatics nor yet chaff blown by the wind but let us be ὡς ὁ φρονιμος διαρισειεν and not as any one else διαρισειεν. (P. 111)

Aristotle's cautionary presence in the background is validly prophetic, but it does not disguise the profound spiritual discouragement that Arnold's language conveys. His harshness toward his older contemporaries (Carlyle as a "moral desperado," Tennyson as "dawdling with [the Universe's] painted shell" [p. 63], Browning as "obtaining but a confused multitudinousness" [p. 91]) is the harshness of frustration—that of a young writer who had turned for guidance to the literary leaders of his generation and found them wanting. These external metaphors gradually turned inward—"our own selves, and the sickening consciousness of our own difficulties"—but the inward route itself had not yet been found. And so, this young poet, who knew that he was floundering without quite knowing why or what to do about it, flailed rather recklessly at those who had induced his problem (e.g., Byron, Keats, Shelley, and the Romantics generally) and those who had failed to correct it (e.g., Carlyle, Tennyson, and Browning). Though he gradually developed, intellectually, a fundamentally sound aesthetic, he failed to create satisfactory poems. They gave him little pleasure in the making. Even as late as December 1852, when he finally felt that he knew what was wrong with "this set" of his poems—the most recent of which were contained in *Empedocles on Etna and Other Poems* (1852)—he expressed the "doubt whether I shall ever have heat and radiance enough to pierce the clouds that are massed around me" (p. 126).

The cloud mass that hung over Arnold at this time was concentrated around *Empedocles on Etna* and, somewhat less densely, around *The Scholar-Gipsy*; the literary instrument with which he pierced the cloud mass was *Sohrab and Rustum*; and the sunny white light which he thereby released in his poetics and in his nature radiates in the first instance from the Preface to the First Edition of *Poems* (1853). Taken together, then, these four literary documents provide the basis for an insight into one of the most crucial turnings, not just in the personal and poetic life of an indispensable nineteenth-century poet, but in the history of nineteenth-century poetry itself: what happened more or less overtly to Arnold is a key to one of the relentless subterranean stresses of nineteenth-century poets and poetry generally. On literary history's more public side, we are face to face here with a clash between Romanticism and Classicism so deeply rooted in poetic personality and yet so aesthetically and culturally barometric that it assumes some of the inexhaustible fascination of poetry itself, clear enough at one level but as evasive at another as history wedded to myth or fact merged with metaphor. The Arnold at the center of this drama is simply not susceptible to the easy categorizations that modern critics, whether sympathetic or hostile, have customarily sought to impose upon him; neither is the Arnold who emerged, intact and re-spirited, from it. So it is not too much to say that this complex literary event of the late 1840s–early 1850s has had persistent relevance throughout the twentieth century in that it determined the peculiar character of the critic who has been and still is the gadfly to every twentieth-century school of academic critics, who have not been able to argue him out of the way and whose latest strategy of dismissiveness but ill disguises the fact that, for a host of reasons, he is still their critical σκρύπυλος.

III

The literary climate that Arnold inherited in the second half of the 1840s was cluttered with poetic miscellanea. The monumental figures of Romanticism were all long dead, though

Wordsworth had yet to breathe his last; as they had dropped away one by one, such coherence as they represented or such illusion of coherence as their magnificent, many-faceted literary energy had seemed to give, through literature, to the space they occupied for some twenty-five years collapsed in the vacuum created by their departure. As Arnold issued forth into the world (1822), the Romanticism of incomparable poetic talents passed out of it; even that fine glow of critical theory and enthusiasm that had been ignited by Romanticism among quite minor figures like Arthur Henry Hallam and that still gives the 1820s a curious critical vibrancy had lost all its warmth. So what Arnold in his contemporary situation was faced with was a remnant Romanticism without genius—the rubble of Romanticism fallen into the hands of third-rate poetasters who used it as they must, rigidly and myopically, extravagantly and dogmatically. Carlyle was certainly an exception, and Arnold yielded to Carlyle's influence at a depth that, if he ever fully recognized it, he never fully admitted. Besides, Arnold's problem was poetic in a quite specialized sense—the actual making of poems—and for this Carlyle was an entirely inappropriate mentor. Tennyson and Browning were exceptions too, but they were still trying to sort out analogous matters for themselves and hence could hardly have been expected to serve as satisfactory guides to a young contemporary with such imperious needs and such a distinctive personality.

It is essential that one not romanticize the Romanticism or post-Romanticism that Arnold looked around and saw, as a prospective poet, in the 1840s. Indeed, if Romanticism is an archetypal state of mind rather than a subject matter or a particular set of metaphors, it was a very unromantic Romanticism that he was faced with. Only in Newman was a relatively pure species of Romanticism at work organically, while the Brontës and Dickens were employing partial and derivative aspects of Romanticism, and Tennyson and Browning were struggling to transform a Romanticism that, though it had served their apprenticeships well enough, positively impeded their majorities. Otherwise, as Arnold saw it, even the deeply fallible but truly grand Romanticism of Wordsworth, Byron, and Keats had foundered on its faults—on the personal/poetic incoherence of Clough, the "Spasmodic" caprice of Alexander Smith, and the formlessness, sentimentality, subjectivity, and miscellaneous image-making and abundant psychologizing of contemporary poetry generally. It is not surprising, then, that as a young writer looking for guidance, Arnold turned away from contemporary poetry in despair and returned to the true founders of nineteenth-century poetic experience and to the writers who had guided them.

For the time being, then, the major Romantic poets became Arnold's chief literary referees, and much the young writer found there to admire. His fundamental seriousness of purpose, though still somewhat inchoate, responded vigorously to their seriousness, and his lively sense of curiosity was profoundly stimulated by their extraordinary literary variety. Their faith in the incomparable distinctiveness of literary experience and in the indispensable role of literary experience in modern life found easy companionship with his similar faith. He could register in himself their imaginative force without envy, and he could scrutinize their use of Classical subject matter in distinctly modern ways without intimidation. In short, he could appraise their monumental achievements without anxiety because he recognized that much that they had done, he simply did not have the power to do. He could be generous towards them because what they had done so well hardly needed to be done again.

But in order to understand the way in which Arnold's response to the Romantics as guides to the young writer became programmatic in his poetry, one must recognize and bring forward to the issue three very basic elements in his nature. First, he was innately poetical—not profound, perhaps, or grand or deeply moving (to reverse his own appraisal of the age and turn it back upon him), but innately poetical. To be an authentic poet was his great spiritual ambition, and he abandoned the practice of poetry only after that practice itself had taught him what his limitations were and had processed him to the clear recognition that he could be a great adjunct to poetry rather than a great poet. Second, he was innately critical—that is, from earliest maturity he gave evidence of a critical consciousness that, with a sort of spontaneous inevitability, converted experience into a judgment of experience, sight turning as if automatically into insight. He was a language man *par excellence*, and his language perpetually sought out objects of intelligence with which it could construct reasonably accurate models of verbal meaning. Third, his temperament was fundamentally sanguine. He was not an idealist of the sort bred by German Romanticism, and he had serious reservations about the ultimate usefulness of Carlyle, just as he was basically sceptical about what he considered the exaggerated place in the formation of modernism assigned to German Romanticism by John Stuart Mill. But that his sanguinity was muted makes it no less real. When he was most self-conflicted, he may have felt hope at a rather desperate level; but to be self-conflicted was an unacceptable state for Arnold, as his letters to Clough, taken as a whole, clearly illustrate. And though he could identify imaginatively at a very intimate level with those spiritual aliens for whom the threat of moral paralysis was one of the harrowing metaphors of modernism, as many of his poems right up to and including *Empedocles on Etna* show, these were metaphoric experiences, imaginatively or formalistically auto-biographical rather than literally so. It would be simply unreasonable to expect absolute consistency from a young poet caught in the confusions of his time and nature and lacking a fully clarified poetics, but the overwhelming direction or drift of what Arnold is doing in those crucial poems is clear enough: he is creating these extraordinary metaphors of spiritual experience in order to critique them. He has not yet found an encompassing and sustaining idea of the world, and this is his failure; but his critical consciousness is rather acutely aware of the false postures to which, in an age still trying to find its answers in Romanticism, the most sensitive are paradoxically the most susceptible. So he seems to have been limited for the time being to the creation of Romantic structures and solutions with which his language could work at a subtle poetic level in the exhibition of their inadequacy or positive falseness. Perhaps it was not the true, imaginatively authentic Romanticism at the center of the archetype itself—say, Wordsworth and Keats at their severest and best; but it was the Romanticism that, at a belated hour, tended to spill into the general life and to offer to young writers desperate for guidance models of spiritual and imaginative response that were not quite trustworthy.

Finally, two considerations of a somewhat less deeply personal kind may help one maintain a steady perspective in tracing the subtle course of Arnold's poetic performance during the years leading up to *Empedocles on Etna* and the self-revelation it embodied for him, a course made subtle for the critic because Arnold was not himself quite conscious of their implications. One is the substantial presence in his work almost from the beginning of Classical subject matter and his tendency to turn that Classical subject matter toward modern relevance. These were, of course, obvious characteristics of the Romantic poets— both the subject matter and the poetic formulation being pervasive in their works—and in this Arnold was simply following their lead. But this form of Classicism did not prevent his ultimate aesthetic-spiritual crisis. Indeed, it may have contributed to its violence in that it functioned for a time as a plausible self-deception, an ingratiating halfway measure that temporarily blinded him to the perception that genuine Classicism was a far more radical metaphor than this. Thus we are alerted to avoid succumbing to a delusive quibble over Arnold's intermediate and final Classicism—what might be called cosmetic versus core Classicism—and to be prepared to recognize, when the shift comes, the profound implications of an aesthetic-spiritual position removed in kind from a mere dilettantish preference of the ancients to the moderns. The second consideration is analogous to the first. To say that Arnold throughout these pre-*Empedocles* years was a persistent critic of Romanticism is not to say that he was a wholly adequate critic of it, at either the poetic or the personal level. In fact, the evidence leads to the conclusion that he was both *persistent* and *inadequate*. Even while, in poem after poem, he was positing Romantic answers to excruciating spiritual problems and critiquing their inadequacy, he was himself drifting in the direction of the Romanticism of the day.[11] He was in that sense a self-deceived dilettante, bringing a soulful intensity to a perceptual inadequacy. Despite all of his programmatic critiquing, all of the very real and traceable operations of his acute critical consciousness, he was in effect "add[ing] zest to [his readers' and his own] melancholy or grace to their dreams." A poetic process so delicately balanced that for several highly creative years it deceived Arnold himself obviously presents delicate problems for the student of Arnold, and one may have to relax one's hold on categorical unequivocalness in dealing with it. But, then, Arnold was caught within the frame of his own poems as we are not; at this distance in time, we can look with considerable emotional detachment at the truly fascinating humanness of the failed strategies of a poet-critic of Romanticism who was himself unconsciously enervated by the very Romanticism he was attempting to critique. We have the decisive advantage of a retrospective view of Arnold's earlier poems conditioned by his own climactic recognition of what was "all wrong" with them.[12] Thus again we are brought to *Empedocles on Etna* and the Preface of 1853, in which Arnold critiqued its *poeticalness*. We can be fairly encouraged to free Arnold's critical metaphors from a reference peculiar to that poem only and to see them as relevant to his whole career as a poet up to that time.

Notes

1. *The Poems of Matthew Arnold*, Miriam Allott, ed., 2nd ed. (London and New York: Longman, 1979), p. 208, emphasis added. Doubting such "shadowy autobiographical significance" is clearly easier for some than for others. All references to Arnold's poems are to this edition and are given wherever possible in parentheses in the text.
2. Preface to the First Edition of *Poems, The Complete Prose Works of Matthew Arnold*, R.H. Super, ed. (Ann Arbor: University of Michigan Press, 1960), volume I, p. 4. Except where specifically indicated, all references to Arnold's prose are to this edition and are given in parentheses in the text wherever possible.
3. The phrase is from Thomas Hardy's Preface to *The Dynasts*.
4. *The Complete Poems of Thomas Hardy*, James Gibson, ed. (New York: Macmillan, 1976), p. [6], emphasis added.
5. There seems to be a valid analogy between Arnold's role here and the role Newman played as leader of the Oxford Movement. In neither case did the circumstances call upon them to become direct leaders of a popularly based movement, but while their appeal to an upper echelon of experts both enabled and required them to hone their special subjects severely, they could hope that their views would undergo responsible

translation as they traveled further and further through the ranks of those who were non-expert but yet available to their overall apprehensions.

6. The uniqueness of Arnold's poetic program is further reinforced by a comparison with the less coherent and less persistent way in which other nineteenth-century poets dealt with the issue. Despite the colossal relevance of the Preface to *Lyrical Ballads* and *The Prelude* to the redemption of poetry, Wordsworth couched his exposition in very personal, more literally autobiographical terms, and his celebration of Nature is ultimately more primary than his celebration of poetry. Byron was less serious, Shelley less pragmatic, Keats less public. Tennyson paired perceptions in a more dramatically noncommittal way and moved the subject to a more parabolic distance. Browning fragmented it among several *dramatis personae* and dealt with only a part of it even in *The Ring and the Book*. Rossetti played it too narrowly against specific artistic conventions with which he was out of sympathy; Swinburne, in his incomparably confrontal way, subjected it to the harrowing of hell rather than the winnowing of wisdom; and its full relevance to Hardy is not yet sufficiently understood.

7. *The Letters of Matthew Arnold to Arthur Hugh Clough*, H.F. Lowry, ed. (London and New York: Oxford University Press, 1932). All references to these letters are to this edition, pages being cited in parentheses in the text wherever appropriate. The three prefaces are taken up in later discussions.

8. The most extended commentary on Arnold's poetry that bears some significant relationship to my own approach to the subject is contained in A. Dwight Culler's *Imaginative Reason: The Poetry of Matthew Arnold* (New Haven and London: Yale University Press, 1966). But though we pass through the same field and see the obvious aspects of the same topography, we look at our essential subject with very different critical eyes. Professor Culler persistently sees Arnold's poetry as autobiographical, Arnold's own voice as its mediating voice; as his title suggests, he follows the evolution of heightened but essentially rational statement as the primary focus of his critical interest in Arnold's poetry. In these crucial matters, my own critical emphasis is quite different from Professor Culler's. On the issue on which we may seem to have most in common, our differences are in fact most dramatic. While it is clear to both of us that Arnold, in his poetry as well as in his prose, is a persistent critic of the Romantic tradition, it seems clearer to me than to Professor Culler that this issue is invasive of Arnold's poetic texts, of his actual poetry-making, at the most fundamental level; that it was an illusive program uncertainly apprehended that he followed; and that this programmatic illusion was a persistent source of vaguely understood aesthetic-spiritual distress, a pain that climaxed in a crisis of spirit, a recognition of self-deception, and a resolution that deepened and enlarged his ultimate Classicism in an explosive way. This leads to very different emphases between Professor Culler and me as to the background and literary

character of the Preface of 1853, the special significance of Arnold's literary endeavors in the years immediately following its publication, and the peculiar integrity, *at the strict level of literariness*, between the critic-poet of the 1840s and 1850s and the poet-critic of the 1860s and 1870s. So while we tend to place Arnold in the same field of vision and may appear to see a vaguely similar poet in the distance, Professor Culler and I have close-up views of Arnold that are radically different. Professor Culler's approach is basically moral-descriptive while mine is aesthetic-analytical. And though our readings of many individual Arnold poems and of the chief coordinates in the development of Arnold as a poet are fundamentally different, it would serve little critical purpose to put those individual readings into contention since the controversy would be endless and ultimately incoherent at such an *ad hoc* level. We exhibit critical enthusiasms that are rather clearly distinguishable from one another because we find the excitement of poetry in different poetic centers.

9. I have accepted Professor Lowry's tentative dating of many of the letters since I have not identified any case where contention over uncertain dates would be germane to my argument.

10. Another analogy to Newman's spiritual history suggests itself. When Newman saw his face in the mirror of the Monophysite heresy and dubbed himself "a Monophysite," he was recognizing something profoundly true and profoundly metaphoric. Likewise, there was nothing mechanically literal, in the autobiographical sense, about Arnold's discovery of a deep truth about the direction he had been following in "my Empedocles." The poem was unequivocal proof, impossible to deny, that, despite all the elegance of his thoughts about poetry and all his *ad hoc* efforts to critique, in individual dramatic lyrics, some of the representative false leads of Romanticism, he had himself drifted with the currents of the age and had, as illustrated by his most ambitious poetic effort, become "a Romantic." Thus both Newman and Arnold discovered that they were implicitly in rebellion against the very principles that they most highly prized.

11. Again there is an unavoidable analogy to Newman's personal history: Newman's drift toward Liberalism despite all his instincts and articulate preferences for the opposite direction corresponds to Arnold's comparable drift toward Romanticism, and their respective realizations of the false track they were following were comparably intense.

12. *Letters to Clough*, p. 126.

2.

The Main Tendency
of Arnold's Poetry before 1853:
Exploratory Readings
of Some Major and Minor Texts

The critical purpose of the unusual methodology of this chapter is to enable a significant number of Arnold's major and minor poems to reassume their individual integrity or autonomy in the hope that the reader will thereby get a crisper and clearer view of Arnold's way of creating imaginative structures. Such a perception, indispensable to any genuine appreciation of Arnold's imaginative intuitions and craft, is very often obscured by the subordination of the poems as aesthetic totalities to some thematic argument or network of arguments. The method also dramatizes the mimetic character of Arnold's poems and brings their personative qualities into sharper focus.

Poems like Dover Beach *and* Stanzas from the Grande Chartreuse, *which were outgrowths of the period before 1853, though published later, are included. Certain other poems that unquestionably belong to this period are treated elsewhere.* Tristram and Iseult *and* Empedocles on Etna *are given a separate chapter (Chapter 3), and*

The Scholar-Gipsy *is paired, for purposes of comparison and contrast, with* Thyrsis *(Chapter 4).*

Mycerinus

Mycerinus provides the reader with a very satisfying poetic experience. It turns upon a public myth that echoes at one level or another every reader's awareness of the justice/injustice of his experience of events in conflict with the way in which events may actually happen. Thus the poem provides the reader with an adequately developed action (or "Exhibition") through which to examine in an empathetic way and at a new imaginative depth perceptions that were already his own or become his own through participation in the poem's metaphor of interpretive action. *Mycerinus* is a poem of Classical *mimesis* enriched by a dense texture of psychological meditation.

Behind *Mycerinus* stand two literary texts—Herodotus' account of the story, cited by Arnold in a note,[1] and Wordsworth's *Laodamia*, which is also a poem about the "justice" of the gods' dealings with humans and is the source of the stanzaic pattern used by Arnold in the first part of his poem (ll. 1–78); and these two texts are given an interwoven relationship in the poem. Wordsworth, who drew upon a plenitude of Classical sources in attempting to shape the action of his poem, never could satisfy himself that his disposition of Laodamia's fate was quite right. Between 1815, the first published version, and 1845, when he finally let the matter rest, he substantially altered the stanza crucial to this issue at least three times (he left four different printed versions) and seriously sought outside advice as to how to handle it.[2] Although Arnold could not have known some parts of this history and probably did not know other parts of it, he almost certainly would have recognized—and by the witness of his own poem did recognize—the overarching poetic issue as, not whether a poet's particular disposition of a moral issue was right, but whether or not resolute and dogmatic disposition of particular moral issues was the poet's responsibility. It is on this larger poetic issue that *Mycerinus* stands as a critical gloss on *Laodamia*:

dogmatic rigidity is returned to imaginative solution in Arnold's poem. The action upon which the moral question will turn having been framed with much formal complexity in ll. 1–78, dogmatic rigidity is erased through the use of a much more open-ended form in ll. 79–127. Thus the "moral profundity" of a genuine poetic "action," of which Arnold will speak with much urgency in the years to come, is freed from the moral disposition that a poet may take from his sources or from his own time-frame.

The interweaving of the text of Wordsworth and the text of Herodotus also takes place at a somewhat metaphoric level. Even without Wordsworth's helpful notes pointing to his Classical sources, Arnold would certainly have seen the modern poet's use of ancient materials as a subject of almost limitless interest for the young writer with an acute critical consciousness attempting to shape his own career as a distinctive poet. The Romantics had not made greater use of ancient materials than the Neoclassical writers, but they had certainly altered that use, shifting the critical issue from *what* to *how*. Ironically, Wordsworth's difficulty was not primarily with Laodamia, as he perceived it to be, but with Protesilaus: having accepted as imperative Euripides' characterization of Protesilaus' unimpeachable rectitude in *Iphigenia in Aulis*, he felt compelled to imprison Laodamia in that rectitude despite his obvious discomfort in doing so, and the stern judgment of Virgil in *Aeneid VI* had reinforced this apparent necessity. Wordsworth's difficulty, then, was rooted in a faulty use of his ancient sources: he had felt it necessary to take both his action and his interpretation of that action (both the incident and the moral) from his sources, and this had entangled him in a confused and sterile poetic situation. Herodotus, on the other hand, was a historian, not a poet, and he had not imposed on the story of Mycerinus a moral imperative, but had recorded quite dispassionately only the incident, Mycerinus' thoughts being an integral part of the incident. So Arnold as a poet was creatively free: he could convert the myth from history into poetry through the intuitions of the imagination and the associations of the fancy without having to rationalize any moral judgment other than that inherent in the action itself.

Thus *Mycerinus* is an illustration of an appropriate use of ancient materials by a modern poet, and the text of Herodotus is interwoven with the text of *Laodamia* in the sense that Arnold incorporates the Classical text into his exhibition of the fault at the heart of the Romantic text.

There is another sense in which *Mycerinus* may be seen as critical of Wordsworth—namely, as the exponent of a simplistic moral psychology. But to see this as a fully operative dimension of *Mycerinus*, the reader will have to set aside the tendency of critics of Arnold's poem to oversimplify the complexity of its moral probings. Though the voice of the narrator-commentator in the second part of *Mycerinus* opens up and reinforces complex possibilities, so does the voice of Mycerinus himself in the first part. At the beginning and at the end of his address to his people, Mycerinus is haughty, righteous, and declamatory. In between he entertains—at a rhetorical distance that gradually weakens into "'though something would I say—/ Something—yet what I know not'" (ll. 68–69)—thoughts that are self-indicting on the one hand and god-exonerating on the other. It is possible, he acknowledges, that he has made a supreme error in judgment and that what he is momentarily and intensely suffering from is merely the collapse of his own metaphysics, his own self-willed myth ("'some better archetype,'" l. 22); it is possible, too, that the gods in whom he has put his trust are no more potent than Hardy's subalterns and, like man, are mere puppets of "'a tyrannous necessity'" (l. 42). Thus he embarks upon an odyssey of wondering, like the chidden children in Hardy's *Nature's Questioning*, and he ends up, despite the vast difference in the tone of his voice, essentially at the position adopted by the speaker in Hardy's poem: "No answerer I." The power of his divination self-destructs in the light of a million possibilities that "'may be'" (l. 41). So just as we see that the Byronic defiance with which Mycerinus begins and ends his monologue is ultimately theatrical and therefore self-indicting, we see, too, that the speculations into which he is drawn have much more to do with Hardy's

> web Enorm,
> Whose furthest hem and selvage may extend

> To where the roars and plashings of the flames
> Of earth-invisible suns swell noisily,[3]

than with Wordsworth's neater and less imaginative moral package.

The Strayed Reveller

Whatever metaphor one may choose to give perspective on the place of *The Strayed Reveller* in the Arnold canon, most serious students of Arnold will see the poem as occupying a crucial space in Arnold's poetic development, as an expression of his distinctive poetic consciousness, and as adding an indispensable dimension to his overall poetic achievement. *The Strayed Reveller* is an inspired lyrical drama-in-miniature—liberated in its form, free in its verse, delicately teasing in its critical and imaginative implications. It was the title poem of his first volume and hence the primary text with which Arnold came before the world after he was entirely on his own as to both form and subject. In all these senses, *The Strayed Reveller* is major Arnold.

Subject and style are inseparable in *The Strayed Reveller*: they interpenetrate and reinforce each other at every point, and as soon as the reader begins to talk about the poem's action, he realizes that much of his perspective on it has been shaped by the poem's style. A deceptive simplicity characterizes both its story and its style: very little seems to happen in the former, and the latter seems self-elucidating. But apparent simplicity is one of the chief imaginative illusions in Arnold's poetry. Like his mentor Sophocles, he draws his fables in simple, severe lines; sparseness is such an identifying mark of his rhetoric that any rotundity of rhetorical gesturing within a poem is a trustworthy indication that some *dramatis persona* is giving off signals of falseness. Thus in reading an Arnold poem, as in reading a Sophoclean play, we must take maximum advantage of a minimum of metaphors, not assuming (as in reading Carlyle's rhetoric of Romanticism, for example) that what we miss at one point will be reiterated at several other points. We must expect that every metaphor, however seemingly casual,

has potential significance for the ultimate shape and significance of the text. Thus, when we come to the point of rendering
for ourselves the subject or action of *The Strayed Reveller* as a
way of getting at the poem's initiating imaginative intuition, we
have to be adequately comprehensive, neglecting none of the
slender text's suggestions. What we find is that Arnold's myth,
despite its illusion of simplicity, is very rich in its implications,
even carrying its subject beyond the possibility of thematic
closure.

A talented and ardent youth with all the dewy freshness of
the early world still upon him (morning as metaphor) sets out
to join his fellows in the celebration of the rites of Dionysus
(Dionysus as root metaphor for the reveller's identity). Curiosity
draws him off track to the palace of Circe (shrewd, worldly
wise, witchlike goddess who knows how to reveal the dark
underbelly of human reality), where, with all the boldness of
a typical Dionysian, he drinks from Circe's cup and experiences
the deep feelings of terror of one who has entered a strange
sanctuary where unfamiliar rites are performed. Circe is hos-
pitable and reassuring, inducing him to follow his natural bent
and drink yet more. The youth does so, and Circe calls Ulysses
to witness this curious event.

Ulysses, who is crafty, suspicious, and observant, at first
suspects the goddess of having lured the youth into the palace,
but she assures him that she has not. In the meantime, Ulysses
observes the rich cluster of images by which the youth is
unequivocally identified with Dionysus as Dionysus is identified
with Pan: the reminiscence of Ampelus, the vine and ivy, the
fawn-skin, the wine stains, the disheveled drunkenness (images
as oblique metaphors of identity). It is now getting very late
(evening as metaphor), and the youth wears a different aspect
from the one he had worn in the morning—more dissolute
and self-revealed at a shabbier level. Ulysses has, in a general
way, already understood the matter, but he is the archetypal
inquirer (character as metaphor of the critical consciousness);
and so he not only asks the youth who he is, but also insinuates
the field of interest around which he would like the answer to
be shaped. If you are the follower of "some divine bard," he
says, "then hail!" (ll. 117–128). The rest of the poem's action

is made up of the reveller's account of what old Silenus has taught him[4] "at noon" (l. 246, noon, Pan's sacred hour, as metaphor). The reveller's account provides a highly resonant contrast between the situation of the gods, who know all and suffer nothing, and that of the "bards," who know all and suffer all, ending with the youth's assertion that he has seen much and suffered nothing, but is fully in tune with Nature:

> Ah, cool night-wind, tremulous stars!
> Ah, glimmering water,
> Fitful earth-murmur,
> Dreaming woods!
>
> (ll. 281–285)

Various readers of *The Strayed Reveller* will undoubtedly identify exciting aspects of the poem not included in the above sketch, and this is as it should be: the basic critical point is that one can hardly hope to discover the initiating imaginative intuition of Arnold's poem by over-simplifying the myth (subject, action) of which it is both the cause and the result. Measured by this more comprehensive statement of its myth, an interpretation of the poem that gives as its primary object the simple contrast between the Olympian (detached) and the Romantic (excruciatingly involved) views of poetry is obviously an inadequate, even seriously reductive, simplification. The suggestion that Arnold is himself complicit in the reveller's intoxication borders on the absurd. The poem creates a myth of poetic/human history (the metaphors of morning, noon, and night) by which the inception, fullness, and exhaustion of the old Panic-Dionysian dispensation are lightly traced, and the abandoned pathos of the reveller is that of an ingratiatingly nostalgic anachronism, an attractive but depleted image. Dionysus-Pan is, so to speak, brought face to face with Apollo-Christ, and Ulysses is their arbiter. All of the primitive orgiastic secrets, brutal or graceful, are now known (Circe has been an authority on them all along), and the chaotic frenzy must now submit to the moral imperatives of the Homeric epic. This is what makes the presence of Circe and Ulysses as the critical consciousnesses evaluating the reveller's disquisition so imagi-

natively crucial. Circe is fully qualified to measure the inadequacy of the reveller's Olympianism, knowing that the life of
the gods is inextricably bound up with the lives of men and
that they suffer, in an exemplary way, the same pains of
competition and disappointment that men suffer; Ulysses is
too shrewd and experienced to accept the identification of the
epic hero's pain with the epic poet's pain. He would recognize
its usefulness as an analogy but its absurdity as an equation.
Moreover, Circe and Ulysses, though with very different mental
attitudes, would both see the failed linkage in the reveller's
argument: after all, she is about to instruct Ulysses in the
secrets of how to survive the rigors of hell, and he is about to
undertake the journey. Thus they would see as essentially
fruitless and inert the reveller's equation of the poet's pain with
the world's pain. The really fruitful link is between pain and
moral perspective, and the poet who is literally absorbed by
pain can hardly be an adequate critic of life. It is not absorption
which he requires, but empathy—identification at a critical
distance—and this brings us to the very threshold of the moral
grandeur of Homer and the long literary tradition, with its
widely varying degrees of adequacy and inadequacy, rooted
there.

Stylistically, the primary reality of *The Strayed Reveller* is its
form as a lyrical drama to which the Classical unities of time,
place, and action have been conscientiously applied. It is a brief
sequence of contrapuntal voicings in which the myth is converted to language and language releases the myth. If it has
the large interpretive implications suggested above, then this
validates the Classical principle that the simplest language,
properly used, is capable of generating imaginative insights of
a most rich and resonant sort. The groundtone of the drama
is established by the prologogic speech of the reveller himself:
he struggles with the inner pleasures of inebriation to prove
that he has a firm grasp on external reality. He asserts that he
sees Circe standing there with all the three-dimensional solidity
of a stage prop (ll. 7–13), and because he can fully "prove"
what time of day it is, is master of the metaphor of time (ll.
14–22). Even the *vers libre* that he introduces as the poem's
prosody is a metaphor of his precarious placement between

drunken chaos and formality, between looseness and order, between prose and poetry. Circe's first line, "Whence art thou, sleeper?" (l. 23), is, on the other hand, crisp, clear, and assured. It is a no-nonsense question that sets in motion the machinery of the drama on both levels (what are your physical origins? what is your symbolic meaning?) while it plants an equally double-edged judgment. The characterization "sleeper" is also both physical and psychic: the reveller has been sleeping off his wine while time has been passing him by.

The reveller's reply to Circe's blunt question is a marvel of metaphoric richness rendered in a voice that is both expository and lyrical, responsive and diversionary, sure and acutely uneasy. He lives at the top of the valley, he says, and, being an enthusiast in the ranks of Dionysus (Iacchus), he started early to the celebration ("the rout") of the Dionysian rites, but was diverted by curiosity and in a state of awesome terror to look in upon Circe's palace, where he drank from the cup and went to sleep. In a matter-of-fact, short-ranged sense, this is an answer to Circe's question, but by epical standards, whether Homeric or Biblical, it is no answer at all. Lacking even a fragment of genealogy or of social-familial place, the reveller does not exist as a person. He is only a sensuously visible state of consciousness, an expression, not of an individual (Ulysses, for example), but of a vague, inchoate state of a world. This expository vagueness on the part of the reveller, suggesting that what he is takes precedence over who he is, is compensated for by the dense fabric of imagery—lyrical in its overtones, symbolist in its aesthetic implications—that very considerably deepens and reinforces, at a more imaginative level, the tendency of the exposition. He is a traveler from the world of Pan, with its firs, chestnuts, and fawn-skins, from the "dawn" and "valley-head" of time on his way to participate in the Panic world's utmost development of pre-civilized ritual—the religion of Dionysus, natural, imaginative at a premature level, violent, and inadequate to the age of the heroes that is now dawning. Out of his primitive darkness (his "dark valley," l. 42), he sees Circe's palace, the strange, ominous house of change ("Smokeless, empty!" l. 45) where the age of the heroes, in the person of Ulysses on the eve of his journey to the underworld, is being born. When Ulysses comes on stage, his strong sense of identity will counterpoint the reveller's personal anonymity, just as, by extension, the moral imperative at the center of the age of the heroes will define the human role in an entirely new way and lodge man's identity, not in raw, sensual nature, but in moral values.

When Circe speaks again, all her cool crispness is gone. She is indulgent, ingratiating, reassuring. She recognizes the event in the making, and she knows that the reveller can play his role satisfactorily only if he is a bit intoxicated. So although she did not lure him to her palace, she lures him to her bowl. The "dark seeds" in her "red creaming liquor" (ll. 57–58) are the shadowy past out of which the well-defined future will spring, and she wants Ulysses to witness the stunning event in the making. The reveller, of course, succumbs readily to Circe's suasions and finds her wine "More soft, ah me,/More subtle-winding/Than Pan's flute-music!" (ll. 65–67), an evaluative lyrical image that not only reinforces the reveller's identification with Pan but also suggests that he is a barometer of the change that is in the offing. Circe reads this speech well, and the imagery with which she summons Ulysses tells us that man's age of "glad animal movements" is coming to a close: he need no longer weary himself with hunting (l. 72) or beguile his hours by "range[ing] the woodland" (l. 73) because the day has brought the beginning of a new era.

Ulysses can hardly be expected to understand how fully his own destiny and, through him, the destiny of man is implicit in the simple sight before him—a sleeping youth in a half-naked state of drunken disarray. So he lightly taunts Circe with her witchery and her well-known habit of luring men to a swine-like fall from humanness. But the shrewd and curious observer is dominant in Ulysses, and, as has already been said, he reads the images rightly and identifies the reveller as "some youth beloved of Pan,/Of Pan and the Nymphs" (ll. 80–81). "Who is he," Ulysses finally inquires, "What youth, Goddess, what guest of Gods or mortals?" (ll. 90, 94–95), and this sets the stage for the dramatic revelation in which the poem will climax. Who is he—that is, what does he signify—and is that significance more germane to the gods or to men? At this point, Circe reflects the agitation of the pregnant situation and insists only that she has not manipulated it in any fundamental way, "lured him not hither, Ulysses" (l. 97).

The reveller's speech following his symbolic awakening as Ulysses makes his approach "from within" shows that the future is already emergent and visible in the mediatorial figure of "This spare, dark-featured,/Quick-eyed stranger" (ll. 102–103) from beyond the waves whose growing fame—already a legend in his own time—has sharpened the eye of the reveller and enabled him to recognize the visible images of *homo agonistes*: "His sailor's bonnet,/His short-coat, travel-tarnished,/With one arm bare!" (ll. 105–107). This is none of the brood of Pan, worshippers of Dionysus; this is "The wise Ulysses,/Laertes' son" (ll. 112–113). Ulysses is in turn gracious to the strayed reveller, yielding him imaginary credentials that suit the sweetness of his voice by fancying for him a legendary history devoted to the highest poetic emprise:

> songs
> Of Gods and Heroes,
> Of war and arts,
> And peopled cities,
> Inland, or built
> By the grey sea.
>
> (ll. 123–128)

It is a graceful strategy on the part of the quick-witted Ulysses, whose authoritative eye has already identified the youth generically as a son of Pan and not as a celebrant of the heroically hard-won victories of civilization. But the strategy, besides its worth as a courtesy returned, enables Ulysses both to define the moral position from which he will listen to the reveller's ensuing disquisition and to influence in a degree the subject and the tone of that disquisition.

Ulysses' specific question to the reveller has been, who are you? ("I am Ulysses./And thou, too, sleeper? [ll. 114–115]), and we have to take the reveller's answer as a parabolic response to that question. I am a spokesman, he implicitly says, for the best of my age—for Pan and Silenus and Dionysus. But as a spokesman for his age, he is also an addition to it: he is a style, an interpretive voice and a premonition, not adequate to the future certainly, but not wholly dead-centered in the past. The way in which he celebrates the privileged position of the gods is a model of propriety and decorum—formal, detached, austerely respectful—but cold, as if he is being implicitly critical without being explicitly judgmental or as if, in giving them their full due, he is giving them more than any human can think they have a right to. So while he over-simplifies the situation of the gods, there is a critical subtext implicit in his over-simplification. On the other hand, he brings great warmth of feeling to his exposition of the ambiguous privilege of the bards: to suffer in proportion to their knowledge. "But oh, what labour!/O prince, what pain!" (ll. 210–211). There is over-simplification here too, but it works in an opposite direction: by over-stressing the poet-pain issue, he reduces it to a species of melancholy pathos, having omitted the moral insight that is the worthiest end of poetry and the justification for such sympathy as the poet feels for the perennial distresses of mankind.

In the end, the reveller, despite a consciousness that seems to be groping towards the future, does not in fact recognize the moral imperative of conscientious man and confesses that his daily imaginings are essentially free from pain. His is yet a world of "natural magic" without "moral profundity," and so his last verbal gesture is an exact balancing of his first:

> Faster, faster,
> O Circe, Goddess,
> Let the wild, thronging train,
> The bright procession
> Of eddying forms,
> Sweep through my soul!

>   (ll. 1–6, 292–297)

He cannot tell us who he is because, as we understand identity, he does not yet exist: he is a tender, ingratiating member of the tribe of Pan, but still only an anonymous member—a strayed reveller, not yet a moral man.

Fragment of an 'Antigone'

Coping with death is the poetic idea examined in *Fragment of an 'Antigone'*, a fragment when considered in relationship to Sophocles' play but quite complete in itself when seen in the aesthetic context of Arnold's own poems as developed in this essay. It is a poetic voicing through which the reader, like the author, is enabled to critique the adequacy of the idea that it posits. Being in itself so unpretentious, it has a normative value in that, since it clearly does not challenge Sophocles in any respect, it suggests a way of gaining proper perspective on Arnold's later, more ambitious Classical emulations—*Sohrab and Rustum, Balder Dead,* and *Merope.* Arnold is not there challenging Homer, Virgil, and Sophocles, respectively, any more than he is challenging Sophocles in this fragment: he is simply trying to capture in his poems an exemplary suggestion of "the grand moral effects produced by style"[5] in the chief Classical writers. Those "grand moral effects" are inseparable from the adequacy with which an author treats the ideas that he chooses to deal with. Moreover, Arnold's choice of the Classical chorus as his model for such poetic voicings is a brilliant stroke which is critically very useful. Except at the end of a Greek tragedy, where they customarily articulate such reconciliation as the total action has achieved, the chorus's reactions to the incidents and situations as they evolve and its interpretations of those situations, though always serious at an oratorical level and reflective of representative human responses, are not to be considered infallible. Arnold's use of this model suggests that dynamic fallibility rather than dogmatic infallibility is also a *donné* of his poetic voicings, which are dramatic rather than depositional.

The total action of *Fragment of an 'Antigone'*, and hence its movement of consciousness, is from rebellion to reconciliation, from wilfulness to acceptance. The provocative extra-textual events that are an initiating assumption of Arnold's poem (the dire consequences of an irreconcilable collision of conflicting laws maintained with equal rigor by their exponents) stimulate both the chorus and Haemon to extravagant if perfectly natural responses. The poem's more muted internal events (the gradual assumption on the part of the chorus of a more moderate and serious critical role and Haemon's responsiveness to the chorus's lead) bring the matter to poise.

The chorus's first chant is an impassioned endorsement of Romantic Prometheanism. Drawing the gods themselves into an alliance with man in a defiance of Fate, it portrays man as adrift in life, the victim of a thousand externally induced shocks, the victim of his own penchant for error, and inevitably the victim of death. It applauds *any* control he carves out for his own happiness within the context of "the ties of blood," ties that he cannot himself originate but which, if reverenced, will give him the strength he needs to endure. But reverence for the ties of blood is, ironically, the source of Haemon's pathetic plight. In a paroxysm of grief, he becomes the hysterical exponent of romantic love (Romantic passion) and the ally of Creon in his own distraught condemnation of Antigone, though the epithets he uses ("cruel," "too-bold," "headstrong," "pitiless") insinuate that he is in fact indicting the very thing he is advocating—cruel, pitiless romantic love.

The chorus's second chant moves toward modification of its initial Romantic philosophy of defiance. The story of Eos-Aurora's ill-fated passion for Orion, the fulfilment of which would have "postpon[ed] an eternal law" against the godlike immortality of mortals,[6] shows that the gods are subject to the same eternal laws as men are in the ultimate disposition of fundamentals.[7] Moreover, since it was a fellow goddess who felled Orion, as it was a fellow man who felled Antigone, the interference of Fate in the matter is equivocated except in the most rigidly ideological and doctrinaire view of the short-ranged experience. Haemon's second speech shows that he has undergone the moderating influence of the instructive action recounted in this second choric chant: hysterical rebellion has become a more subdued unwillingness to succumb and some confusion about the role of the "envious Gods" rather than of Fate in bringing about his bitter situation.

The third choric chant then completes the curve of the poem's narrative: in the myths of both Amphiaraus and Hercules—the man of vision and the man of action—it was not the fact of their deaths that chiefly moved Zeus, who "preferred Fate to his strong desire" (l. 97), but the quality of their deaths.

Thus the poetic idea of death is processively enlarged—and in that sense made considerably more adequate—in *Fragment of an 'Antigone'*; Romantic Prometheanism and its analogues in other aspects of a passionate Romantic rebelliousness are subjected to a critiquing that draws principally on other Classical myths that subject them to a correcting perspective. Prometheanism is not made to appear less archetypal, only less singularly compelling. This suggests an even more oblique and fascinating interest of the poet in *Fragment of an 'Antigone'*: the huge import the choice of an action has on the character and significance of one's poems *and one's thoughts* (the myth of Antigone as contrasted with the myth of Prometheus, for example) and the way in which myth itself works in processing our imaginative and moral concerns. As myths find analogues in our thoughts, our thoughts find analogues in myths; the disposition of our thoughts, like the disposition of our poems— their destructive or constructive character—depends on the myths through which we elect to process them.

The Sick King in Bokhara

The Sick King in Bokhara is another fine example among Arnold's poems of the victory of style. One can fairly think of Arnold's attitude toward Sophocles as actually monitoring his motive in composing the poem: "Nay in Sophocles what is valuable is not so much his contributions to psychology and the anatomy of sentiment, as the grand moral effects produced by *style*. . . ."[8] The poem touches several complex, epic-like themes: the responsibilities of kingship, the austere sanctities of the law both as an expression of public order and as an imperious need of the inner man, the interpenetration of men by a common oneness of which the grave is only the ultimate symbol. But Arnold has subdued these large, timeless themes to the most unpretentious of elegiac dramas. In *The Sick King in Bokhara*, subject or action, structure, and language are compressed to their utmost simplicity and directness, and it is in that sense that the poem can be called a victory of style and seen as an implicit critique of the flamboyant formlessness and linguistic extravagance of the "Spasmodic" tendencies of contemporary poets and of such precedent texts as Shelley's *Prometheus Unbound*. In light of the growing seriousness of his thinking about the role of form in poetry, it is reasonable to surmise, too, that Arnold adopted this particular form for *The Sick King in Bokhara* in conscious imaginative preference to alternative literary forms available to him—the choric fragment of his *Fragment of an 'Antigone'*, for example, or the dramatic lyric shaped as a dramatic monologue, a form that was often congenial to Arnold's purposes and one that was becoming the dominant form in contemporary poetry. However, the fragment was not quite equal to the complexity of the subject or action of this poem, and the dramatic monologue would have put the emphasis in the wrong place—on "psychology and the anatomy of sentiment." Arnold knew as well as anyone that "psychology and the anatomy of sentiment" were crucial to an art that aspired to be a "complete magister vitae,"[9] but he became increasingly convinced that an art that succumbed to life could hardly serve as an adequate criticism of life and that an over-weighted emphasis on "psychology and the anatomy of sentiment," which he found to be a chief tendency of the Romantics, often led to a distortion of a poem's action and, hence, of its affect. So the form he adopted for *The Sick King in Bokhara* serves as an illustration of the appropriate relationship of action (*imitation*) to sentiment (*expressiveness*) and supplies an implicit critical corrective to the Romantic tendency to place disproportionate emphasis on the latter.

Few readers would fault *The Sick King in Bokhara* on the adequacy of its treatment of the moral and psychological implications inherent in its total action. There is a grim magnificence about the mullah, and the young king absorbs into a psyche that has heretofore been undistressed the stern instructiveness of the poem's life-shaking incident, responding to it at a truly anguished level. Moreover, though the "meaning" of the poem is subtle and multifaceted, it is projected with a directness and clarity that reveal the poet's fundamental faith in the resonant impressiveness of the action itself. These qualities of directness and clarity in the treatment of ideas in poetry were what Arnold found in his Classical models and what he expected of himself. He was deeply concerned that the idea-content of a poem be adequate to the field of perception in which such ideas could be reasonably expected to function, and he can surely be credited with such adequacy in the working out of *The Sick King in Bokhara*.

But there are two dimensions of the poem that have more direct stylistic implications, and they should perhaps be seen as having primary relevance to what Arnold's critical imagination was attempting to achieve. One is the conversion of the prose account of the incident that he found in Alexander Burnes's *Travels in Bokhara* into poetic style.[10] The two accounts are remarkably close even in details, and what Arnold has chiefly added are dramatic structure, diction, prosody, and such expansion of psychological or perceptual details as seemed to him relevant to specific characters centered in the particular action upon which the poem turns. These are essentially stylistic matters, and *The Sick King in Bokhara* is, like *Mycerinus*, an exemplification that the subtle difference between prose history and poetic myth is fundamentally a matter of style.

The other interesting stylistic strategy of the poem is Arnold's placement of a normative poetic voice in the text itself, a voice that establishes the stylistic criteria that hold details of the poem in place. This is the voice of Hussein, "teller of sweet tales, [his] own,/Ferdousi's, and the others' . . ." (ll. 11–12). It is Hussein (ll. 30–132) who, in an entirely self-effacing way, puts the controlling action into proper perspective, and it is he who gradually evolves the prosodic formula by which the counterpointing voices of the Vizier and the King bring the action to its expressive climax. Thus Hussein becomes a sort of Aristotelian implant who verifies what Arnold would eventually enunciate as the summary import of Greek theory and practice: "All depends upon the subject; choose a fitting action, penetrate yourself with the feeling of its situations; this done, everything else will follow."[11] That "everything else" is style, and as an exemplary illustration of a poetic theory, *The Sick King in Bokhara* seems to overleap the great poetic crisis Arnold had yet to face and to find imaginative companionship in *Sohrab and Rustum.* Both are essentially expressions of style (subject or action, construction, diction and rhythm, psychology or sentiment maintained at a proportionate level, and the poetic attitude that fuses all of these elements together), and both are compelling symbolic statements that the truly distinctive manner in which poetry makes its application of ideas to life is defined primarily as style.

Five Early Sonnets

The Sick King in Bokhara was followed in *The Strayed Reveller* volume of 1849 by five sonnets. These sonnets derive a constructive character from being sonnets and from the way in which Arnold, like Hardy after him, adopts and builds on the Miltonic-Wordsworthian precedent of stretching to their utmost the public, critical, dramatic potentialities of a poetic form that, in the nineteenth century as at other times, was customarily used for private, emotional, confessional ends.

There is a unifying literary purpose in this group of sonnets. *Shakespeare* is not a traditional Romantic laying of unction to the soul of Shakespeare, but a celebration of the supreme objectivity of England's (perhaps the world's) greatest poet and thus of objectivity itself as the poet's supreme goal. Shakespeare, despite all the tangential and distracting uses made of him by the Romantics, is an embodiment of the Classical ideal of full self-knowledge combined with complete self-effacement. His "heaven of heavens" was the heaven within him, and by maintaining in his literary works such a high degree of personal anonymity, he frustrated the archetypal Romantic search for personal equivalents in poetry ("'A true allegory of the state of one's own mind in a representative history. . .'")[12] and turned the reader's eye toward poetry's austerer and more primary function, the revelation of "All pains the immortal spirit must endure,/All weakness which impairs, all griefs which bow. . ." (ll. 12–13).

As *Shakespeare* emphasizes the indispensability of Classical form to the realization of poetry's highest purposes, so *To the Duke of Wellington: On Hearing Him Dispraised* emphasizes the

Classical role of the heroic protagonist in the disposition of human affairs. Wellington was not a Romantic hero setting a Titanic personality against the inevitable developments of time; nor did he, like the "feeble sons of pleasure," merely "vex the patient ground," "spinning sand" (ll. 3, 6, 7). Rather, he was a modern Odysseus who accepted the "general law" (l. 8) of the universe as it in fact is; he "saw," like Odysseus, "one clue to life, and followed it" (l. 14); and, like Odysseus "Laborious, persevering, serious, firm" (l. 10), he pursued his "track, across the fretful foam/Of vehement actions without scope or term,/Called history. . ." (ll. 11–13). The sonnet *To the Duke of Wellington* thus gives perspective on the kind of "action" or "subject" that the modern poet, like his ancient equivalent, might choose if he truly wished to achieve poetry's high purpose of reconciling men, amid the perennial bedlam of contemporary contradictions, to his universe by reminding him of its long rhythms and heroic exemplars.

Written in Butler's Sermons enlarges in another way Arnold's critique of some of the chief vagaries that have led to a kind of chaos in modern literary experience—namely, an overwrought psychological emphasis that, despite its doubtful tenableness, has destroyed the unity of poetry's effect through concentration, not on the action itself, but on the poet's commentary on the action, on what *he thinks* about the action. Thus an action is not allowed to "subsist as it did in nature,"[13] but is suspended in an endless activity of only relatively trustworthy psychological astutenesses. In the case of *Written in Butler's Sermons*, we have external evidence that strongly suggests this was the perceptual frame of reference in which Arnold conceived the poem. Writing some thirty years later under the indicative title *Bishop Butler and the Zeit-Geist*, Arnold made two relevant comments: (1) "we at Oxford used to read our Aristotle or our Butler with the same absolute faith in the classicality of their matter as in the classicality of Homer's form"; and (2) "The truth is, all this elaborate psychology of Butler's. . .is unsatisfying. . .What he calls our instincts and principles of action, which are in truth the most obscure, changing, interdependent of phenomena, Butler takes as if they were things. . .separate, fixed, and palpable. . . ."[14] Both the non-classicality of Butler and the deleterious effects of his misconceived "elaborate psychology" make him a crucial representative of the modern "men" who "Rend in a thousand shreds this life of ours" (ll. 3, 4). But Arnold's sonnet is subtler than that—clever at a much more devilish level. While one can accept the metaphors by which the concept of a subterranean human unity is set against this shredding of modern life (the deep foundations of ll. 5–8, the underwater arms of ll. 9–10, the common pediments upon which the mountain peaks rest of l. 11), it is impossible to make any serious sense out of the fanciful imagery of the final tercet. This is the climactic point of the poem: even when certain Romantic Modernist poets— Shelley, for example—perceived the difficulty inherent in this process of human disunification, they rendered it poetically in such attractive, fanciful, and impenetrable imagery that it was impossible to know exactly what their perception was or to get a fundamentally satisfying sense of their subject from the capricious way in which they handled it. Thus *Written in Butler's Sermons* is a complicated poetic experience that moves from a poetry of statement on modern misperception of the true nature of man to a highly sophisticated literary critique of the Romantic poet's ineptness (his over-fanciful imagery obfuscating even his underlying conceit) in dealing with it.

Written in Emerson's Essays is one of the most calculatedly histrionic of all of Arnold's poems. It is, in fact, so stagey that one can apply to it with considerable composure the phrases with which Arnold characterizes the poet in *Night comes. . .*:[15] his "rash and feverish melancholy," his "feignings of fantastic grief," his "false breath" and "shallow music" (ll. 5–8). But since there can hardly be any serious doubt about the depth and genuineness of Arnold's personal response to Emerson's *Essays,*[16] we must deal with the sonnet as embodying a metaphoric voice put to a poetically theatrical purpose. The final line of the poem—"Dumb judges, answer, truth or mockery?"— seems to provide the clue in that it turns the question upon the reader in its rawest, most dichotomized form. The answer is, of course, *both*. There is a "new, and moving, and unforgettable" truth in Emerson that is, in fact, captured at the poem's center:

> the will is free;
> Strong is the soul, and wise, and beautiful;
>
> The seeds of godlike power are in us still;
> Gods are we, bards, saints, heroes, if you will!—
>
> (ll. 10–13)

But there is the mockery of inflated insincerity in the *persona*'s posturing that in turn makes a mockery of poetry itself, especially for those bearers of a "wistful incredulity" (l. 7) whose need for a believable revelation is greatest. The speaker is an embodiment of the most extravagant form of the "Egotistical Sublime," a Spasmodic poseur, and the critical awareness of *Written in Emerson's Essays* is a variation on and extension of that of *Written in Butler's Sermons*: the effectualness of poetry ultimately depends on style, and no style can hope to succeed that imposes a mist or a thunderclap between the subject, however worthy, and the audience.

The stridency of the voice of *In Harmony with Nature*—with its name-calling rhetoric and extravagant exclamation marks— immediately alerts us to the poet's critical or deflationary intention; since the subject itself was one of the recurrent concerns of Romanticism, it is a fairly safe assumption that Romantic attitudes toward Nature will be the poet's critical focus. But he has worked it all out with extraordinary skill. First, he has imposed upon the poem's experience a thoroughly disagreeable dogmatic personality who disqualifies himself as an arbiter of the issue by virtue of his confrontal dogmatism. Second, the speaker's iron-bound ethical humanism is just as sentimental and unserviceable as his soft-headed naturalism, and together they would create a great fissure between man and his universe. Man is not adequately described by such evaluations as "sick of blood," "would fain adore," "hath need of rest," "would be mild, and with safe conscience blest"; and to call Nature "cruel," "stubborn," "fickle," and "unforgiving" is not only to be pathetically fallacious but also to ignore the vast field of animation that Nature and man in fact share.

Third, the speaker's vocal stridency serves as an ironic gloss on his humanist manifesto, suggesting that the calm strength he lacks is the very thing he might have learned from Nature. Finally, the competition with Nature that he prescribes for man bespeaks a gross misunderstanding both of the role Nature has historically played in men's lives and of the true meaning of "harmony."

Such dramatic debunking of one point of view does not, however, imply the poet's endorsement of its opposite. Rather, it serves as a stunning illustration of the profound complexity with which the whole subject is fraught; it is critical of analogously assertive and sentimental points of view. Arnold felt that the moderns, especially the Romantics, had wandered from the sanity of the ancients on this crucial issue, and he would, in the future, allow himself to be instructed in the matter by Spinoza, who had instructed Goethe;[17] but in *In Harmony with Nature* he chose only to create a critical caution against this aspect of the chaos to which Romantic Modernism had shown itself deeply susceptible.

What Arnold accomplished in these five sonnets is, then, truly astounding. Using a modest but difficult form that was deeply woven into the fabric of English poetry and had undergone a particularly brilliant renewal in the hands of two of the Romantic poets, he critiqued some of the most fundamental poetic issues on which even the great Romantic poets had seemed to wander uncertainly and on which their latter-day successors were foundering: the indispensability of a controlling form (*Shakespeare*); the importance of a poem's "action" or "subject" to poetry's highest purposes (*To the Duke of Wellington*); the danger inherent in an over-elaborate psychological emphasis that, even if the psychology itself is not fatally faulted, diverts the poet's eye from its primary object (*Written in Butler's Sermons*); the deceptive attraction of a strong talent for rhetoric and imagery that imposes between the subject of the poem and the reader the impediment of over-fanciful language (*Written in Butler's Sermons* and *Written in Emerson's Essays*); the poetic ineffectualness that results from a poet's imposition of his own personality, however intense, upon his subject, however primary (*Written in Emerson's Essays* and *In*

Harmony with Nature); the chaos that results if the poet's ideas on man in his universe are, despite their abundance, simply inadequate (*In Harmony with Nature*). We can, of course, see herein some of the main tendencies of Arnold's future mind, but the future must not be allowed to steal the present. To an unprecedented degree, Arnold found the uses of poetry in the uses of criticism; and if we can allow his specialized metaphors somewhat wider range, we will see him implanting in poetry, in a quite fresh and distinctive way, the modern critical consciousness.

The New Sirens

The New Sirens examines with exemplary imaginative freshness the myth of pleasure in the lives of men, especially but not exclusively of men on whom the idea of pleasure makes of necessity imperious demands—poets, for example. Obviously, such an examination, if it would add anything to the basic idea, involved highly significant philosophical and historical-cultural implications. *Ascesis* versus *voluptas* and many variations on self-restraint versus self-indulgence had provided poles between which Western civilization had moved, in both broad and narrow gauges, from pre-Socratic to post-Benthamite times— Epicurus vs. Plato, pagan Rome vs. medieval Rome, the Renaissance vs. the Reformation, post-Renaissance naturalism vs. post-Renaissance supernaturalism. The archetypal contention of the two in the unconsciously evolving fabric of culture had just been dramatically confirmed by the simultaneous rise in the second half of the eighteenth century of Wesley's gospel of *ascesis* and Bentham's gospel of *voluptas*. And while the metaphors of *The New Sirens* are admittedly honed in a somewhat severer way through the characters of the *dramatis personae*, including especially the character, frame of reference, and psychic movement of the speaker, these larger reverberations are drawn into the poem's specifically aesthetic fabric by its reminders that the old sirens drew men to destruction while the new sirens, less gross but not less inimical, draw them to the death-in-life of spiritual atrophy. Still, even while one recognizes the philosophical and cultural sophistication that Arnold brought to *The New Sirens*, one can recognize, too, that it is an experiential rather than a philosophical poem, that thought has been subordinated to personality, and that the imaginative difficulty Arnold had in composing the poem, like our imaginative difficulty in understanding it, stems from his very effort to avoid discursiveness and to make imagination the master of thought.

The New Sirens has a fascinating extra-textual history as well as a textual history of essentially extra-textual significance, and this is important to a consideration of what actually happens in the poem's language because it may predispose the reader on such vital questions as the poem's "meaning" and comprehensibility (i.e., its ultimate poetic finish). First, we know that Arnold tinkered with the text of the poem from its initial composition in the late 1840s until he prepared the Library Edition of his poems for publication in 1885 and that he told Clough [in March 1849?], "I have doctored it so much and looked at it so long that I am now powerless respecting it."[18] And yet, the revisions that we know about, though certainly significant, are relatively insubstantial, mostly alterations of individual words and a few phrases rather than any large reconceptualization. So even though he accepted Clough's characterization of it as "a mumble,"[19] Arnold apparently meant that he felt that he had mumbled his precise intention in his use of specific words and phrases, though by the test of published revisions even they are not particularly numerous. Second, that he provided for Clough such an elaborate prose outline of the poem's continuity[20] suggests that behind his diffidence regarding his workmanship there remained a steady faith in the poem's essential rightness and value. But the existence of this prose sketch has a profounder literary significance. In it, Arnold assumes the role of reader of his poem, and that seems to give the document an authority it does not in fact have: having assumed a role analogous to that of any other reader, his reading is subject to the same detached scrutiny to which other readings are customarily subjected. One might fairly expect to find readings of the poem that one would consider superior to Arnold's reading. What Arnold's sketch provides that has great if relative value is not a reading of the poem, but a *preparation* for a reading of it—implicit testimony that the progress of aesthetic civilization (more narrowly, "the progress of poesy") is the field in which the poem is functioning; that the ancients and the moderns (more narrowly, the Classical writers and the Romantics) are the enclosing epochal metaphors; that the transmogrification of myth is one of the chief conceptual concerns of the poem (more narrowly, that myth is just as imperative among the moderns as among the ancients); that, despite the epic analogies suggested by both the subject and the epochal frame, the poem is a dramatic lyric in which everything that happens takes place in a registering consciousness, the narrative movement being a movement of that consciousness (more broadly, that arche-typal myth perpetually re-enacts itself, not only in cultural history, but in the individual consciousness attuned to history). These are very large preparations indeed, and to the degree that Arnold privately translated his own metaphors into such conceptual terms, they were enough to make a persistent, ambitious, but essentially modest young poet very uneasy. Third, Arnold wrote to George Smith of Smith, Elder about the poem [in September 1875?], "I don't thoroughly under-stand it myself, but I believe it is very fine and Rossetti and his school say it is the best thing I ever wrote."[21] This is quite different from Arnold's initial tendency to apologize for the poem, and perhaps it represents an upsurge of that original faith in its quality that he had originally found it impossible to explain. Fourth, he reprinted the poem in *Macmillan's Magazine* in December 1876. This was probably an act of homage to George Sand, who had died earlier that year and for whose novels Arnold had both a youthful and a life-long enthusiasm. This suggests that he still thought it "very fine" and worthy of an object of such deep imaginative devotion. Finally, Arnold wrote to C.E. Swinerton on January 24, 1885, as follows: "the mythological Sirens were . . . beautiful and charming creatures, whose charm and song allured men to their ruin. The idea of the poem is to consider as their successors Beauty and Pleasure as they meet in actual life, and distract us from spiritual Beauty, though in themselves transitory and unsatisfying."[22]

Setting aside differing interpretations of its details, this extraordinary extra-textual history seems to confirm that *The New Sirens* is one of the truly focal poems in the Arnold canon. Thus any inclination to treat it lightly or to draw strength from Arnold's remarks for the view that it is not quite comprehensible and hence in some degree negligible would be a serious critical error. It is a poem that, despite its roots in Classical subject matter, is not quite Classical. It is from the pen of a young poet who had consistently built his poetic canon on a critical consciousness that pointed to the inadequacy of the Romantic apprehension of life and hence of the Romantic view of literature. In *The New Sirens*, too, there is a serious critiquing of the Romantic predilection for a "life of Sensation," for a sensuous Beauty and a sensuous Pleasure that, even if they do not directly collide with the principle of "spiritual Beauty," enervate the spirit's will to grapple with the latter's austerities. But the narrative consciousness of *The New Sirens* does not complete a Classical curve: he reaches an insight, a recognition which he does not vent in action. The lamentation which he utters first in ll. 113–114—"Pluck, pluck cypress, O pale maidens,/Dusk the hall with yew!"—is repeated twice in intensified fashion in the final stanza (ll. 269–270, 275–276), and this is as far as he can carry it. Thus the critic of Romanticism, its critical measurer, himself drifts in the direction of Romanticism, and his critical consciousness is not enough to correct his imaginative tendency. Down the road a few years are *The Scholar-Gipsy* and *Empedocles on Etna*, the mirrors in which the poet will see his face, but he does not quite see it in *The New Sirens* because he has not yet undergone at its excruciating depth the discomfort that will make it necessary for him to see it. Moreover, he has not yet fully developed that representative, metaphoric modern consciousness that, though not literally himself, is so all-absorbing that it absorbs himself. It has begun to emerge, but it is not yet so fully drawn and so compelling that it demands that, if he would be authentic, he too must identify with it. But Arnold did make two symbolic gestures that were prophetic: he maintained his faith in the poem at one level and his uneasiness regarding it at another, and he dropped it from his canon for a long period of years, restoring it long after his crisis had passed and at the urging of another important poet, Rossetti. Thus the pattern of his response to *Empedocles on Etna* is already evident, though the high intensity associated with the later act is absent.

None of this is meant to suggest that *The New Sirens* is not a worthy poem or that the poet failed to accomplish his purpose in making the poetic idea that he adopted more adequate than he had found it in the poetry of his Romantic predecessors and contemporaries. On the contrary, Arnold's art shows great subtlety and finesse, and his critical consciousness refines and enlarges its subject matter quite admirably. The poem has a distinct symbolist character akin to that which had increasingly marked the poetry of Tennyson, and this is far more important than the isolated verbal echoes from Tennyson that readers customarily identify. Its movement is a musical movement, appropriately impeded by its trochaic rhythms and unusual enough to invite the reader to acquire the taste necessary for its full enjoyment. Its form is that of a lyrical ballad, lyrical intensity subsumed to action, and the final pentameter of each stanza not only expands the lyrical feeling but also reminds us of the poem's origins in the secondary or highly self-conscious literary ballad. Hence, though it is in no literal sense *like* Tennyson's *Recollections of the Arabian Nights, The Lady of Shalott*, and the *Mariana* poems, it is attempting to achieve its poetic purpose in a manner analogous to the manner in which they try to achieve theirs. While the critical consciousness of the poem is evident in its thought-linkages, that consciousness works its way through a dense fabric of allusive images that lead the reader's reflections in many suggestive but inconclusive directions and that characteristically leave open the question as to whether the image is primarily in the thought or the thought primarily in the image. The *persona* of the poem is so characterized as to prevent him from rough-hewing the critical issue even in the face of his clear critical insights. The poem's final refusal of closure, its failure to convert clear recognition into clear resolution, suspends thought in a very special experience of thought and demotes theme in favor of, at least metaphorically, an inexhaustible imaginative contemplativeness. So while *The New Sirens*, like *Empedocles on Etna*, was unsatisfactory by the criterion of Classical high seriousness to which Arnold would ultimately and ardently subscribe, it is a well-wrought poem in the mainstream of Romantic Modernism.

The poetic idea at the center of *The New Sirens*—the relative calls on human allegiance by thought, with its austere spiritual implications, and feeling, with its emphasis on sensuous delight however refined—is given expanded adequacy in several ways. One is the fabric of allusion by which such figures as the saint of Christian moral insight (Christ, ll. 21–22) and the saint of pagan moral action (Ulysses, ll. 43–44) are drawn into the poem's frame of reference. But the two most important ways are elaborately experiential rather than conceptual. The abstract merits of the arguments take on quite a different character when subjected to such realities of life in this world as age, mutability, decay. The god-like implacability of youth must inevitably yield to the laws of mortality, and any over-prolonged defiance of that fact simply leads to grotesque behavior and profound depression of spirit. Further, the youth cult in which the pleasure principle is essentially centered is prone to subtle self-deceptions: its adherents see its newest form as different in kind from the primitive grossness of its older aspect when in fact it is simply a subtler, more civilized form of the same abandonment of man's spiritual vocation (the new sirens versus the old); they tout it as a positive philosophy when in fact it is an *ad hoc* decision of those too soon despairing of the slow progress of "a purer fire" (l. 140 in the context of ll. 139–146); they assert their unequivocal allegiance to this life style when in fact it is an elaborate rationalization (ll. 73–88) punctuated with haunting reminders ("Still they gall you, the long hours,/And the hungry thought that must be fed!" [ll. 129–130]) of the alternative reality of their natures. Once they become locked in to their life style, through doctrinaire defensiveness and continued habit, they succumb to the most fatal self-deception of all—that there is no turning back:

> O, loose hands, and let it be!
> Proudly, like a king bewailing,
> O, let fall one tear, and set us free!

> (ll. 224–226)

This extraordinarily modern deepening of the issue to the center of personality is in turn glossed by the failure of the speaker, the agent of these insights, to himself undergo the full conversion that the insights would seem to dictate. This is an implicit recognition that he perceives what is far easier to say than to do and that the issue at the heart of the poem is so archetypal because it constitutes such a truly torturous and perennial human dilemma. It is all very well to analyze, the poem suggests, but the leap from analysis to action is a matter of far greater magnitude. Thus, Arnold's most Romantic poem to date both critiques the Romantic emphasis on feeling and recognizes the imperious demands it makes on the imaginative spirit of man.

The Forsaken Merman

In its form, *The Forsaken Merman* seems to occupy the precise breaking-point between a dramatic lyric and a lyrical drama, and the reader's decision as to whether the action (*imitation*) or the lyricism (*expressiveness*) is more primary to the poem's imaginative disclosure will determine in which of those two formal directions he will be inclined to move it. Though the issue is subtle, it is by no means trivial since, like the issue of whether Sohrab or Rustum is the protagonist of Arnold's Persian poem, it must significantly affect one's appraisal of the character of the poem and the precise dimensions of its success. If the reader opts for a predominant lyricism, then his critical emphases should probably be on the poem's fairy-tale feature, its tonality, the marvelous way in which the images are washed by vocal approximations of the sounds of wind and wave, and the note of sadness that the merman's lament induces as the poem's primary affect. If he chooses to place primary emphasis on the poem's action or plot, on the other hand, the fairy-tale is converted into parable, the stylistic refinements, while still admirable in themselves, are judged to a larger degree by the critical ends they serve, and the note of sadness, if it remains intact, becomes anchored in a different place, namely, in the failure of a character or characters to cope with some basic demand of the story line or myth.

The poetic scope of *The Forsaken Merman* is considerably expanded—deepened and made more adequate as a poetic experience—by the perception that it is primarily a plot poem. Then Margaret's desertion of the merman and their brood takes on greater symbolic significance, the role of the reader as critical arbiter of the poem's complete action becomes better defined and strengthened, and the poem's expressiveness, centered entirely in the merman, is subjected to the poem's total parable of meaning and not left fluttering as an emotional thing in itself.

Some of its more conspicuous metaphors establish the field of awareness in which the poetic idea of *The Forsaken Merman* is functioning. The mermanization of Margaret and the humanization of the merman suggest that at some moment in mythical time man and nature enjoyed a fertile union and poses the question as to what caused their severance. That the merman is the speaker represents a reversal of the usual construct—nature's attitude toward man rather than man's attitude toward nature—and thereby returns the question, as usually posed, to solution; there is a wry irony in the merman's perception that it is man rather than nature who has been "cruel" (ll. 140–143). In an earlier variation on this song of the merman (nature's hymnal), "cruel" had been "faithless" (ll. 120–123); the irony of this cuts deeper than wryness when one considers that it is a fearful faith that has made Margaret faithless—fear of eternal damnation if she fails to make her Easter duties in a church-centered civilization that puts prayer and work foremost among its values. The inevitable answer to the question posed, then—an answer that the merman does not consciously recognize but unconsciously and primitivistically insinuates through story and image—is that as man began to develop an ascetic supernaturalism, he began also to sacrifice to it a sensuous naturalism; that the more he sophisticated his civilization, including especially his religion, the more he became fixated on the imperious system itself and thereby alienated from his primitive origins. Severed at the level of self-conscious conviction and ritual, perhaps, but not freed from the recurrent importunities of an archetypal racial memory, the misunderstood reminiscences of the collective unconscious that gropes in the darkness of man's civilized state toward linkages that, though rejected and almost forgotten, yet haunt him with an inarticulate myth of a return to some lost Edenic past. Perhaps there is some residue here of that premature eighteenth-century Romantic cult of the noble savage, but the emphasis is quite different and much more ingratiating. It is, rather, a tentative exploration through fable of that pervasive and perennial intimation of man, typically released by contact with nature in her benignest aspects (e.g., ll. 125–135) and often untenably sentimentalized, that man is somehow divided against himself because he has forsaken, in his obsession with an ever-less-satisfying civilization, the life-giving natural waters by which his roots were initially nourished.

This, of course, is not what the merman *says*; it is rather what a reader might postulate as a reasonable conceptual translation of the much more exploratory and sensuous groping after the meaning of the event projected by the merman's voice, images, and short-ranged, laboring consciousness; the counterpoint thus released between two "readings" of the event—ours and the merman's, both authentic and yet almost ontologically separated from each other—is the most exciting imaginative intuition generating the poem's idiosyncratic distinctiveness. Thus Arnold's choice of the merman as speaker is ironic, finally, at that subtle edge at which irony threatens to spill over into solemnity, just as the ontological issue is both posited and undercut: in his primitive way, the merman has elusive insights that customarily escape us, and it is possible that his nature and ours are connected at some forgotten subterranean level. As he attempts to critique this august personal event, an event that has "left lonely for ever/The kings of the sea" (ll. 142–143, var. 122–123), the merman expresses many of the typical responses of the deserted lover who still loves the lady who has enshrined herself in an alien world: this is the last time he will plead with her; she will be sorry; she is faithless and cruel; she should return, if not for his sake, then for the children's; she has rewarded the generosity of his act with the coldness of her own; in the future, he may at least come with the children and observe her from a fair distance. Thus "Nature never did betray/The heart that loved her. . . ."[23]

But the merman's more poetic intuitions, intuitions which he does not understand but toward which he makes abundant verbal gestures, are that the event with which he is attempting to cope exceeds the here and now and subsists ultimately in the all-encompassing metaphors of time and space. Thus the "Now . . . Now . . . Now . . . Now" of ll. 2–6 plays against the reiterated question, "When did music come this way?/Children dear, was it yesterday?/Children dear, was it yesterday?" (ll. 46–48), with its repetitions in ll. 30 and 63, insinuating into the reader's awareness the awesome and evasive metaphor of time, time as one of Carlyle's "modes of consciousness" and one of Einstein's "stubborn illusions." Space has an immediately visual aspect lacking to time, and the merman makes the transition to the one from the other through his sense of the contrast between the restless, dynamic, ever-moving world of the sea and the encased, static, "sealed" world of the town. His natural world has almost limitless depth ("Down, down, down!/Down to the depths of the sea!" [ll. 85–86]) and a circumference as large as the globe; the two metaphors of endless time and limitless space merge in the image of the whales—"Where great whales come sailing by,/Sail and sail, with unshut eye,/Round the world for ever and aye" (ll. 43–45). The world of the town, on the other hand, is an austerely restricted space— "narrow paved streets," "little grey church," "small leaded panes" (ll. 57, 70, 71, 75)—with little more depth than the depth of its "graves" (l. 74). From Margaret's perspective, it is a joyous world, busy with people, children at play, full of religion's promises, flushed with "the blessed light of the sun" (ll. 89–93); but the sun inevitably goes down, the activity stops, and alternative memories of time and space invade her consciousness with a suffusive melancholy. The merman does not bring these poetic intuitions to term in any conclusive generalization, of course, and neither should we. We should wonder rather than resolve, "muse on, never know," as Years says in Hardy's *The Dynasts*; this suspends the largest poetic idea

probed by the poem in delicate, primitive, imaginative rumi-
nation rather than imprisoning it in one of civilized man's
highly developed but restrictive ideological constructs.

Thus *The Forsaken Merman* is one of Arnold's most accomplished critiques of Romantic inadequacy: it demonstrates by
example that Romantic expressiveness can be fully enjoyed
without the sacrifice to it of Classical action; and it measures
Romantic ideas of man's relationship to Nature by returning
the more hackneyed versions of those ideas to poetic solution
and reconstructing the basic questions involved in a new,
inexhaustibly probing, symbolistically evocative way.

In Utrumque Paratus

As events would have it, *In Utrumque Paratus* supplies a fulcrum
for the century. Even if, as has been demonstrated, [24] Arnold
was drawing upon his reading in Plotinus for his conceptual
metaphors of the descent and ascent of man (man as ultimately
the expression of a divine idea or man, with his distinguishing
consciousness, as the apex result of a wholly naturalistic process), he was using the thoughts of the Neoplatonic philosopher
to give more encompassing scope to the issue of man in his
relation to his universe. The hieratic view—man as an ema-
nation from the Fountain of Deity and destined to reascend
there (ll. 1–14)—had, with Judeo-Christian modifications of
imagery, been acculturated in the contemporary poetic mind
principally by Wordsworth, with whom such lofty poetic ideas
were closely associated. The opposite view, which, fed by the
scepticism inherent in an increasingly rationalistic age and by
the uniformitarian tendencies of multiple theories of evolution,
was undergoing rapid development in the 1840s and 1850s,
would reach its imaginative climax in the new century in the
poetry of Thomas Hardy, especially in *The Dynasts*, of which
Arnold's poem seems uncannily prescient:

> But, if the wild unfathered mass no birth
>   In divine seats hath known;
> In the blank, echoing solitude if Earth,

Rocking her obscure body to and fro,
Ceases not from all time to heave and groan,
Unfruitful oft, and at her happiest throe
   Forms, what she forms, alone. . . .

(ll. 22–28)

Crucially Hardyan too is the emergence in man of a distinguishing consciousness ("O seeming sole to awake, thy sun-bathed head/Piercing the solemn cloud/Round thy still dreaming brother-world outspread!" [ll. 29–31]). And the sophistication of this consciousness into a sort of perceptual self-decreation ("Yet doth thine inmost soul with yearning teem./ —Oh, what a spasm shakes the dreamer's heart!/'*I, too, but seem.*'" [ll. 40–42]) strikes one of the central notes that the reader will hear in the voice of that exacerbated modern psyche Hardy places at the center of his imaginative world.

    Thus we can safely say that *In Utrumque Paratus* considerably enlarges the field in which the issue of the origins and destinies of man is to be contemplated and, through that enlargement, makes of it a more adequate poetic idea. It subjects a hieratic Romanticism (say, that of Wordsworth) to a more circumspect Classicism (say, that of Plotinus) and emerges with a balancing and prescient Modernism (say, that of Hardy). But Arnold's poem has its own consciousness and its own voice, and the explicit judgment that the speaker makes focuses on yet another penetrating idea: the ethical, psychological, and behavioral implications of the notions one holds about one's place in the universe. As the hieratic view induces psychological passivity ("Thin, thin the pleasant human noises grow,/And faint the city gleams" [ll. 15–16]), the secular view induces psychological aggression ("Who hath a monarch's hath no brother's part" [l. 39]). The egotism of an exclusive secular humanism can become even more conspicuous than the egotism of an exclusive supernaturalism. It would be profoundly ironic if an ebullient secular humanism, which also promises its full share of human distresses for the future, should diminish or destroy man's feelings of genuine fellowship with his secular universe.

    The poetic character of *In Utrumque Paratus* is determined by the peculiarities of its speaker rather than by its naked thoughts. Stripped of his generative personality, those thoughts collapse into a customary contrast between supernaturalistic and naturalistic perspectives on man and his universe, with the usual prudent caution that, since we cannot be sure, we should be circumspect ("prepared for both possibilities"). But the poem is no ordinary reflection of a rather ordinary point of view because the speaker, like the speaker in Donne's *Holy Sonnet VII* ("At the round earth's imagined corners") or in Hopkins's *The Windhover*, is an extraordinary personality capable of both ecstatic and terror-stricken responses to perceptual reality and of giving to his perceptual responses a verbal reality that is intense and richly textured. Like many of Arnold's poems, *In Utrumque Paratus* is a vocalization of consciousness, a projection into the peculiarities of language of a highly individuated personality who speaks in a certain way because that is our only key to the depth and authenticity of his thoughts, feelings, and sense of self.

Resignation

The text of *Resignation* simply does not sustain the customary view that the poem is an explicit statement of Arnold's own views of the human condition or of the exemplary role of the poet in human life. Moreover, to see it as a direct rebuttal of Wordsworthianism is to deny the greater part of its masterful imaginative qualities. Its formalistic ties with *Tintern Abbey* are clear enough.[25] But its critical gloss on Wordsworth's philosophy is positioned at such an oblique angle by being rooted in the solipsisms of an imaginary character that it works by suggestion, not confrontation, by experience rather than abstraction; the chief analogy it sustains is that, as this speaker's views on Nature, human life, and poetry are very personal and relative, so are Wordsworth's.

Resignation is a discourse under the guise of a conversation, and this is one index to the character of the speaker, a formal expression of his temperament and personal need. Another is the *exemplum* upon which the discourse is constructed: "*To die be given us, or attain!/Fierce work it were, to do again*" (ll. 1–2). It

is a motto of very curious import as to both manner and meaning. Tonally, it could hardly be more pompous and rhetorically overbearing as the beginning of a conversation poem; substantively, it says that to one who has competed and failed, a new beginning is virtually unthinkable. It dichotomizes life somewhat fiercely, and its tropes are rather Faustian—"*To die . . . or attain!*" Coming so soon after the subtitle of the poem, "To Fausta," this releases in the reader's critical imagination the possibility that the speaker is a failed Faust speaking to a troubled Fausta, a Faust full of "doubts" and "discouragements" (Preface of 1853) attempting to translate his own experience of life as an unsuccessful over-reacher into the perspectives of a listener who occupies a place much nearer than his to the human norm. There is nothing here that would justify taking a formal allegorical view of the poem, but the Faust motif does have the effect of placing the speaker in a modern parabolic field of very large scope and of alerting us to be critically scrupulous in appraising what he says. Moreover, the Faust motif is sustained at an invasive rather than a Titanic level: the speaker is not finally to be measured against Marlowe's protagonist or Goethe's, but to be seen as the persistent presence of one temperamental metaphor of the age, archetypal at the dismantled distance at which Hardy would use his mythic archetypes. It surfaces non-insistently in such leitmotifs as the speaker's categorical views of human nature, his perception of the gipsies as essentially clods, his myth of the poet as gifted beyond all other men, superior even to the hero and analogous only with God, and his air of benign patronage toward his listener.

At the center of the speaker's discourse are the sequences on the character of the poet, and they present that character under three different aspects—the poet as *vates* (ll. 144–169), the poet as pastoralist (ll. 170–198), and the poet as passionless anatomist of the passions, leading to an analogy between the poet and God (ll. 231–260). These are very well said, and it is clearly the poet's intention to make them ingratiating. The sequence on the poet as pastoralist is especially taking. But there is just as clearly a latent intention that undercuts each sequence even while it builds, revealing a critical flaw in the

speaker's apprehension that contains an echo of the mythical Faust and in a degree dehumanizes him. In the vatic sequence, his detachment is too aloof. Though he may have done much—

> Though he move mountains, though his day
> Be passed on the proud heights of sway,
> Though he hath loosed a thousand chains,
> Though he hath borne immortal pains,
> Action and suffering though he know
>
> (ll. 148–152)

—his proper "station" is "high" above the crowd from which he can look down without saying to himself "*I am alone*" (ll. 164, 169). The echo of Faust's contemptuous serviceability is unmistakable, and the haughtiness that has been stripped from the exposition is still residual in the imagery and the dramatic gesture. In the pastoral sequence, there is a reminiscence of Faust's alliance with a higher Destiny and his defiance of the shocks the ordinary flesh is heir to—"if not in vain/Fate gave, what chance shall not control" (ll. 196–197)—and his over-pathetic celebration of a pastoral world finally climaxes in dehumanized images—

> That life, whose dumb wish is not missed
> If birth proceeds, if things subsist;
> The life of plants, and stones, and rain,
> The life he craves—. . . .
>
> (ll. 193–196)

Thus the speaker's pastoralism sins on both sides—from exaggerated tenderness and exaggerated hardness. In the final sequence—that of the passionless anatomist of human passion who, by a special gift, knows the most elusive things in a way that others do not and who can thus *a priori* forego human longing for love and power—echoes of the mythic Faust almost overwhelm us. This sequence reaches its apogee in a theological perspective from which the moral imperative of *homo agonistes* has been wholly eliminated:

> in His eye,
> To whom each moment in its race,
> Crowd as we will its neutral space,
> Is but a quiet watershed
> Whence, equally, the seas of life and death are fed.
>
> (ll. 256–260)

The speaker, having disclaimed for himself the role of poet (ll. 245–246), is not a Faust-figure even at the parabolic distance posited here, but he is a *persona*, a spokesman for the subliminal Faustianism that has invaded the culture which he represents.

To the degree that one accepts the critical perspectives developed here, *Resignation* becomes quite a different poetic experience from that customarily described by the commentators, and Arnold becomes quite a different poet. Without the sacrifice of any of their idiomatic idiosyncrasy, both the poem and the poet are seen to be moving successfully in that atmosphere of aesthetic reorientation which marked the generation of Tennyson and Browning and which led directly, through the turning which Hardy ultimately gave it, to what is called modern poetry. *Resignation* is primarily a poem of experience, not of argument; though its idea content is exceedingly high, thought has been made subordinate to the greater authority of imaginative intuition. Whatever relationship the speaker and his subdued but sufficient collocutor may originally have had to literal historical fact (Matthew Arnold and his sister Jane, for example), that relationship has been converted from history to myth and enabled to function imaginatively in a manner that is different in kind from whatever interpretive construction one may put upon the literal historical fact. Through a process usually called imaginative impersonation (which is really personification stripped of the imperiousness of abstraction and dressed in the illusion or fiction of approximate realism), the characters have become metaphors, generic points to which certain typical, eternally repetitive patterns of the human plot (situations, responses) can be seen to draw and by which they can be to some degree illuminated. And whatever construction one may put on the relationship of *Resignation* to *Tintern Abbey*, it is obviously not critically useful to imprison Arnold's poem in Wordsworth's in a more graceful manifestation of the same sort of critical literalism. The continuity of art—for example, the making of literature out of literature—is an endlessly fascinating object of study, but he would be a poor poet for whom literary rootedness became more primary than literary rebellion, and he would be a poor critic who confused a literary point of departure with a literary destination. Although it is reasonable to say that *Resignation* critiques *Tintern Abbey* in certain explicit formalistic ways and in certain obliquely implicit substantive ways, Arnold's poem ultimately draws much closer to poetic experiences like those contained in Browning's *Cleon* and *Bishop Blougram's Apology* than to that of *Tintern Abbey*. At its center is a distressed human psyche for whom a rather imperious intellectual *persona* is presumably attempting, with some ambiguous degree of empathetic sincerity, to provide guidance. As it turns out, however, we discover much more about the speaker's problem than about the listener's, the speaker's discourse gradually evolving as an *apologia pro vita sua*. Moreover, Arnold's speaker shares with Browning's the peculiarities of a cultural role that is subtly insinuated into his discourse, as in theirs, through images and rhetorical gestures. As Cleon is a remnant of the Golden Age of Greece and Blougram is a remnant of the Great Age of Faith, so the speaker in *Resignation* is a dismantled Faust and, as such, a remnant of the Titanic Age of Romanticism. All three of them work among the broken spars of eras that, though still magnificently visible, are past; although the stoical "resignation" of Arnold's title is the psychological, intellectual, and moral condition to which each must aspire if he would find peace, none is in fact quite resigned. There is something rather sad about all of them, and in Arnold's poem sadness is a large part of the consciousness of the piece. All the energy has gone out of this latter-day Romantic Faust, and he can hardly do more than "add zest to [his] melancholy or grace to [his] dreams";[26] and his view of the poet is not one to "*animate* and *ennoble*" because the mind that generates it is profoundly discouraged by a deeply troubling sense of "The something that infects the world" (l. 278).

Faded Leaves

The strict autobiographical reading of *Faded Leaves* very quickly
succumbs to the realization that the five short monodramas
that make up the sequence of dramatic lyrics project a highly
generalized profile of a young man suffering the tortures of
unrequited romantic love. His is a very different personality
from that of the speaker-protagonist of the *Switzerland* poems—
less volatile, less self-destructive, subject to a narrower gauge
of attitudinal and emotional swings—but he is not effaced
thereby, only differentiated. The theory, based on very fragmentary and largely speculative external evidence, that these
poems capture a specific period of interruption in Arnold's
courtship of Frances Lucy Wightman, his future wife, has a
vivid interest for students of his life; but that it is essentially a
non-critical interest is strongly supported by the fact that the
poems are strengthened rather than diminished as poetic
experiences if the theory is totally ignored.[27] The poems move
the protagonist from deep frustration over the "belov'd's"
negligent inattentiveness in the intensely dramatic first poem,
The River, to a full consciousness of the hopelessness of the
situation in the last, *Longing*;[28] what they dramatize as a whole
are the representative strategies by which he attempts to cope
with the unrequitedness of his love. In *Too Late*, he indicts the
shallow insincerity by which he was entrapped: "—Thy heart
is mine! —*True, true! ah, true!/*—Then, love, thy hand! —*Ah
no! adieu!*" (ll. 7–8). In *Separation*, he disdains the faded leaves
of memory, "the steadfast commandment of Nature" (l. 5), and
declares his preference for wrenching the fate that all humans
must suffer by having either eternally self-renewing pain with
eternally self-renewing memory or no pain at all at the cost of
no memory at all. This, of course, is a highly Romantic gesture
of his consciousness, equating eternal passion with eternal pain,
and constitutes a gross simplification both of his own organic
humanness and of the role of time in human development. *On
the Rhine* is the *Wanderjahre* panel, in which the Romantic seeks
in the sublimer aspects of Nature a counterpoise to his "turbulent youthful glow," a "joy . . . in their calm" (ll. 24–25). He

has found his "effort to forget" (l. 1) as vain as "the agony of grief" (l. 6); having admitted that an "iron knot" of fate separates them as well as that she does not love him (ll. 7–9), he explores the pleasures of Romantic melancholy. What he is doing is both suffusing his consciousness with tender memories of her and wishing his youth away in a euphoria of sublimated responses to scenes of Nature that suggest the joy of an ageless age that has passed beyond the turbulence of youth. But he is also "crossing himself," in Samuel Butler's trope, getting himself out of himself and something else into him, and it is, for all of its Romantic ambiguity, a positive movement toward recovery. There is a witty conceit at the heart of *Longing*, and this completes the poem's narrative-emotional curve. The speaker finally admits that he has long been re-playing a goddess-myth that has had no truth in reality—that this imaginary angelic "messenger from radiant climes" (l. 6) has never in fact come to him at all (l. 9) and that, if she has been only so kind to others as to him, she can hardly be said to have "smile[d] on [her] new world" (ll. 7–8). With a devilish irony, he then pleads with her to

> Come now, and let me dream it truth;
> And part my hair, and kiss my brow,
> And say: *My love! why sufferest thou?*
>
> (ll. 10–12)

It is the cleansing gesture: though such a ritualistic visit might be the fulfilment of a romantic fantasy, it would be a Romantic travesty of her true character, and his emphatic recognition that this is a just if bitter insight frees him of the incubus of a prolonged fantasy or soul-sick imagining. It is in that sense that her coming to him in his dreams enables him to "be well again!" and that the night can be said to "more than pay/The hopeless longing of the day" (ll. 1–4, 13–16).

It becomes virtually impossible, then, to equate what actually emerges from a careful reading of the texts of the five lyrics that make up the dramatic narrative entitled *Faded Leaves* with the temporary interruption of Arnold's eventually successful courtship of Frances Lucy Wightman. We have no hard facts connected with the presumed historical event, only bits of hearsay propagated by tradition, and they are not enough to persuade any mind not already wholly disposed to accept them literally and to exaggerate their evidential significance monumentally. But we do have the five poems, and they create a specific dramatic narrative. They trace through five lyric phases or positionings the progress of a mildly self-torturing Romantic from a crisis of the heart brought on by emotional enslavement to a worldly coquette to at least the threshold of purgation and self-redemption. Their basic method is monodramatic, and their speaker is an imaginary, metaphoric *persona*. The poems have their own subject or action, their own structure, their own diction and rhythm. It is the critic's task to submit those poetic clues to as uninhibited a scrutiny as possible and then to yield to the tale *they* tell, not to some tale that we borrow or imagine or impose vaguely and disrespectfully upon them. The one procedure at least shows serious critical intention; the other is mere gossip.

Switzerland

The closest thing we have to a canonical text of the *Switzerland* poems is the final arrangement that Arnold gave them in the 1877 edition of his poems: *Meeting, Parting, A Farewell, Isolation. To Marguerite, To Marguerite—Continued, Absence, The Terrace at Berne*. It is upon this order that a study of the aesthetic procedures working through them must be based.

The poems constitute a narrative curve of some ten years' span, and at the center of the curve is an action or mythic fiction. The crux of the action is a choice that the speaker makes—or rationalizes having made—between two ways of life, the ordinary life of romantic domesticity and a life of austere solitude dictated by an overwhelming sense of a special vocation. Thus the conflict with which he is faced is rooted deeply in the idiosyncrasies of his character, and what we are invited to watch is how this carefully individuated *persona* copes with this eccentric but still representative metaphor of human choice or action. The lineaments of an experimental mono-drama begin to emerge in the *Switzerland* poems, analogous to if not quite like Tennyson's *Maud*.

Meeting is a monodramatic prologue to the piece. It takes place entirely within the speaker's strange consciousness and ruptures explosively the lyric texture established in the first two quatrains. When inclined to make a usual, self-gratifying choice, he hears a "tremendous voice" "in tones of ire" (ll. 11, 10) counseling rejection of that choice. In the final quatrain, he addresses a plaintive cry to the "guiding Powers" asking that he be spared this special ordeal. *Meeting* is an odd little poem considered separately, so much characterization and dramatic foreshadowing being packed into its unpretentious quatrains, but the oddness seems justified by what it accom-plishes with such extraordinary succinctness. The voice that we hear is not that of a divided self in any ordinary, analytical-descriptive sense, but a torn psyche, like that in *Maud*, on the threshold of madness. He not only "hears voices," but feels his life wrenched by a contrarious destiny so strong that he cries out in anguished protest.

Parting is an extraordinarily impressive dramatic lyric, one of those heightened orchestrations of verbal gesture at which the nineteenth-century poets were so accomplished and of which Tennyson's *Maud* is the classic example. The full range of the speaker's voice is given exposure in counterpointing lyric exercises that reach from a soaring energy that threatens to spill into bombast to modulations so delicate that they almost dissolve into animated silence. These are the lyric metaphors of his troubled state, emotional extremes so profound that they seem to defy reconciliation and to foretell either a tragic or a shabby outcome of the event. In the one, we hear the refined but ordinary human longing for romantic fulfilment; in the other, the echoes of the Romantic over-reacher—the echoes of Faust, Manfred, even Empedocles at the height of his self-destructive exaltation—flood the speaker's images and tone. The pathos of the speaker's character and hence of his situation is picked up unmistakably in the final movement, in which he confesses his incapacity to rise out of his sundered situation:

> Forgive me! forgive me!
>   Ah, Marguerite, fain
> Would these arms reach to clasp thee!
>   But see! 'tis in vain.

(ll. 59–62)

But he then abruptly rationalizes his failed humanness by a retreat into cynicism: their pasts are so different, she has given her love to others, it is mere sentimentality to think that one heart ever understands another. In the end, still echoing Faust, Manfred, and Empedocles, he invokes the wild forces of Nature to transport him away from human fellowship to a lonely asylum on the "high mountain-platforms" (l. 85).

In *A Farewell*, the speaker's volatility enters a new phase. He has returned, some time having elapsed since the volcanic eruption of the preceding scene, and they have been reunited in a love-rendezvous, passionate though brief. Now it is the gradual waning of her passion for him that he must deal with, and he does so in a fascinatingly strategic way. First, he concedes that he is not really lovable, but he does so with a curious reservation—because "something in [his] depths doth glow/Too strange, too restless, too untamed" (ll. 19–20). Thus, even in a mood of calm, analytical reflection, he protects the Titanic emotional individuality that has both defeated him and provided his route of retreat from personal reconciliation and moral victory. Next, he undertakes a rather elaborate analysis of the conflict inherent in the masculine-feminine principle. Women, who are gentle, seek strength in the male as compensation for the "blind gusts" of emotion that sway them (ll. 21–28). He, too, who has been subject to such emotional extremes, has longed for "trenchant force,/And will like a dividing spear" (ll. 33–34). He has, plagued with an overplus of the feminine principle, "praised" an overplus of the masculine principle, though experience of the world has taught him that love, the feminine principle, is even rarer than energy, the masculine principle, though it is rare too. As he has "learnt" this "truth"—that the ultimate bent of the heart is "to be gentle, tranquil, true" (ll. 47–48)—"time and fate" will also teach it to her. That is their human denominator—what neither knew,

what both must learn. But then the speaker creates a magnificent myth of human despair: his new-found gentleness com-
bining with his recurrent impulse to flee into sanctuarial
isolation projects a vision of eternity in which these buffetings
of worldly stress are all ended and, having seen their "true
affinities of soul" (l. 56), they may "greet" each other "across
infinity" and "maintain" together "The hush among the shining
stars,/The calm upon the moonlit sea!" (ll. 79–80). It is ingratiatingly beautiful—and quite false, an exquisite dehumanization (desexualization), but a dehumanization nonetheless. The
speaker's longing for peace is so all-engaging and his capacity
(his force, his will) for human conversion so inadequate that
he substitutes for the distasteful struggle of moral self-renewal
a beautiful imagining in which de-creation of the old self and
re-creation of the self in an acceptable way are effected through
the miracle of sublimative myth. It is the wilfulness of dream
rather than the wilfulness of moral action; although the old
Faust metaphor has been somewhat celestialized, remnants of
the old Faust are still visible. There is the undertow of contempt
for "the mass" of people (ll. 57–58), the unredeemed persuasion
that he is essentially "good" and "generous" though he appears
to be full of "pride and guile" (ll. 62–64), the familiar tendency
to rationalize away the "still joys of such/As hand in hand face
earthly strife" (ll. 67–68), the essentially egotistical dependence
on "a vast regret" and "contrition sealed thrice sure" (ll. 71–72)
to redress the unredressed moral balance, and the disguised
but recurrent perversion of the medieval principle of *contemptus
mundi*:

> The gentleness too rudely hurled
> On *this wild earth of hate and fear*;
> The thirst for peace *a raving world*
> Would never let us satiate here.
>
> (ll. 85–88, emphasis added)

A Farewell, then, brings the highly concentrated dramatic process of the *Switzerland* poems to a new, apt, and necessary point.
The odd, prologogic overture of *Meeting* had established the
fundamental conflict in the character of the speaker, and the
counterpointing movements of *Parting* had reinforced this

conflict with great virtuosity through the most ambitious of lyrical dilations. *A Farewell* moves lyrical force to lyrical understanding and, in a much more subdued and reflective manner, lets us see into the strategic maneuvers of the protagonist's consciousness by watching him attempt to cope with a change in fortune that comes from outside that consciousness.

As *A Farewell* is the turning-point in the drama, so *Isolation. To Marguerite* and *To Marguerite—Continued* are its climax. The titles themselves tell us that they are two stages of a single movement, the one providing the dramatic continuity and the dramatic preparation, the other the full lyrical exposure that must be conceived of dramatically if one would allow the poet's text to maintain its own integrity.

The speaker in *Isolation. To Marguerite* is now finally alone. The affair with Marguerite is over, and he begins with a recapitulation of its demise. It was an unsuccessful experiment in constancy that foundered on the miscalculation that his constancy made her constant, whereas our feelings, being entirely controlled from within ("Self-swayed," l. 11), are not susceptible to the influence of another's feelings. Having accepted as compelling this highly Romantic theory of feeling, the speaker then instructs his own heart in the existential loneliness which is the inevitable outgrowth of such a theory. It is a superbly literary moment when the self-chastening speaker, as a gesture of his isolation, employs the utmost resource of the monodramatic form by directly lecturing his own heart and draws upon Keats's *Endymion* for the most esoteric and ambiguous of metaphors with which to condemn himself to total isolation: "'Thou hast been, shalt be, art, alone'" (l. 30). Then suddenly, as a sort of organic outgrowth of his Luna-Endymion analogy, a crucial disclosure breaks through: it is not isolation *per se* that he opts for, but freedom from mating—"Or, if not quite alone, yet they/Which touch thee are unmating things—" (ll. 31–32). It is wholly consistent with the speaker's character—his cumulative imagery throughout the drama, his wide tonal swings—but it is explosively ironic too: this sophisticated man of feeling is afraid of feeling; this supreme Romantic is in flight from the intricate involvements of human romance, from sexuality; the love which he needs and which he has applauded at an abstract level is the very love of which he is afraid and, being afraid, on which he refuses to take a chance. So, as is his wont, he decreates it. He is willing to share part of his life with men "happier" by having "*dreamed* two human hearts might blend" (ll. 36–38), which he sees as their unconscious strategy for breaking out of their isolation; but this asexual social compromise is made possible only by *his* superior insight into *their* self-serving delusion. Such men, "although not less/Alone than thou," he tells his isolated heart, simply do not know "their loneliness" (ll. 41–42). Though gracefully phrased, the tone of superiority is still in place, and the speaker's self-deception is complete.

It is out of this total and complex dramatic action that the poem's climactic aria of human anguish, *To Marguerite—Continued*, emerges, as far removed from the historical voice of Matthew Arnold as literature can make it. It is the authentic *cri de coeur* of an inauthentic but wholly barometric man—an emblematic Romantic, a diminished Faust, whose soul-distress is so poetically penetrating because, even while we identify with it, we know that it is in a large degree self-induced. So far, too, from being the simple statement of a simple but intense idea, it is the heightened upwelling into verbal gesture of the character, personal history, intellectual misgivings, physical isolation, imperious sexual longing, and self-defeating toughness of a deeply torn but imperial man—modern, certainly, but perennial too. As the text says, his is "a longing like despair" (l. 13). But even in his desperate state, he cannot look within—this modern Romantic man who professes such a doctrinaire belief in "Self-sway"—for some partial reason for his plight, but must externalize the cause in a vaguely conceived abstraction—"A God, a God [my] severance ruled" (l. 22). It is a matter of the very first literary importance in one's study of the development and precise character of Arnold as a poet to note the fundamental difference in imaginative affect that this dramatic framework gives to *To Marguerite—Continued*. It is not a lyrical "allegory of the state of [Matthew Arnold's] own mind," but the climax of a poetic action rooted in an intense, exacerbated modern psyche whose "story" we know and with whom we can feel a commensurately intense empathy. He is not a representation of the author, but a representation of ourselves, and we witness his terror as we would witness our own, with this difference—we have the illusion at least of understanding him more fully and more formally than we understand ourselves.

Absence and *The Terrace at Berne* gradually impose upon the turbulent center of the *Switzerland* poems the detaching distance of time. The former embodies a time still relatively close to the climactic event and reflects a dual mood—a willingness to forego the "Once-longed-for storms of love" (l. 14) but a reluctance to allow the warming glow of remembrance to dissolve into a forgotten past (ll. 17–20). The speaker feels that he is making some progress "towards the light" (l. 13), but he has the customary impatience with a transition stage between youth and maturity that seems to fill the soul with "petty dust" (l. 9) rather than with "A nobler train/Of wiser thoughts and feelings" (ll. 6–7). *The Terrace at Berne* lends to *Absence* the quality of a "false dawn"—the hope that things may, after all, turn out better than one had feared. In the final lyric, however, our earlier fears that the whole matter might end rather shabbily are realized in a mildly distasteful way. The speaker is ten years older, and we would expect him to be emotionally distanced from the whiplashes of the past. But there is a quality of negligence about his detachment and a tendency to adulterate memory with disquieting fantasies. Did Marguerite become coarse? perhaps a French prostitute? old, ugly, spiritless? It is, after all, only ten years later; if he measured her as he measures himself, such ugly projections would hardly be thinkable. It is almost as though he is invoking a therapy of distaste to rid himself of the true memory of her (and thus of himself at that period in his life), denying her even the "shadow durability" (l. 43) that was a Classical metaphor of immortality. As his earlier life had lacked social or horizontal organicism, so now he denies it the need for historical or perpendicular organicism:

> Like driftwood spars, which meet and pass
> Upon the boundless ocean-plain,
> So on the sea of life, alas!
> Man meets man—meets, and quits again.
>
> (ll. 45–48)

The simile, the tone, and the sentiment are alike chilling. We are left with the chastening recognition that the speaker's earlier Romanticism has been converted, not into a positive and stabilizing truth, but into a shrunken, self-protective, and sterile cynicism.

Seen in the manner suggested here, Arnold's *Switzerland* poems, despite their highly idiosyncratic distinctiveness, are drawn into the mainstream of nineteenth-century poetic innovation. Like Tennyson's *Maud*, they constitute a monodrama that moves the consciousness along a series of lyric voicings that gradually yield to the lyrics the character of an intensely registered dramatic piece. Like Tennyson and Browning, Arnold places at the center of this drama a hero so fallible that he brings to his lyrics the exacerbated stresses suggestive of a species of madness. He is, as he is in Tennyson and Browning, not a model, but a barometer of human experience in one of its representative manifestations; the reader is pressed into the co-creative role of scrutinizing his images, listening attentively to his vocal gestures, and evaluating the metaphoric significance of his actions in order to appraise, in a necessarily tentative way, the insights of which all these taken together are an approximative disclosure. It is highly instructive to remember that, though Arnold was moving ever more steadily toward a reaffirmation of a full faith in Aristotelian principles of poetic substance and poetic construction, these were no impediment whatsoever to his ability to absorb into his own poems the tensions and techniques that make of them, like those of Tennyson and Browning and Swinburne and Hardy, "the modern expression of a modern outlook."

A Ring of Perspectives on Human Life: Six Short Poems

That it is critically more profitable to see Arnold's dramatic lyrics as a "ring" of perspectives analogous to Browning's use of that ordering metaphor in *The Ring and the Book* is well illustrated by a small cluster of short lyrics that he composed, it is conjectured, in late 1849–early 1850: *Consolation, Human Life, Courage, Self-Dependence, Destiny, Youth's Agitations*, and *The*

World's Triumphs. One advantage of this way of looking at the poems is that we are relieved thereby of the need, essentially negative in its impact, to emphasize the contradictions even in juxtaposed poems, an emphasis that implies that the author was an incompetent thinker and did not know what he believed and leaves us with a frustrating sense of the poetic inconsequence of such inadequately mastered ideas. A vastly greater advantage is that, once the rigidifying authority of the author is stripped from the poems, they become fields of imaginative terrain in which our own role as active explorers is defined and we can enjoy being as watchful and acute as possible in attempting to identify the textual signals by which to discover the *poems'* discoveries. This in turn leads to the ultimate excitement of participation in a world in motion, imaginatively ordered but maintaining itself in solution, in which we can perceive the metaphoric equivalent of what our own world might be—a dramatic state of imaginative being in which form is not mere mechanism and feeling is not mere froth, but in which our imaginations lead us to the realization that we can be reconciled to a thousand difficulties without the profound discouragement of a paralyzing doubt.

The speaker in *Consolation* pronounces an *apologia pro tempore*, a self-detaching concept of the whole not unlike that of Pope's *Essay on Man*: "*Whatever is, is right.*" The tone is one of quiet equanimity, the illustrations catholic, the moral outlook even-handed and just. It is an old-world voice antipodal to the importunate urgencies of the contrary voices implied in the examples that it cites—the furious voices of religious sectarianism, belligerent partisanship, rebelliousness against fate, and the imprecatory extravagance of romantic love. Whether or not its attitudinal model is Sophocles, as one would suppose, its references to the Muses and to the Goddess of Destiny anchor it firmly in Classical perspective.

Human Life, on the other hand, projects a very different *persona* from that of *Consolation*; the difference is not so much in the speakers' philosophies, which are reconcilable, as in their temperaments. The speaker of *Human Life* gets no consolation from his philosophy. He evinces a nervous sort of petulance ("Ah!" "Ay!" "No!") that, even while it accepts the rule of "some unknown Powers" (l. 26), has an angry edge to it, as though the abstract "joys," "friends," and "homes" (ll. 28–30) that are yielded up intellectually are clung to emotionally. He both accepts fate and would play with fate: all our randomness is but fruitless self-deception since we do not chart our own course, and our claim to having consciously contributed to the fulfilment of the law of our own nature is really an idle boast. Moreover, he hovers precariously on the edge of a genuine moral dilemma:

> Let us not fret and fear to miss our aim,
> If some fair coast have lured us to make stay,
> Or some friend hailed us to keep company.
>
> (ll. 10–12)

Deploying in his allusion the example of Aeneas, he suggests that we may use our predestined condition as an excuse for self-indulgence. Though the speaker confronts this notion with verbal gestures of moral outrage—"Weakness! and worse, weakness bestowed in vain!" (l. 15)—he really does not deal adequately with the central issue itself. "Man cannot, though he would, live chance's fool" (l. 18). Perhaps; but how is a man who has been disqualified even as a reader of his own "inly-written chart" (l. 5) to be expected to distinguish between the suiting and the "unsuiting consort" (l. 16), the appropriate and the inappropriate joy, the natural and the unnatural friend, the destined and the undestined home? There are ways out of this dilemma, as most readers of the poem would know, but the speaker does not find one, and it is his personality that stands in his way. He undertakes to deal with an issue of his own contrivance argumentatively but ends up disposing of it assertively; instead of deriving a sense of quiet mastery from an argument well framed, he spasms nervously around a topic on which he has very strong views but very inadequate ideas.

The perspective shifts yet again in *Courage*, and again the imaginative basis for the shift is the personality of the speaker. That he is a *persona* who looks at life from the peculiar angle of a distinctive character is made irresistibly clear by the way in which his opening statement, with its bored, impatient

weariness over the reiterative principle of renunciation, echoes
Faust:

> Arnold: True, we tame our rebel will:
> True, we must bow to Nature's law:
> Must bear in silence many an ill;
> Must learn to wait, renounce, withdraw.
>
> (ll. 1–4)
>
> Faust: *Renounce! renounce! 'tis all one hears!*
> *That is the song that ceaselessly*
> *Is ringing, ringing in our ears:*
> *That every hour with hoarse insistence*
> *Repeats throughout our whole existence.* . . .
>
> (*Faust*, I, 1549–1553, Shawcross ed.)

Such moral austerity is all very well, he says, but it is also a
bore; and what *his* imagination requires is that a fiery, passionate meteor invade all this moral grayness and give life something a bit more energizing than a dwarfish prudence. It is
Faust's rebellion against the "huddling sheep" (l. 8) that he
sees all around him, even the "boldest wills" giving way, in the
face of intimidating "Fate and Circumstance" (l. 6), to the self-
effacing doctrine of renunciation. It is an expression of weakness, not strength, he thinks, the doctrine of renunciation
being a moral "disguise" given to a "faltering course" (ll. 25,
26). Instead of sheepishly yielding to "Fate and Circumstance,"
the second Cato and Byron defied them, and most importantly,
defied them with *style*. Thus Cato "raised [his arm against
himself] dauntlessly" (ll. 13–16), and Byron's "fiery courage"
had its distinctive "glow" even as the sun has its (ll. 20, 21–24).
It is an attractive, well-rationalized expression of Romanticism
that draws its strength from the reader's capacity to identify
with the speaker's rebellion against dull prudence and to
admire the tropes in which he articulates that rebellion (*his
style*). But the issue at the heart of this personality-drama, in its
turn "disguised" by that fascinating personality, is the issue,
not just of rebellion versus acceptance, but of what principle
he will opt for to conduct his affairs—feeling or reason? force
or understanding? Romanticism or Classicism?—and what

option, continuously pursued, represents the higher or truer form of human courage.

Self-Dependence is an extraordinary poetic exercise in verbal gesturing. It creates a language man; and although one end result is the creation of a very distinctive personality different from those reflected in the other poems, the verbal manner in which that creation takes place holds for the reader a special fascination. As in most of Arnold's interesting poems, a complex spiritual state is counterpointed to an illusion of poetic simplicity, and the maneuvering of the poem's psyche within a severely stripped narrative fiction provides the poem's movement toward disclosure. At the heart of the poem is the Delphic precept "Know thyself," and the question that the poem explores is how one can internalize such a precept and make it effective in one's own life. It is one of the most conscientious of moral questions, and its very presence as the moral crux of the poem defines the moral seriousness of the speaker. But seriousness is not enough.

The poem begins with the weariness born of a prolonged effort to come to terms with the precept: "Weary of myself, and sick of asking/What I am and what I ought to be. . . ." (ll. 1–2). Who am I? and is that the me I should accept? The poem's fiction is that the speaker is sailing rapidly into the future ("Forwards, forwards," l. 4) without any adequate moral or imaginative instrumentation to deal with that future. So his mental state is a blend of eagerness and anxiety, urgent longing and desperate fear; this, together with his situation at the prow of a moving ship, his existential loneliness, his despair of finding a trustworthy answer in himself by himself for himself, his past experience of discovering sources of calm and self-renewal in the waters of the great ocean and in the stars of the great firmament, and his present sense of a vast but serene activity in the cosmos ("intense, clear, star-sown vault of heaven," "the lit sea's unquiet ways," "the rustling night-air," [ll. 13, 14, 15]) provide his motive for flinging his imprecation at the universe and a credible psychological basis for his receiving, under the rubric of "a willing suspension of disbelief," the special answer that comes to him. It is a cluster of visual, emotional, and situational metaphors analogous to those that generate the epiphanic moments in Tennyson's *In Memoriam* and Pater's *Marius the Epicurean*. What he reaps, of course, as do Tennyson's and Pater's protagonists, are the rewards of his own imaginative conscientiousness. Having worked his way as far as one mode of inquiry will carry him, he takes a leap into a different mode; what he discovers is a correspondence between the two modes—the moral reason and the imagination—as there is a correspondence between the microcosm (himself) and the macrocosm (the universe). From one point of view, the poem's fiction is quite irrational—a dialogue between a troubled psyche and an untroubled universe that completes a narrative curve for the psyche. But, from another point of view, it is not irrational at all; when one has conscientiously exhausted one mode of inquiry, it is entirely reasonable to take a leap into a different mode, and it is entirely reasonable to expect that, by discovering the proper mirror, one can get a perspective on the self that will not come simply of concentration on the self in unrefracted isolation. This metaphor has another correspondence in the poem that shows that, while keeping his Delphic text intact, the poet has been exploring the question of how one can internalize such a precept and make it effective in one's own life. The answer is that by *being* oneself, one can get to *know* oneself: "Resolve to be thyself, and know that he,/Who finds himself, loses his misery!" (ll. 31–32). This is the way, presumably, in which the psyche avoids endless abstract self-harrowing and finds through *being* a measurable way of *knowing*.[29] Finally, the "misery" that the individual loses through finding himself according to the precept is simply the misery of not knowing what one is and what one ought to be.

Self-Dependence, then, is unlike any other poetic text in this cluster. It is a dramatic lyric in which a Classical precept is shown to be wholly convertible into life relevance by an intensely self-conscious Romantic sensibility that has no way of purging its own Romantic malaise other than by moral conscientiousness reinforced and facilitated by imaginative openness to the natural magic of the universe. The view of Nature, like the Delphic precept, is severely Classical (as Nature fulfils the law of its being, man should be instructed thereby to fulfil his);

although this insight is filtered through a Romantic sensibility (Nature's internal monologue—ll. 16–28—being a dramatic externalization of the speaker's own thoughts and feelings), the speaker manages to keep a saving distance from the more extravagant forms of the pathetic fallacy and to prevent his view of Nature from getting lost in the spilt natural religion of Romanticism.

Destiny has all the brutal thrust of an epigram launched by a speaker whose view of human life is wholly cynical. In fact, he overleaps more than a generation and begins to use tropes that Hardy would acculturate more fully a half-century later. Man's view of his destiny is irredeemably altered the moment "sport" is assigned as the motive of the gods; if his "strife" is both "endless" and "aimless" and is centered entirely in his very nature as man, then he cannot break out of his horrendous magic circle, but exists eternally as a metaphor of pathos exacerbated to the nth degree by the intensity of his consciousness and the unrealizability of his dreams. That is the vision of man's future held by a deeply distressed Romantic who locks man so severely into his own nature that he cannot hope to enjoy even the liberating terrors of Apocalypse and for whom a Prometheus-figure is not waiting in the wings. His position is ultimately untenable, of course: he has simply read his Aeschylus in a literal, doctrinaire way and ignored the possibility that, however tragic his situation, there is a severe and precarious myth by which man can be liberated and returned from his stultifying pathetic state.

Finally, the two sonnets *Youth's Agitations* and *The World's Triumphs* create *personae* very different from each other and from other *personae* in this cluster as a whole. The speaker in *Youth's Agitations* is a scintillating ironist rather than a cynic, and it is in that capacity that he reaches toward Hardy's theme of the distress of growing up and the "modern disease of restlessness" ("discontent") that conditions our lives whether we grow up or not. The conceit of the poem is curious—a youth projecting himself ten years into the future and acknowledging that there really is no cure for what ails him, that human life is such that one should not care greatly for it. In tone, sentiment, and ironic turning, it is a dramatic lyric that might easily have come from Hardy's own pen and that would fit easily into Hardy's poetic canon. *The World's Triumphs* is the deliberative articulation of an exceedingly bitter *persona*, also of the Hardy type. The dialogue that he creates between the world and "her foe" presents the world as so massively resistant to change that she shreds those heroic spirits who would correct her injustices and warns others not to try. It is the maddening recognition of a young idealist that the worldly system is not amenable to even gradual modification and that a violent eruption is the only way available for dealing with it.

These six short poems, then, contain wildly inconsistent ideas, and the voices they release come from personalities with very contrary centers. They are in a large degree dramatic or personative, and the poet has created them as so many imaginary persons not himself; they are dramatically conceived and embody imaginary points on a ring of perspectives whose common denominator is simply varying perspectives on the human condition.

Memorial Verses

There was undoubtedly something of the ebullient high spirits of the sense of a job well done in Arnold's statement to Clough that he had "dirged W.W. *in the grand style*,"[30] but the poem fully qualifies for that description as Arnold would clarify its meaning more than a decade later.[31] Its seriousness of purpose, a manner at once simple and severe, the detached nobility of apprehension that distributes the poem's cultural metaphors in a field of intensely personal imaginative emotion—all these cast the speaker of this highly accomplished "triple Epicede" in a public role analogous to the roles in which he has cast Byron, Goethe, and Wordsworth. He becomes a poetic metaphor responding to poetic metaphors: as each of them confronted the "doubts, disputes, distractions, fears" of an "iron time" (ll. 43, 44) in an intensely heightened but fascinatingly representative way, so the speaker frames the issue as to how he and the generation that now succeeds them will deal with the "condition of modern Europe" question in their turn. As the poem's metaphors define the speaker's field of imaginative interest (modern poetry's ways of coping) and his own role therein (the poet-successor's overview and perception of alternatives), so also do they designate his audience (the young writer in search of literary models and a proper focus for his endeavors).

For the young writer seriously engaged with his role—and in that sense himself a refraction of the role that the speaker assumes—Byron is the most alluring and deceptive model of all. He was more of a body-linguist than a serious poet, and only "Titans" have any chance of authentic imitation of his example. It was what he did rather than what he said that evoked throughout Europe the oratorical imprecations of a tragic chorus—the "Shivering heart" and the "reverential awe" inspired by the fatal struggle of a pre-Olympian god-figure, a precursor of Prometheus without a Promethean purpose. The young writer can hardly deny the pull of sympathy ("pity") toward Byron, but he must recognize the terror ("fear") too; in the end, if he is seriously engaged in his role, he can hardly avoid the suspicion that, by the austere standards that alone make tragedy cathartic, "the fount of fiery life/Which served for that Titanic strife" (ll. 13–14) dissipated itself like the lava of Etna under which Typho still defiantly groans. Byron's example is instructive, but the originality of his personal style was unique and hence essentially inimitable, and one who tries to role-play Byron is doomed to fail of a constructive purpose.

To move from Byron to Goethe is to move from the Titans to the Olympians, from godlike caprice to godlike conscientiousness, from raw if grand force to cultivated, detached understanding. That the example of Goethe can in fact be imitated to a significant degree, the poem itself confirms. The speaker is acting out in large part, though in a minor degree, a Goethean role: he, too, is, in a generic sense, a "Physician of the iron age" (l. 17), which is the inevitable role of the serious modern writer, and thus in turn says to his audience, *"Art still has truth, take refuge there!"* (l. 28). But though his admiration for Goethe is solemn, sincere, and purposive, there is reserve in his view of Goethe as a fully serviceable model for the young writer in this belated hour. Europe's *ancien regime* has been overthrown; the "weltering strife" in which that dispensation expired is past. Though Goethe was the supreme witness of the "fitful dream and feverish power" in which that great human drama was enacted, the times are altered and require of their writers, not less wisdom, but less godlike postures:

> And he was happy, if to know
> Causes of things, and far below
> His feet to see the lurid flow
> Of terror, and insane distress,
> And headlong fate, be happiness.

> (ll. 29–33)

It is not an explicit judgment, certainly; but since it poses the question about the Olympian gods that has been troublesome to man throughout the Western mythic tradition (are they happy?), it casts an implicit shadow of a doubt on the degree of relevance Olympianism has for the young writer of the present and the future—on the possibility as well as the propriety, in altered times, of a posture that admittedly worked well in an *ancien regime* and even during the period of its death struggle. But as Titanism has ended, Olympianism has lost a degree of its relevance too.

The movement from Goethe to Wordsworth is a movement from one order of being and one concept of the poet to quite another; paradoxically, the movement toward simplicity is a process of enlargement. Wordsworth "put ... by" all the contentious mythological machinery of Titans and Olympians in which our "mortal destiny" is both embodied and beclouded (ll. 68–70)—a worthy enough subject for a Titan like Byron and an Olympian like Goethe, a grand and inexhaustibly serious subject—and returned poetry to its earliest symbol (the lyre), to its earliest practitioner (Orpheus), and to its earliest purposes: the redemption of Nature to benign vitality and the reconciliation of man to a universe that he can actually see and hear and touch and smell and taste and love. Older even than Zeus himself, Orpheus embodies a power that will outlive all Houses of Cadmus and Danaus, all Trojan Wars, all Reigns of Terror, all benumbment of the soul by an era, all dark and desiccated days. That is the power Wordsworth restored to poetry, the simultaneous rejuvenation of both Nature and man:

> for there was shed
> On spirits that had long been dead,
> Spirits dried up and closely furled,
> The freshness of the early world.
>
> (ll. 54–57)

Wordsworth, then, becomes the most trustworthy model for the young writer because only Wordsworth, in all the centuries of English poetry, successfully completed the myth of the return to the origins and pristine purposes of lyric poetry symbolized by Orpheus. That what Wordsworth did is harder of accomplishment than what either Byron or Goethe did is both explicitly stated—

> Ah! since dark days still bring to light
> Man's prudence and man's fiery might,
> Time may restore us in his course
> Goethe's sage mind and Byron's force. . . .
>
> (ll. 58–61)

—and confirmed by the long time it took in the coming. So the final questions of the speaker assume the character of a very simple but very large challenge to the young writer in search of a model and of a constructive field of imaginative endeavor:

> But who, ah! who, will make us feel?
> The cloud of mortal destiny,
> Others will front it fearlessly—
> But who, like him, will put it by?
>
> (ll. 67–70)

There is no need to make a peremptory, black-and-white choice concerning Arnold as the speaker *in propria persona* of *Memorial Verses*. The speaker is a poet-critic in an act of generic role-playing, and in that sense the poem is "in a large degree dramatic or personative." The speaker is absorbed into the poem's metaphors; the more aware we become of their complex frames of reference, the more deeply absorbed he becomes, so that at some point the text speaks for the speaker, and his literal historical identity becomes a diminished question of a largely extra-textual interest.

The Buried Life

The Buried Life delineates a *persona* who is subtle, alluring at a subliminal level, and both exquisitely and disquietingly ambiguous. *The Buried Life* takes its place as one of Arnold's most accomplished dramatic lyrics, competitive in poetic poise and finish with such minor masterpieces in the same genre as Browning's *My Last Duchess*, Swinburne's *The Leper*, and Hardy's *A Broken Appointment*. As in *Dover Beach*, a dramatic monologue is formally established and then allowed to elide into a monodrama. But here the audience is not made faceless, as in *Dover Beach*, by the rhetorical fury of the speaker. Rather, she is, by implication, sufficiently developed as a character in the first twenty-nine lines of the poem to serve as a wry, critical presence in the text, a sceptical observer of the dramaturgical gesturing of the speaker. The subject of the poem is identity, and "his own identity" (l. 34) is what we are invited to examine about the speaker. We need to determine if he is "Tricked in disguises" (l. 21)—what those disguises are, what he is as distinct from what he would appear to be—and we are encouraged and directed in this imaginative quest by her sceptical detachment from his self-indulgent soul-knitting. She is characterized by "mocking words," a spirit of "jest," and "gay smiles" (ll. 1, 4, 5, 7, 8).

A reader hardly needs to be wholly sensitive to the subtle and pervasive use Arnold makes of voicings throughout his dramatic lyrics to recognize that there is some melodramatic posturing going on in the opening lines of *The Buried Life*, a calculated querulousness of voice, an exaggeration of language, a self-referential tendency that is just a mite too transparent:

> Light flows our war of mocking words, and yet,
> *Behold, with tears mine eyes are wet!*

> *I feel a nameless sadness o'er me roll.*
> Yes, yes, *we know* that we can jest,
> *We know, we know* that we can smile!
> But there's *a something in this breast,*
> To which thy light words *bring no rest,*
> And thy gay smiles *no anodyne.*
> Give me thy hand, and hush awhile,
> And turn *those limpid eyes* on mine,
> And *let me read* there, love! *thy inmost soul.*
>
> (ll. 1–11, emphasis added)

The sentiments, the exclamation marks, the epithets, the images, the implicit body-language, the vagueness, the struggle of temperaments, the ego-assaults—all put the issue of the speaker's sincerity into serious question and place the reader in the position of a carefully alerted observer of a *persona*-process that promises to play the speaker's sense of self against our own critical estimate of who he is and what, metaphorically, he represents.

Subtle, alluring at a subliminal level, both exquisitely and disquietingly ambiguous—these are real dimensions of the speaker's appeal to even the critical reader, and putting them securely in place was an indispensable part of the poet's intention. We can all identify with his longing for authenticity; with his impatience with the false daily maneuvers of action and language; with his despair of success in the satisfaction of a racking need to track his true self to its ultimate origins; with his temptation, as a consequence of that despair, to cast himself both frantically and willy-nilly upon the busyness of life; with the ultimate failure of such strategies of despair and the inevitable resurfacing of an imperious need to know who he truly is. We can also identify with the general tendency, conventional even if valid, to equate the penetrating resonances and suffusive elations of romantic love with the *vrai verité* of spiritual authenticity—with a surcease of psychic turmoil, a new and satisfying sense of personal poise, and the elevation of emotional uplift into hieratic metaphors. All this we can intensely identify with because it represents an archetypal patterning of a typical human need and a typical human response to that need.

But if we see ourselves in the speaker's fiction, in his skillful outmaneuvering of the less attractive daily ploys of action and language, we are invited at the same time to see ourselves in the wry light created by expectations, arguments, and verbal gestures used by the speaker in very questionable ways. For example, romantic love assumes for him so much of the character of a magic wand—so formulaic a way of achieving what he "thinks" (l. 96) of as the spiritualization of life—that one has a nagging doubt about the true motive of his heartfelt disquisition in the romantic fiction in which it takes place, a disquieting suspicion that seduction itself may be the goal of his seductiveness. This motif is somewhat diffused in the final movement of the poem—as is, perhaps, his interest—but it is relatively explicit in the transition from the first to the second verse-paragraphs (say, ll. 9–14), where, having held her hand and looked into her "limpid eyes" for a moment, he gestures impatiently that the formula is not working:

> Alas! is even love too weak
> To unlock the heart, and let it speak?
> Are even lovers powerless to reveal
> To one another what indeed they feel?

Further, there is something sophistical in his elaborate and fanciful explanation of why fate buried the authentic self so deep. If it is true that man's "genuine self" is thereby protected from his "capricious play" (ll. 35–36) and if, in spite of man's sense of "Eddying at large in blind uncertainty" (l. 43), he is yet forced "to obey/Even in his own despite his being's law" (ll. 36–37), the river of his life relentlessly pursuing its way and "driving him on with it eternally" (ll. 40, 44), then this whole elaborate ritual of self-conscious self-seeking is essentially an exercise in futility conducive of little more than a self-harrowing/self-massaging melancholy. It may be a way of spending "our fire and restless force" (l. 49) on "the mystery of this heart which beats/So wild, so deep in us" (ll. 52–53), but it is not necessarily the right way. Finally, the speaker suspends his dilemma in such a medium of verbal vagueness—"a nameless sadness," "an unspeakable desire," "the mystery of this heart," "nameless feelings," "vague and forlorn," "airs, and floating echoes," "somewhere in our breast," "flying and elusive shadow" (ll. 3, 47, 52, 62, 72, 75, 84, 93)—that one can more easily yield to the lull of his soulful language than define the specific nature of his problem, can either luxuriate in the tepid waters of his misty Romantic melancholy or withdraw to a critical vantage point that saves one from succumbing to a state of feeling that, however subliminally alluring, is fundamentally pernicious.

The speaker of *The Buried Life* is an embodiment, a literary metaphor, of that irrepressible self-consciousness that was recognized on all sides as one of the demons of the age, a source alike of its distinctive energy and its characteristic confusion, of its delicacy of perception and the painful paralysis suffered by some of its finest spirits. That Arnold fully appreciated the two-sidedness of the issue is firmly insinuated by the precarious equipoise to which he brings them in this poem. He was aware, too, that the inward-looking eye (l. 86) was one ritualized way of trying to implement the Delphic dictum "Know thyself." But Socrates, whose voice is antiphonal to that of the speaker in *The Buried Life*, had stressed reason rather than emotion as the proper instrument of self-knowledge, and his eye had looked outward, to man in his historical and social relations, as the proper field of human investigation, making it a philosophical and moral pursuit rather than a psychological one. The Romantic revision of this Classical procedure had been to some degree fruitful, but its abandonment of objective, external referents had led to a degree of imprisonment in the self, to an intense emotional and psychological isolation, that made the Romantic search for the buried life both magnetic and haphazard, essentially solipsistic and not a little sad.

Stanzas in Memory of the Author of 'Obermann'

Stanzas in Memory of the Author of 'Obermann' is a hallmark of Arnoldianism, one of the dozen or so poetic texts through which one looks at Arnold and reflects upon the character of his poetry. Arnold classified *Stanzas in Memory of the Author of 'Obermann'* as an elegiac poem, and its memorial quality monitors its tone of somber lament as well as the vocal swells of celebration through which the eclipsed, disquieting heroism of Obermann is acknowledged and the anguished debt of the speaker paid. But the poem is also a lyrical ballad, a dramatic narrative recounting the sentimental journey of a soul to the shrine of one of its literary guides to spiritual perspective and probing, in a muted fashion, the semi-redemption that it achieves there. Hence, *Stanzas in Memory of the Author of 'Obermann'* is an elegiac action poem, and its action is both the source of its structure and the chief metaphor upon which its disclosure depends. The events of the poem are separated from any vaguely analogous event in the author's own life by the conventions of the elegy and the sentimental journey. Moreover, poetic action has its own laws quite independent of the vagaries of an unpoeticized historical sequence: once interpretively enriched images are put formally into place, they dictate the rules of inevitability by which a dramatic narrative will process the insight or intuition that led initially to their choice. This is what makes any poem worthy of the name exploratory rather than depositional, idiosyncratically dynamic rather than customary and static; by its effect of putting the author in a locus analogous to that occupied by a comparably sensitive reader, a poem's self-processing action draws him further away from the literalness of assumed authoriality and gives him a generic rather than an individual and historical character in relation to the poem. This is what defines poetry with a center in action or myth and distinguishes it from "A true allegory of the state of one's own mind in a representative history . . ." (Preface of 1853).

But there are less theoretical pieces of evidence to show that Arnold is no more complicit in the poem's process of witnessing than any other reader who can fully identify with "the feeling of its situations." One is the mirroring role that Senancour's literary text plays in the poem. It is not to Senancour himself, but to the imaginary hero of Senancour's novel, that the speaker responds. These are the "leaves" that he turns, and it is the illusion of reality created by the novel's language that he "feels." The "fever" is "in these pages"; it is "through these pages" that "the virgin mountain-air" blows; "the bells/Of the

high-pasturing kine" are heard "as you read" (ll. 21, 26, 31–32).
This is what makes Obermann so compelling: he is a type of
respondent to life (like Wordsworth, like Goethe) who has been
made intensely penetrative through his translation into spiritually invasive language. The implicit analogy, powerfully reinforced by the depth to which the speaker initially identifies
with the fictional hero of the novel and the distance he
gradually establishes from him in the course of the poem, is
that as Obermann is to Senancour, so the speaker of *Stanzas in
Memory of the Author of 'Obermann'* is to Arnold—the imaginary
protagonist of a fictional narrative, a human type, a literary
metaphor. There is a second analogy operative within the first:
as the speaker of the poem ultimately measures the protagonist
of the novel, so also is he subject to measuring. Thus the poem
is not a "true allegory of the state of [Arnold's] own mind"—
which would make it a solipsistic tautology, true because it is
"true"—but an imaginative action established at a fictional level
in order to enable a critical consciousness to function; in short,
a poem whose motive is a "criticism of life" or "the application
of ideas to life." And there is yet a third analogy: though
Obermann is not Senancour, literature not being life except
"at the remove of form and idea," this does not exclude
Senancour from full imaginative empathy with his hero. Arnold
can identify strongly *and critically* with the speaker of *Stanzas*
without being literally identified with him.

Like Arnold, the speaker is a young writer in search of
guidance, as his critical attitudes toward Wordsworth and
Goethe and his critical quest for a literary alternative make
clear. He is a critic-poet who, through the experience of the
poem's illusions, makes some fundamental discoveries about
the difficulties a poet faces. For example:

> Some secrets may the poet tell,
> For the world loves new ways;
> To tell too deep ones is not well—
> It knows not what he says.
>
> (ll. 41–44)

> Ah! two desires toss about
> The poet's feverish blood.

> One drives him to the world without,
> And one to solitude.
>
> (ll. 96–98)

These are not discoveries that Arnold makes, but discoveries that he imagines his protagonist as making as he verbalizes for himself the significance of the experiences that the poem provides; the degree of their cogency is internally rather than externally monitored. The poet is to be held accountable only for their validity as relevant and constructive dimensions of characterization—as metaphoric verbalizations that give us a profounder understanding of the imaginary consciousness being defined and enlarged by the poem.

Though *Stanzas in Memory of the Author of 'Obermann'* may be seen fruitfully as a representative episode in a much larger quest—a sort of *Wanderjahre* like that of the hero of Carlyle's *Sartor Resartus* and of Goethe's *Wilhelm Meister* and *Sorrows of Young Werther*—it is, poetically, a complete action, having a well-designed beginning, middle, and end: he comes, he witnesses at a multiplicity of levels, he departs. Also, true to its character as a heightened dramatic episode, it preserves the Classical unities of place, time, and action. Finally, it is not only a mirror of consciousness but also a movement of consciousness: the external narrative has an internal correspondence, and the protagonist, within the scale of his meticulously defined personality, leaves the scene of the action measurably altered.

The speaker brings to the concrete landscape imagery with which the poem begins an eye that sees what it is inclined to see. He comes with the novel *Obermann* in hand and in heart, and the images of terror, turbulence, decay, and confusion that he consciously registers (ll. 1–10), though the images are actually there, are read so strictly according to his mood that they reflect a controlled species of the pathetic fallacy. This is the basis of his peculiar identification with Obermann, an identification which is so strong that he seems to hear the fictional figure actually address him:

> Fly hence, poor wretch, whoe'er thou art,
> Condemned to cast about,

All shipwreck in thy own weak heart,
For comfort from without!

                                                    (ll. 16–19)

That is how he sees himself and how he imagines Obermann
as seeing him. Obermann's "air of languor, cold, and death"
(l. 15), his "fever," and his wounds (ll. 21, 23) are the speaker's.
Thus the idyllic pastoral side of Obermann (ll. 25–34), though
it surfaces in images that are also concrete and very different
from those of the opening landscape, is enveloped by the
speaker's psyche in his own "sobs"—in "I know not what
ground-tone/Of human agony" (ll. 35–36). His Obermann is
only half real, an icon manufactured out of his self-conscious
identification and the self-enlargement of his own pain.

The speaker's peculiar weighting of the meaning of Obermann explains how he finds a place for him in a trinity of
contemporary sages that is completed by Wordsworth and
Goethe. His eulogy of Goethe is impeccable (ll. 55–62), but it
is all admiration and no identification. What he *says* is that
Goethe reached too Olympian a height to be emulated, but
what he *implies* is that Goethe's freedom, sanity, and clarity of
vision are the exact opposites of the imprisoning, unhealthy,
misty perspective with which, in a fury of self-pity, he defines
himself. He is the product of a blasted youth, the pathetic
victim of an unsheltered and harassed childhood (ll. 69–78).[32]
The speaker's attitude toward Wordsworth is a good deal more
dismissive. Even his sympathetic metaphors vibrate with irony,
and his direct indictment is unequivocal: "Wordsworth's eyes
avert their ken/From half of human fate . . ." (ll. 53–54). It is
a crucial clue both to the speaker's character and to the
imaginative process in which Arnold has involved him. Setting
aside the question of whether or not the judgment of Wordsworth has merit, it is an echo of Byron's judgment, and it aligns
the speaker with a latter-day species of Byronism. He, too, is
averting his eyes from "half of human fate," the very half that
Wordsworth saw with the greatest imaginative luminosity; it is
the half of Obermann—the idyllic pastoral side—that he has
submerged in a tide of sentimental pathos.

When the speaker turns to his eulogy of Obermann, it is a

deeply faulted eulogy—a paean to pain, a celebration of death rather than of life, a diapason of despair, a metaphor of hell: "Thy realm of thought is drear and cold—" (l. 107). Then something very dramatic happens that induces the narrative's turning-point and reveals the speaker's central tension even if, by virtue of the speaker's character, it fails of a full *peripeteia*. As if to redeem Obermann from the negativism that his own language has imposed upon him, the speaker begins to dilate on the "pleasures" to be found in the book, and in the process of doing so (ll. 109–128), he is led gradually to the very brink of what can fairly be called the alluring temptation of the Wordsworth metaphor:

> Heard accents of the eternal tongue
> Through the pine branches play—
> Listened, and felt thyself grow young!
> Listened and wept—*Away!*
>
> *Away the dreams that but deceive*
> And thou, sad guide, adieu!
> (ll. 125–130, emphasis added)

He would, but he will not, wants to but cannot. Still, the speaker's tendency is implicit in the speaker's tension; despite his gestures of verbal protest, we can measure this response to the reconciling visions and voices of Nature against his earlier response (ll. 25–34) and recognize a significant though incomplete movement. That he connects his rebellion against this inner susceptibility or spiritual tendency so intimately with his decision to leave these sacred precincts strongly suggests that he must continue his Romantic quest elsewhere, since even the degree of movement he has undergone makes the uses to which he came to put Obermann no longer possible.

There is both clarification and ambiguity in the poem's denouement. The strong sense of an ill-fated life that had been the chief anchor of his self-pity is residual in his perception of a "rigorous" obligation to the world as a mandate of "some unknown Power" (l. 133), and the pathos of his plight is given another massage: "Can neither, when we will, enjoy,/Nor, when we will, resign" (ll. 135–136). Since he no longer "obeys" Obermann's "spell" (ll. 157–159)—that is, the imperious, self-flagellating image that he had himself created out of half of Obermann—he must find other grounds for a "transfigured" image that he can to some degree internalize. This becomes the image of "The Children of the Second Birth," through which Obermann is salvaged from the extreme and self-defeating position summed up in the earlier pronouncement that "He only lives with the world's life,/Who hath renounced his own" (ll. 103–104), and the speaker can be reconciled to Obermann and to himself in the role in which he will now cast himself. But here, too, the speaker's penchant for rather grand Romantic gesturing is transfigured rather than abandoned:

> Christian and pagan, king and slave,
> Soldier and anchorite,
> Distinctions we esteem so grave,
> Are nothing in their sight.
>
> They do not ask, who pined unseen,
> Who was on action hurled,
> Whose one bond is, that all have been
> Unspotted by the world.
>
> (ll. 149–156)

It is a rather too magnificent celebration of human detachment that is not without its difficulties for one reflecting on the import of its images, not the least of which is the godlike role it assigns to the "Children of the Second Birth";[33] but it is undoubtedly high-minded, and it does provide a modified *mythos* in which to center Obermann, in which to become self-centered, and through the creation of which the speaker is freed to make "A last, a last farewell!" (l. 184).

The very importunateness of this final utterance makes very curious demands upon the reader. The poem's whole process dictates that we see it as chiefly self-referential, but the exact note on which the action of the poem is concluded, like the exact note on which it was begun, is an indispensable tonic metaphor, as the insistent, repetitive language ("A last, a last") signals, and an intricate element in the design of the poem's ultimate disclosure. Since the speaker has ceased to identify Obermann with himself at the soul-blending level of intensity with which the poem began, it cannot be a valediction to himself. Indeed, the later process of the poem—its creation of an alternative *mythos*—depletes even the extravagance of the emotional outburst that the first "adieu" released in the speaker: "I go, fate drives me; but I leave/Half of my life with you" (ll. 131–132). Any sense in which this can still be true is very different from the sense in which it was originally meant. A misguided or false self may be buried near the abandoned Baths of Leuk, but none of the living self is left there.

What the speaker takes with him on his return to the world is the important thing, not what he leaves behind. What he takes are the faint beginnings of a restorative reconciliation with Nature and the memory of an event so archetypally self-defining that it may always serve as an objective correlative for understanding his inner life history. The pastoral sequence with which the poem moves to its close (ll. 161ff.) is markedly different from any of the preceding ones—from the morbidity of the initial landscape, the doctrinaire insensitivity of the second, the eruptive rebellion of the third. It is no longer the stimulus to false dreams, but a source of peace and reconciliation that reaches beyond the grave and unites urban centers with "stern Alpine dells" (l. 182) in the image of the "blue Seine" rolling "her wave" "between granite terraces" in the "Capital of Pleasure" (ll. 177–179).[34] The Byronic metaphor that had initially sustained his violent but crippled energy has yielded, at a threshold stage, to the Wordsworthian metaphor which had fueled his dismissive defiance. The speaker has begun to learn, besides, a very large and humbling truth about himself—namely, the massive force of his own fallibility and the correlation between his Romantically volcanic passion and his proneness to self-destructive error. It is this which gives such importunate intensity to his final utterance—the recognition of a sad and sobering wisdom reinforced by the equally painful recognition that alienation from this icon of his afflicted spirit is the price that he must pay for it.

But the speaker's final characterization of Obermann—"O

unstrung will! O broken heart!" (l. 183)—is at once so heartfelt and so ambivalent that it re-opens the question of the design of the poem's ultimate disclosure. There are disquieting over-tones to his exclamations, as if the erstwhile devoted disciple has become the indulgent patron of the master. One is even reminded of the ironic vibrations released earlier by the speaker's patronizing images of Wordsworth—the gray old man with his "sweet calm." The irony is magnified several-fold when one recalls that the idyllic pastoral to which the speaker now implicitly subscribes has been a pervasive but rejected presence in Senancour's *Obermann* text all along and that the *persona* of the "unstrung will" and "broken heart" has been a one-sided image manufactured by the speaker himself, another example of his seeing what his eye intends to see.

This would seem to be Arnold's subtle way of preserving the poem's integrity as essentially a process of action and character and of undercutting the possibility of bringing it to an easy Romantic closure. Although the speaker has moved toward some significant alteration in the content of his response, his personal patterns of behavior have not significantly changed: he has taken on some new ideas, not a new character. And whatever ideas he becomes available to in the future will, like those of the past and present, have to undergo the trial of personality and will be strengthened or adulterated accord-ingly. *Stanzas in Memory of the Author of 'Obermann'* is a highly attitudinal poem. Attitudes toward Nature, the human situa-tion, spiritual models, the character of poetry, and so forth, are a large and indispensable part of its subject matter. But its ultimate imaginative disclosure transcends all of these, is pro-cessive rather than topical. Like the poetry of Tennyson, Hardy, and the best work of twentieth-century poets, it subjects thought to the experience of thought, distances ideology to personality, and gives poetic habitation to the most Classical of all principles—namely that unless a man knows himself, what-ever else he may know is relatively minor. The living center is in the self, and unless the center is secure, nothing else can hold together and continue to exist.

Stanzas in Memory of the Author of 'Obermann' has the charac-teristic note of honesty that Arnold brought to his Romantic quest-poems of the early 1850s. Its protagonist struggles with his own fallibility, creates his own crippling delusions, postures and protests and equivocates. He only half-discovers that he is trying to live literature instead of living life and that his dissatisfaction with both Goethe and Wordsworth is that it is impossible to live their literature. A grossly simplified Obermann does seem to work for a while, but it too inevitably collapses under the special pressures of life in this world, and though the protagonist does seem to accomplish a shift from his self-harrowing image of Obermann to a more reconciling image of Nature—to close his *Obermann* and open his Wordsworth, so to speak—the inner tendency that led to his delusion in the first place has not been touched, and we are not blinded to the very real possibility that his fundamental fallibility will lead him astray again and again. He is like a young man who has taken Goethe's insight that *"Art still has truth, take refuge there!"* too literally and tried to make art a substitute for rather than a guide to life. We recognize it as an understandable response on the part of a sensitive young man at his disheveled moment in cultural time, but we also recognize as an ingratiating fallacy an attempt to "live in art" or to "live literature." The weakness of the poem—the fault of Arnold's poems generally at this time, as he himself would eventually assert—is that it does not exhibit an antidote or counterpoint commensurate with its exhibition of the malaise or misdirection, is strong on diagnosis and weak on cure and in that sense makes poetry as paralytic as its subjects. But the delineation itself is firm and specific and provides, at both the historical and the metaphoric levels, one of our most trustworthy poetic identifications of one crucial symptom of "this strange disease of modern life."

Lines written in Kensington Gardens

Lines written in Kensington Gardens inevitably reminds the reader of nineteenth-century poetry of Wordsworth's *Composed upon Westminster Bridge*. Both poems celebrate the joy of discovering Nature at a primary, permanent level in the heart of the great city, and inner "calm" is the spiritual quality each speaker seeks to reinforce through the discovery. The hyperbole of aesthetic surprise expressed in Wordsworth's poem—"Never did sun more beautifully steep/In his first splendour, valley, rock, or hill" (ll. 9–10)—has its counterpart in Arnold's:

> Scarce fresher is the mountain-sod
> Where the tired angler lies, stretched out,
> And, eased of basket and of rod,
> Counts his day's spoil, the spotted trout.
>
> (ll. 17–20)

Indeed, Arnold apparently wishes to signal unmistakably to the reader that there is the very deepest sympathy—almost an identity of feeling—between his speaker's love of Nature and Wordsworth's; he does this because he wishes to establish between them a critical difference too.

What Arnold does in *Lines written in Kensington Gardens* is to take a Wordsworthian conclusion and make it the basis for a much more radical poetic imagining: to play it off against Pater's *Apollo in Picardy*, he creates an imaginary portrait of a Pan in Piccadilly; and he does it with a subtlety and a finesse that are nowhere prosaically insistent. The speaker of the poem, for example, is not aware of the role he is playing in the poet's overarching conception. He is more than a metaphor of the sentimental Romantic city-dweller who goes into the park for a momentary tonic, though that metaphor certainly lingers on the fringes of the poem. He is a modern, urban sophisticate with a memory that reaches back to a rural childhood. The action of the poem provides his consciousness with a favored moment that releases those memories of the past and, by storing his maturer mind with fresh images of the endlessly active vitality of Nature quietly performing her often mysterious work, supplies an experience that will function in the future as an internalized mechanism of imaginative insight and refreshment. The speaker is keenly available to the sensuous impingement of the experience—to its sights and smells and especially to its sounds, its "quiet" being repeatedly contrasted with the "roar" and "uproar" of the city that forms ramparts around it. But he is also a modern thinker, a man in an advanced state of civilization, and he inevitably abstracts from the dense fabric of sensuous images a cerebral response—notably, that the activities he has just witnessed, though they are taking place at a center of civilization, are not the product of civilization and betoken a presence in the universe of something more permanent than anything man has made and that this presence continues whether man is around or not. He then goes on—as man's archetypal way is, quite independent of the state of his official creeds—to convert this cerebral response into a hieratic poetic response, a prayer:

> Calm soul of all things! make it mine
> To feel, amid the city's jar,
> That there abides a peace of thine,
> Man did not make, and cannot mar.
>
> The will to neither strive nor cry,
> The power to feel with others give!
> Calm, calm me more! nor let me die
> Before I have begun to live.
>
> (ll. 37–44)

This poetic prayer to Pan is wholly naturalistic and secular: it diminishes all capitals and closely interweaves the personality of the speaker, the experience, and the speaker's psychological extrapolation of the meaning of the experience. Even at that level, it is a radical departure from Wordsworth's overtones of religious revivalism as marked by the presence in *Composed upon Westminster Bridge* of the evocative "Dear God" (l. 13).

But it is at an almost subtextual level that the more radical poetic imagining of *Lines written in Kensington Gardens* operates—namely, that the wholly naturalistic and secular speaker has an analogue in Pan himself, that the reader can trace in him the faint remnant images of Pan and the sons of Pan, and thus that the archetypal myth is still functional and the great god Pan is *not* dead. The speaker, of course, makes direct references to Pan, and this draws the issue forward at an explicit textual level:

> In the huge world, which roars hard by,
> Be others happy if they can!
> But in my helpless cradle I
> Was breathed on by the rural Pan.
>
> (ll 21–24)

This grouping of metaphors brings the goals and origins of life itself into association with Pan—"happy," "helpless cradle," "breathed on"; and the following quatrain insinuates into that association the fear that Pan is dead:

> I, on men's impious uproar hurled,
> Think often, as I hear them rave,
> That peace has left the upper world
> And now keeps only in the grave.
>
> (ll. 25–28)

The madness of modern urban life versus the happiness and peace of the ancient rural world of Pan, the use of the metaphor "the upper world" to describe the land of the living, the wholly current thought that perhaps Pan's peaceful dispensation has ended—these, together with the metaphors already cited, implant rather firmly into the text that Pan is at the center of the speaker's frame of reference. But these allusions, though unquestionably important to the poet's purposes, are, it might be fairly argued, gracefully Classical rather than indispensably integral. They show the speaker at a conscious rather than an unconscious level employing a Panic analogy; since imagery of which the speaker was not himself conscious would be the ultimate test of the poet's intention, this conscious manipulation of the analogy is highly suggestive rather than fully persuasive.

The fact is that imagery having unmistakable reference to Pan *is* unconsciously employed by the speaker in the early, strikingly sensuous quatrains (ll. 1–16), and the speaker is himself one of those images. As he lies there in his "lone, open glade" (with his head propped on one arm to see what he sees and hear what he hears), he assumes one of the typical poses that art has given to Pan; the "black-crowned, red-boled pine-trees" are the trees special to Pan, and the light "green-foliag'd chestnuts" and the "darker elms" of the second stanza of the first printing, omitted after 1852, are standard props in Pan's sacred groves. But his body language is especially goatlike—how he slowly moves his head about, in his reclined position, looking at every movement and listening to every sound, attentive like Caliban at a natural, animal like level:

> Here at my feet what wonders pass,
> What endless, active life is here!
> What blowing daisies, fragrant grass!
> An air-stirred forest, fresh and clear.

> (ll. 13–16)

The speaker is, in a very subtle way, role-playing Pan, and to say, therefore, that *Lines written in Kensington Gardens* is an imaginary portrait of Pan in Piccadilly, though a bit fanciful, is not entirely beside the mark, because at one crucial creative level it seriously plays with the idea that Pan as an imaginative archetype is resurfacing in sketchy but unmistakable outline, perhaps as the supernaturalism that buried him goes itself into the grave. This idea is radically critical of Wordsworth, who never brought his sensuousness to this ultimate naturalistic rooting, but tried to make his ruralism and his supernaturalism comfortable bedfellows.

Three Pindarics: The Youth of Nature, The Youth of Man, The Future

The three pindarics *The Youth of Nature, The Youth of Man*, and *The Future* have the chief qualities of companion poems: they probe in varied but analogous ways large issues of perspective on Nature, man, and the future prospect, and they employ a common genre and prosody that unite them and give them a shared voice.

The Youth of Nature is the most aesthetically heightened, and this is appropriate since it explores the most aesthetically ambitious question of the three: is it Nature herself who "fill[s] us with joy/Or the voice which reveals what" she is (ll. 61, 65)? Are Nature's "beauty," "grace," "charm," "romance" "lost when their watcher is gone?" (ll. 63–64, 74).

It is crucial to observe that the poet has created a dramatic action to enable the poem to make its disclosure. Hence, it is not a poem of statement, but a poem of experience—a fictional dialogic structure in which a speaker puts a question that has been generated and intensified by the setting and by a host of associations that quicken his awarenesses to a state of religious anxiety and in which Nature, in the person of someone analogous to the *Idaea Mater* of Mysia or the *Magna Mater* of Crete, makes a grand oracular reply. Hence the poem puts its pindaric heritage to the highly ritualistic uses accordant with such a significant and epiphanically inducive question.

The action begins on an unidentified lake in the heart of the Wordsworth country, and the speaker enriches the scene meticulously with the feelings associated with Wordsworth— silence, soft loveliness, majestic mountains, and valleys "flooded with haze" (ll. 1–7)—and with the place-names that are iden- tified with Wordsworth—Rydal, Fairfield, Ennerdale Lake, Egremont, Grasmere, the Quantock coombs, Michael's sheep- fold and "the favourite waters of Ruth" (ll. 8–24). This is the feeling, the landscape, the topography that Wordsworth made to inhabit the responsive imaginative mind; and although they clearly seem to survive his death, even that perceptual reality presses upon the speaker's consciousness the question of whether they would have been seen without his eyes and whether the darkness that follows his death, the death of the last of the "sacred poet[s]," is prophetic of a general darkness as the oncoming human state.

The analogy with Tiresias, the speaker reflects, would seem to confirm that it is so. He, like Wordsworth, was "a priest to us all" (l. 53), and, like Wordsworth, he "Died in his enemies' days" (l. 35). He, too, inhabited a lovely natural world of cold bubbling springs, moonlit panoramas, mirroring lakes, and sacred, majestic mountains; but when he died, "reviving Thebes" did not "See such a prophet again" (ll. 36–47).

Having been drawn by his penetrating experiences and his reflections on them to an apocalyptic sense of doom ("the fruit-bearing day/Of his race is past on the earth;/And darkness returns to our eyes" [ll. 56–58]), the speaker utters a piercing apostrophe to the topographical metaphors (moonlight, shadow, lake, mountains) and to the feelings (beauty, grace, charm, romance) associated with Wordsworth's sight/insight and puts to them the question of imaginative essence posed above, elaborated as follows:

> Are ye, like daylight and sun,
> Shared and rejoiced in by all?
> Or are ye immersed in the mass
> Of matter, and hard to extract,
> Or sunk at the core of the world
> Too deep for the most to discern?
>
> (ll. 66–71)

In statuesque language and tonal resonances that seem uncannily prophetic of the grand verbal rituals of the mature Swinburne, Nature "mutter[s]" her Classical oracular reply: "Loveliness, magic, and grace,/They are here! they are set in the world,/They abide . . ." (ll. 79–81); "they are immortal and live,/For they are the life of the world" (ll. 85–86); the singer's themes—"Life and emotion and [Nature]"—are themselves more than the singer (ll. 89–90); all men have some access to them, but no man has ever had complete access (ll. 81–83), the whole of life and emotion and Nature being so much more than the sum of even its most exquisite parts (ll. 75–134 *passim*).

But the tone of Nature's voice is one of stern rebuke rather than of maternal reassurance. Man's apocalyptic response to the death of a great poet—his self-torturing, conventionalized despair (ll. 87–90, 126–128)—is the result of a stubborn, sentimental, elegiac resistance to an obvious but awful truth—that Nature does not live for man—a truth that, once accepted, would free him of his mournful self-flagellation. The best of the Classical poets knew this; the modern Romantics do not, and Nature herself has become impatient with the blindness of man's egotistical pretensions. To the generation that has been so elaborately conscious of itself, she says, "Ye know not yourselves . . ." (l. 103); to the generation that has been so humanitarian, she says, "Your selves and your fellows ye know not . . ." (l. 117); to the generation that claims to have read her own secrets, she says,

> Will ye scan me, and read me, and tell
> Of the thoughts that ferment in my breast,
> My longing, my sadness, my joy?
> Will ye claim for your great ones the gift
> To have rendered the gleam of my skies,
> To have echoed the moan of my seas,
> Uttered the voice of my hills?
>
> (ll. 119–125)

Paradoxically, Nature's austerest, most ego-deflating rebuke is also the most reconciling in that it is the most creatively energizing: what men have seen of her is only a slight metaphor of what there is to be seen (ll. 75–134 *passim*); his poetic voice even at its solemn best hardly "Gives us a sense of the awe,/ The vastness, the grandeur, the gloom/Of the unlit gulf of himself" (ll. 99–103); his greatest bards—"The clearest, the best, who have read/Most in themselves—have beheld/Less than they left unrevealed" (ll. 103–106). Thus man stands at the meridian, not at the end, of poetic possibilities; if he can only bring clarity to his apprehension of the realities of Nature and of himself, the future of poetry as a true criticism of life, emotion, and Nature is inexhaustible.

Two aspects of *The Youth of Nature* not fully encompassed by its arguments are particularly interesting critically. One is the way in which the poem, taken as a whole, resists closure. The point of view rendered by the Nature-spokesman in the second half of the poem, though oracularly impressive, is both philosophically opposed and structurally juxtaposed to the point of view rendered by the Man-spokesman in the first half, which is incontestably impressive too—thoughtful, consistent with its images of place and mood, sincere—and not to be peremptorily overwhelmed and washed out by the admittedly impressive counter-voice. What we have, rather, are two points of view placed by the action, structure, diction, and rhythm of the poem in archetypal contention, and this inspires reflection, not resolution.

The other critically exciting aspect of *The Youth of Nature* is rooted in a speculation justified by the poem's structure and having far-reaching implications for the way we read Arnold's poems generally and especially for the way we read some of his most crucial poems. The speculation is this: if *The Youth of Nature* ended at line 74, how differently would we read it, and what very different implications would we find in it for Arnold as a whole? The critical record makes it safe to say that the wholly ingratiating impressiveness of these 74 lines—their thoughtfulness, consistency, and sincerity—would be, for most readers, so persuasive that they would not even imagine the counter-voice that the poem as a whole supplies. In short, they would *then* read *The Youth of Nature* (ll. 1–74) as they *now* read *Dover Beach* and *The Buried Life*, taking it wholly at face value, the explicit voice of the text being the conclusive voice and the closure it gives to the dramatic experience recorded by that text being yielded to simply and unquestioningly. The speaker would be literalized as *Matthew Arnold in propria persona*, and all metaphoric resonances beyond those used to enrich the setting and feeling would be discarded in the interests of personal statement. But since the abbreviated version (the speculative text) of *The Youth of Nature* would be comparable to the canonical versions of *Dover Beach* and *The Buried Life*, the complete structure of *The Youth of Nature* submits our traditional way of reading those and other Arnold poems to serious question and suggests some alternative possibilities that may be more critically provocative.

The Youth of Man is tightly linked to *The Youth of Nature*. The speaker begins under the pervasive influence of the Nature-spokesman's ringing conclusion to the former poem: the races of men "are dust, they are changed, they are gone!/I remain" (*The Youth of Nature*, ll. 133–134); he echoes elsewhere some of the main positions taken by Nature in her oratorical declamation. It is Nature, not man, who is changeless (l. 95); Nature, not man, embodies the life of the world ("Murmur of living,/Stir of existence,/Soul of the world!" [ll. 51–53]); man's own soul is the microcosm in which he can best see Nature's macrocosm mirrored (ll. 116–118). Indeed, the speaker seems to have capitulated so completely to Nature's hieratic reprimand that he has become more than a touch disagreeable: the thoughtful, consistent, sincere, melancholy Romantic of *The Youth of Nature* has been transformed into an unctuous moralist—naive, inconsistent, insincere, a reformed Romantic "sinner" converted into a bumptious moralistic sycophant. "Behold, O Nature, this pair!" (l. 17) is distinctly reminiscent of the parable of the Pharisee and the Publican in St. Luke's Gospel, and the speaker's deluded presumption that he is now qualified to instruct his instructress is as bizarre as the Pharisee's presuming to instruct Christ.

Moreover, the speaker's unimaginative discourse is so riddled with sentimentality, limp clichés, and rhetorical somersaults that it becomes a paradigm of poetic insincerity. Our first clue to his character is his penchant for exclamation marks—twenty of them, mostly efforts to give his sentiments more dramatic force than they have. Then his characterization of Nature as "Sweet, and forgiving, and good" (l. 15) indicates that he has completely misunderstood Nature's self-characterization and is still costuming her in flatulent sentimental clichés. After that, the clichés flow torrentially: "halo of youth," "Crowning their brows," "sunshine of hope," "rapture of spring," the "ceaseless stroke" of Time's "wings," the "bloom" "Brushed from their souls," eyes that are "Clouded and dim," a heart that is "Languid," pulses that are "Quickened" no more (ll. 19–22, 40–45). The speech he puts into the mouth of "this pair" and that he claims to have heard with his own ears (ll. 23–24) is a mockery of verisimilitude offered as an authentic representation of youth's point of view ("Man, man is the king of the world!/Fools that these mystics are/Who prate of Nature!" [ll. 27–29]; "Nature is nothing" [l. 35]). Those tireless wings of Time that have so devastated them ("They drooped, they grew blind, they grew old" [l. 48]) seem to have left him remarkably untouched. It is not quite clear whether they are literally or figuratively blind, but they do "gaze" and "gaze" (ll. 89, 90), and this moves them back into cliché—to "the Eden of youth," "untold anguish," "the mists of delusion," "the scales of habit," the desert of a "weary, unprofitable length" like their "faded, ignoble lives" (ll. 91, 102–111). The scene (ll. 61–74) in which the old couple stand on a balustraded terrace high above the valley listening to their children at play on the lawn and hearing "the bark of a dog/From a distant farm in the hills" (ll. 73–74) is a Romantic set-piece suffused with sentimentality. The even more Romantic scene of their sudden recognition and redemption is inflated into melodrama by the exaggerated gesturing of the speaker, who may be addressing Nature, himself, or an imaginary audience got up for effect:

> Hush, for tears
> Begin to steal to their eyes!
> Hush, for fruit
> Grows from such sorrow as theirs!
>
> (ll. 97–100)

The speaker does have some better moments than these—the landscape of ll. 75–87 is respectable, the apostrophe to the "Soul of the world" (ll. 51–60) is moving, the final imprecation to youth (ll. 112–118) is high-minded—but these more inspired peaks seem to be remnants of the former sincere, melancholy Romantic and are not quite enough to redeem the unimaginative, stubbly terrain represented by the rest of the poem.

What imaginative intuition would have led Arnold to follow a poetic procedure of this kind in the second of these pindarics? One possibility is formalistic: having employed the grandest of grand manners in the second part of *The Youth of Nature*, he wanted to counterpoint this with a deceptively grand deflation in *The Youth of Man* to give variety to his tonics and to undercut any temptation to fall himself into the trap of oracular inflation. Another possibility is thematic: by moving the speaker of the first part of *The Youth of Nature* into a post-conversional context in which he functions in a deeply faulted way, he could show the severely limited possibilities of such a conversion and the precariousness that results when a representative of one side of an archetypal contention attempts to adopt the opposite position. Finally, he may well have wanted to be reductive of the whole permanence-mutability theme of the Romantics in order to demonstrate to what extremes of sentimental absurdity treatments of it were prone, since it had very little cogency for anyone sufficiently in touch with reality to know the difference between a myth and a fantasy or between a Classical Grecian urn and a Romantic poem about it.

The Future, the third poem in this pindaric trilogy, strikes a middle style. Neither heightened like the climactic second part of *The Youth of Nature* nor confused and cliché-ridden like *The Youth of Man*, it is direct, frankly and explicitly metaphoric, and evenhanded in the presentation of its mildly hopeful insight. If the speaker is the same Man-spokesman who has come through the other two poems, he has achieved a new degree of maturity that has freed him of the turbulence of his earlier states of apocalyptic despair and posturing unction and sees life more steadily and in larger perspective, though not infallibly. He is, above all, an optimistic advocate of contemporaneousness, with the strengths and weaknesses implied by that characterization. He treats the past with matter-of-fact naiveté, the future with matter-of-fact negligence, and he shows but little comprehension of the vast imaginative powers of the bards. His theory of mind is distinctly Lockean—what we know is what our sense impressions teach us—and his tentative surmise about man's future prospects is logical rather than intuitive: as the people on the river of Time have always in the past extracted from what they saw on the shore some basis for order and hope, so is it likely to be with people on the river of Time in the future. And if one were to make the river of Time metaphor retroactive in its application to the whole trilogy, one would say that the speaker in the first poem is Romantic-apocalyptic, that of the second poem Romantic-moralistic, and that of the third Romantic-scientific. The "future" that the speaker of this last poem forecasts is clinical, moderately imaginative, subtly de-spiritualized, unruffled, and literal.

Dover Beach

The most conspicuous features of *Dover Beach* as a poetic text or exercise in language-art are the intensity and volatility of the speaker, the rapidity of the poem's movement from the "sweet" "night air" (l. 6) to the "clash by night" (l. 37), and the speaker's capacity to fix his intense emotional insights in images that are so luridly memorable that they are overwhelmingly impressive and tend therefore to leave the reader defenselessly persuaded that his characterization of modern man's situation is certainly the right characterization. He takes us, as it were, by verbal storm, and the *force* of what he says becomes for the moment our *understanding* of what he says. Somewhat less conspicuous is that the poem is centered in an action, a situation involving two persons, and that there is a formal tension in the poem between the dramatic monologue and the monodrama. This tension is an integral dimension of the manner in which the action is so totally absorbed by the forward-thrusting speaker that the dramatic monologue, with which the poem begins, exists only in remnant form by the time the poem ends.

Having suspended, at least for purposes of fresh critical exploration, our predisposition to see Arnold himself as the speaker of *Dover Beach*, we are free to notice some other things about the poem. For example, the opening landscape is a real landscape: its images are crisp and clear, and it has an independent reality that one can invite another to "Come to the window" to view and feel its benevolent effects. The final landscape, on the other hand, has no external referents: it exists only in the exacerbated consciousness of the speaker and in the tropes with which he tries so intensely and successfully to give it an existence outside his own mind. It is not a portrait of life as life in fact is, but an attitude toward life as, for some reason, he would like his listener to see it in *her* mind. It is a translation of literature into literature—whether Thucydides' description of the Battle of Epipolae, as is traditionally said, or of Tennyson's "last, dim, weird battle of the west" in *Morte d'Arthur*, as seems more likely. And it is a translation of life into literature: it is the imposition on the illusion of a life situation (the initiating landscape, the romantic situation implicit in the poem's fiction) of a cluster of metaphors which must inevitably destroy whatever illusion of happiness that life situation might have prompted. Further, unless one opts for some psychoanalytic motive like post-coital depression, the speaker's volatile movement from quiet, well-anchored serenity to torrential despair is lacking in external motivation. The "Only" (l. 7) to which commentators frequently point is procedural rather than motivational, and we are left with the "tremulous cadence" of the sea as the only external catalyst—the "sound" in which he "find[s]" "a thought" (l. 19)—and are forced to the conclusion that he is moved essentially from within, by some master current of the self. In that context, the poem's second "only"— "now I only hear/Its melancholy, long withdrawing roar" (ll. 24–25)—connects with the first and moves procedure (a habit of mind) to motivation (why he acts the way he does). He is a congenital melancholic and habitually sees life negatively and monistically, beauty itself, as in the initial landscape, triggering psychic gloom. His joy is in melancholy, his highest emotional fulfilment in a species of linguistic or metaphoric despair. Thus he wrenches even the fundamental metaphor of the poem— the ebb and flow of the tide and of time—and hears the ebb only:

> But now I only hear
> Its melancholy, long, withdrawing roar,
> Retreating, to the breath
> Of the night-wind, down the vast edges drear
> And naked shingles of the world.
>
> (ll. 24–28)

It is a moving image, most ingratiatingly framed; but if one follows it through to its ultimate implications, the ingratiation dissolves into a spiritually terrifying spectacle of a gaunt naked world in which tide and time are all gone and only the grotesque distortions of an unmediated cadaver of a world remain. It may be true, of course, but the very shock of it—the existential unacceptability of it—turns the eye that has thoroughly seen it toward some alternative to it.

This is why Sophocles is implanted in the text. The verse paragraph in which the speaker draws an analogy between his thoughts and those of Sophocles (ll. 15–20) has given critics some uneasiness: it seems to be a bald intellectual intrusion into an experiential poetic context, a throwing of thought at music. And such uneasiness is fully justified so long as one sees *Dover Beach* as a direct authorial statement—Matthew Arnold making explicit, discursive connections in a work of imagination that really should be allowed to speak for itself. But fault becomes felicity once the reader accepts the poem as dramatic or personative and perceives that the poet and the speaker have very different intentions in the reference to Sophocles. The speaker merely points to an analogy between what Sophocles was drawn to think of by the Aegean ("the turbid ebb and flow/Of human misery" [ll. 17–18]) and his own belated thoughts in a very different but comparable setting. The poet, on the other hand, thereby invites the reader to ask himself a crucial question: how does the life illusion of the speaker of this poem measure up to the tragic vision of Sophocles? what is the effect on the reader of *Dover Beach* as compared, for example, with that of the Theban plays? It is the central question that many of Arnold's poems ask of the reader, and it certainly demands to be asked of this one. The answer has a quality of unequivocal inevitability about it: to yield to the sentiment of this nearly irresistible structure of image, rhythm, and thought is to yield to an enervating pathos for which there is simply no corrective, a pathos in which desperate endurance is the only action. Thus its near irresistibility must in fact be resisted, and that is what the Sophoclean implant enables us to do: it preserves the integrity of the underlying metaphor (while there is ebb, there is also flow) and gives us the essential clue—namely, the highest standard of literary measuring—of how to detach from the mesmerizing ingratiation of the speaker and to deflect his force into our understanding, to watch his processes at an empathetic distance, both imaginatively involved and imaginatively independent.

The speaker of *Dover Beach* is an embodiment of Romanticism in its most alluring and devastating modern form—existential despair—that Classicism in its most austere and most strengthening ancient form constructively contradicts. We are reminded by his excruciating pain, which panics into self-destructive solipsism, that others have dealt with equal pain with a steadiness and wholeness of view that turns pathos into tragedy and makes pain self-redemptive.

The speaker's Romanticism is reinforced in other ways as well. One such reinforcement is his nostalgia for the Middle Ages, which is insinuated through the "Sea of Faith" metaphor, through such usages as "bright girdle" and "naked shingle" (ll. 23, 28), through a retreat into the sentimentality of the courtly love tradition ("Ah, love, let us be true/To one another" [ll. 29–30]), and through his allusion to the battle in which Arthurianism—and, symbolically, medieval Christianity—is lost. He is a modern equivalent of Julian the Apostate, rejecting a post-Christian world as Julian had rejected a post-Imperial world. Another such reinforcement is the speaker's Romantic confusion over the role of Nature in human affairs. The "world," he says,

> which seems
> To lie before us like a land of dreams,
> So various, so beautiful, so new,
> Hath really neither joy, nor love, nor light,
> Nor certitude, nor peace, nor help for pain. . . .
>
> (ll. 30–34)

As the Classical writers and writers like Spinoza and Goethe knew, and the Romantic writers generally did not, it is not Nature's function to bring joy and love and light and certitude and peace and help for pain to man. Man must find ways of doing that for himself, and any dependence on Nature to do it for him inevitably leads to an imposition on Nature of man's own feelings of inadequacy, an imposition that muddles the whole issue and leads to such Romantic bewilderment as that of the speaker of *Dover Beach*. As Nature is Nature, man is man; and though he may find instructive analogies in Nature, the man who seeks in her a direct curative role must eventually learn, often at a great spiritual price, that she is not what, to such a person, she "seems" (l. 30).

The more traditional reading of *Dover Beach* is much neater, of course; it fits the poem into an ideological category and makes it contribute to an ideological design. But it is not a reading that gives the text, the context, and the subtext of the poem full imaginative room. Ideological neatness is surely not too great a price to pay for the imaginative vigor and subtlety that emerge from a view of the poem as a succinct, complex lyrical drama that critiques in an integrated way one of the most intense spiritual distresses of man.

Stanzas from the Grande Chartreuse

Stanzas from the Grande Chartreuse, like *Dover Beach* and *The Buried Life*, embodies the superbly imaginative creation of a complex metaphor of coping with the stinging distresses of modern life that, despite its genuine, even its profoundly fascinating, metaphoric attractiveness, is self-indicting. The speaker's solutions to the problems which he himself puts in place are, as solutions, simply impossible. His is a myth of the return from which, ironically, there is no return; the Virgilian note of sadness that one hears in the poem is compounded to the nth degree because this modern Aeneas-figure can find neither the motive nor the energy to leave the underworld into which he has journeyed. There is a kind of analogue in Arnold's other Virgilian lament, *Balder Dead*, but Balder at least has heard of the prospect of a better world to which he will one day return, and this makes him analogous rather to the monks of the Grande Chartreuse, to whose ears the organ carries "accents of another sphere" (ll. 203–204). The speaker of *Stanzas from the Grande Chartreuse*, on the other hand, has had no such assurance, holds no such belief; and so his taking up residence "Beneath some old-world abbey wall," where he was not in fact "reared," is an act of wilful choice, not a continuous heritage, and what he chooses is to be "Forgotten," "secret," "Deep, deep" hidden, buried alive (ll. 169–174). In the process of articulating his *apologia pro vita sua*, he gives many "reasons," of course; but they are not really reasons at all, only explanations or justifications. His is a journey into emotional and psychological recessiveness—not a journey into timelessness, but into anachronism; his "reason" is simply *this is the way I am*, as his plea is simply *let me be*. He is not an antagonist, but an exile, turning his back on every metaphor of modernism—the "masters of the mind," the Romantic poets and novelists, the

"Sons of the world," the men of action, the men of pleasure—
and claiming kinship only with the strictest exemplars of
medieval monasticism. He does not share their beliefs, and he
cannot live within their walls; even the nobility of their faith is
lacking to his grief. We may be reasonably sure that the monks
of the Grande Chartreuse would not reciprocate the speaker's
identification with them. There is an ontological gulf between
the austere rigors of their faith and the humid melancholy of
his Romantic *Weltschmerz*; though he sees himself as a child
and them as children, they would feel spiritually depleted by
the significance he attaches to this characterization, as they
would feel severely compromised by his suggestion that the
banners of pleasure "Make their blood dance and chain their
eyes" (l. 188) and that the bugle music "Arrests them with a
charmed surprise" (l. 190); nor would they accept his tempor-
izing ("too late") of their reason for not following a life of
action (e.g., war) or of pleasure (e.g., the hunt). These are *his*
responses, not theirs, and they constitute a most curious
imposition upon human images of the pathetically fallacious
tendency that Romanticism had brought to its apprehension
of Nature.

But that the poet dismantles his *persona* even in the process
of putting him in place—simultaneously insinuates his attractiveness and undercuts his validity—is not in and of itself an
adequate basis for evaluating the poem. It may predispose us
to find the process interesting, but it does not qualify for us
the imaginative character of the manner in which it is worked
out. Nor do various useful ways of characterizing or describing
the poem really get at the essential critical question, which must
be located at the poem's internal center. *Stanzas from the Grande
Chartreuse* is Arnold's poetic equivalent of Carlyle's *Characteristics*, a spiritual profile of his age; it is his muted *In Memoriam*,
with an excruciating difference—a remembrance of things past
that ends either in solipsistic sterility or in the most tenuous
discovery in the dead of the "stepping-stones" or myth patterns
of the future. It clarifies and validates in a most helpful way
Arnold's own sense of his characteristics as a poet. In a letter
to his mother, he said, "It might be fairly urged that I have less
poetical sentiment than Tennyson, and less intellectual vigor

and abundance than Browning; yet, because I have perhaps more of a fusion of the two than either of them, and have more regularly applied that fusion to the main line of modern development, I am likely enough to have my turn, as they have had theirs."[35] These are useful ways of pinpointing the field in which the poem is functioning, of establishing a comparative frame of reference for illuminating it, and of getting reasonably close to the poet's probable intention, but they still do not hit at the center of the critical question.

That critical question is this: with what degree of imaginative adequacy does the poet cope with the challenges and expectations that, on the basis of internal evidence, we can perceive that he set for himself? With what subtlety and comprehensiveness has he set in poetic motion and brought to poetic completion the interpretive implications of the subject that he has undertaken? It is the simplest and severest of all critical questions, and its answer can never be luminously and objectively self-evident since each reader must ultimately answer it for himself and since the individual's answer must depend to some degree upon his sympathy with the poet and his capacity to participate co-creatively in shaping, through the quality of his response, the poem's artistic unity and imaginative integrity. But one can hardly hope to deal with the critical question at all unless he does some careful inventory-taking, empirically observing as many key indices to the poet's imaginative frame of reference as possible.

We notice, in the first place, that it is a "we/I/we" poem, a poem in the confessional mode—that is, internally, formalistically autobiographical—in which the speaker wavers somewhat uncertainly between his individual and his generic identity. While there are aesthetic values to be derived from this—the maximum illusion of highly personal experience, of experience registered with utmost intensity on the individual pulse beats, within a larger metaphoric framework—one can hardly avoid seeing this as an aspect of characterization, destabilizing the speaker and diminishing his role as a trustworthy model. Secondly, it very soon becomes clear that what the speaker sees cannot be divorced from the state of feeling or consciousness in which he sees it. The landscape with which the poem begins is a real landscape, and he initially pinpoints its chief images with painstaking matter-of-factness, but he gradually begins to project internal images onto external reality—"strangled sound," "boiling cauldron," "spectral vapours" (ll. 9, 12, 13). This can be seen as the poet's signal that all images have a symbolic content, but it also alerts us that the speaker's translation of visual image into psychic symbol is another index to his temperament or personality and prepares us to keep in proper perspective his climactic creation of the wholly imaginary dramatic tapestry or triptych with which the poem ends. This is an allegory of the state of *his own mind* having only a tangential relationship to the complex reality it is meant to summarize, and its simple emblematic qualities are only as plausible as he is plausible or simplistic as he is simplistic. Like the speaker in *Dover Beach*, he is monitored chiefly by a master current in the self, and this calls into serious question his capacity to draw us outward toward any insight more universal than that individual self extrapolated symbolically. Third, it is an "action" poem, and the action is indispensable both to its structure or narrative curve and to its ultimate disclosure: what happens in the speaker's consciousness is made possible by what happens in the physical or fictional ritual through which he passes, and hence the feeling gives importance to the action, rather than the action to the feeling. On the other hand, his journey being a journey into metaphor, the action itself assumes a metaphoric character and serves as the chief coherent of the poem's complex hierarchy of metaphors. Being a journey into metaphor from which there is no mythic return, the disclosure as the speaker renders it (as distinct from the poetic disclosure that includes but exceeds the speaker) encompasses only exile, and the title is metaphoric too: these stanzas are the communiqué sent out from this old-world metaphor of physical and psychic space and time by an exile who chooses not to return to the world he has abandoned. Being a journey into metaphor, again, it is a journey into poetry in the large, humanly enveloping sense—a search for the tropes by which a private but imaginatively satisfying sense of one's proper place in time and space can be, at least to some extent, achieved. Since it is a *persona* poem with a destabilized protagonist, we can expect that there will be a significant discrepancy between the *persona*'s disclosure and that of the poet; but we can expect, too, that much of the poem's aesthetic excitement will depend upon the subtle way in which the poet gives a kind of legitimacy to the very position that, in the end, he will undercut. Finally, we notice that the poem's form is the result of a curious fusion of genres. The confessional mode emphasizes its intense lyrical quality and places it in the category of a monodrama, thus enabling it to draw with a minimum of formalistic restriction upon the innermost, uninhibited resources of the *persona*'s psyche. The journey motif gives it a narrative curve and moves it in the direction of the epic, and its epic-like qualities are further reinforced by its analogue in the epic journey to the underworld and by its use of the epic simile, the epic roll call, and recurrent epic apostrophes. Ironically, these epic inflations are put to very fallible elegiac uses, and the Classical epic motifs—the epic battle (the *Iliad*), the epic return (the *Odyssey*), and the epic foundation (the *Aeneid*)—are also specifically contradicted; but they play a part in the poet's imaginative apprehension and are an important key to the discrepancy between the way the protagonist sees himself and the way the poet sees him.

Everything about *Stanzas from the Grande Chartreuse* except the speaker's determination to drop out of modern life induces an atmosphere of imaginative ambiguity. Much of this ambiguity is suggested by the aesthetic procedure itself—the we/I/we self-positioning of the speaker, the external landscape that is absorbed into the landscape of the speaker's mind and adulterated there, the discrepancy between the speaker's and the poet's disclosures, the epic/non-epic character of the narrative. But it is also a conspicuous aspect of the speaker's personal *apologia* and of his effort to clarify the metaphor into which he has become absorbed. For example, it is impossible to identify satisfactorily the "rigorous teachers" who "seized [his] youth,/And purged its faith, and trimmed its fire" (ll. 67–68), the "masters of the mind" who forced him to unlearn and resign much that he had aspired to before (ll. 73–75). Writers like Carlyle, Goethe, and Spinoza are often suggested by the commentators, but they seem wholly false to the poem's imagery: they were not "masters of the mind" dismantling youth's faith, and it is rather grotesque to imagine them as spectral and foreboding presences "pierc[ing] the gloom" with such ghastly whispers as *What dost thou in this living tomb?*" (ll. 71–72, Arnold's emphasis). On the other hand, if they are the rationalists, scientific positivists, and sceptics—the embodiments of the most aggressive current of modern intellectualism—the poem itself gives no hint of their specific identities. We can, of course, fill in the blanks with names like Descartes, Hume, Gibbon, Voltaire, Godwin, and Bentham, but it is somewhat arbitrary to do so; since their anonymity is in such sharp contrast to the roll call of "poets" (Byron, Shelley, Senancour), it seems reasonable to conclude that the poet means them to be as generic and anonymous as the monks of the Grande Chartreuse, metaphors of the modern spirit placed in juxtaposition to metaphors of the medieval spirit in a manner analogous to the way in which the speaker manipulates the landscape of the poem, supplying much of its metaphoric content and giving it a special turning out of the center of himself. This has the effect of casting the same shadow of ambiguity over the "masters of the mind" as envelops the monks themselves, the reader being unable to yield to either metaphor the luminous clarity that the speaker would assign them.

A similar ambiguity attends the speaker's bitter lamentation over the failed spiritual fatherhood of the Romantic poets and novelists. Assuming the role of an epic orphan of his age, one of the world's waifs adrift on the perilous seas of modern life (ll. 121–126), he intones, in a voice that is both strident and sad, a chiding dirge over the spiritual sterility of "the pageant of [Byron's] bleeding heart" (ll. 133–138), the "lovely" but ineffectual "wail" of Shelley (ll. 139–144), and the "stern" but self-enclosed and quite personal maneuvers of Obermann (ll. 145–150). The "masters of the mind" had been his "teachers," stern images in a master-pupil relationship from which he could separate himself despite a significant degree of anxiety and guilt (ll. 67–79), but the poets had been his "fathers" (l. 121), and from them there is no real escape. They failed to fulfil their responsibilities as guides to their "sons" (l. 129), but they left an ineradicable imprint—"we—we learnt your lore too well!" (l. 156). So, in a strange, ambiguous way, this pilgrim from the present to the past, from now to then, this outcast of the contemporary universe, is in search of a metaphor of paternity—of a fatherhood that will keep faith with a future that is now in part the speaker's past, of a hospice that, despite its cold severity, will serve as a substitute home. It is not their faith that he craves, but their fraternity, their stability rather than their metaphysics. And this quality is what is tested and confirmed by the speaker in his final imaginary tableau: the monks reject the allurements of both action and pleasure and hold steady in the "desert" of their "peace."[36]

In the sequences on the "masters of the mind" and on the Romantic poets and novelists, the speaker reaches out toward cultural context in a curiously subtextual way—that is, he sees the outer world of cultural history through the filter of inner, largely emotional need. This quality of contextual subtextuality comes as close, perhaps, as any metaphor to characterizing the subtle dilemma of an imperious ambiguity in which the speaker is caught, a dilemma in which every gesture has its counter-gesture and every thought is eroded by a feeling that subverts it. For example, in trying to clarify his position in relation to the "masters of the mind," through an answer to the self-imposed question "—And what am I, that I am here?" (l. 66), the speaker draws a crucial analogy:

> Not as their friend, or child, I speak!
> But as, on some far northern strand,
> Thinking of his own Gods, a Greek
> In pity and mournful awe might stand
> Before some fallen Runic stone—
> For both were faiths, and both are gone.

(ll. 79–84)

This analogy, which is analytical and historical as well as metaphoric, constitutes the poem's central epic simile, and it contains the long prophetic rhythms of the epic. As the faith of the ancient Greeks fell into decay, a latter-day Greek might have stood in "pity and mournful awe" over the remnants of

his religion. But that religion was succeeded in time by Christianity; though the speaker may now stand, in his turn, in "pity
and mournful awe" over the remnants of the Christian religion,
implicit in the analogy is a basis for believing that it, too, will
be succeeded in time by a new, as yet undisclosed faith—
"powerless" at the moment "to be born," but as inevitable as
the succession of the Greek by the Christian. Analytically and
historically perceived, then, the speaker's situation, even as he
sees it, is not without grounds for hope. But it is not to the
hope that he clings experientially. His eye sinks inward (ll.
91–114), and the analytical, historical, outward-looking position
that he had momentarily assumed is suddenly awash in a
deluge of emotional, psychological introspection by which
thought is subverted by feeling and philosophical perspective
is submerged in a torrent of personal pain:

> Ah, if it *be* passed, take away,
> At least, the restlessness, the pain;
> Be man henceforth no more a prey
> To these out-dated stings again!
> The nobleness of grief is gone—
> Ah, leave us not the fret alone!
>
> (ll. 103–108)

There is a shadowy subtext here too, a suggestion that the very
pain the speaker feels in this trough of worldwide disbelief
reflects both the agony of the starved spirit and the archetypal
human need for a spirit-nourishing faith that will, in time,
bring such a faith into being again. But this is the detached
poet-reader's perspective, not the speaker's, who pleads simply
for time "to die out" unmolested:

> But—if you cannot give us ease—
> Last of the race of them who grieve,
> Here leave us to die out with these
> Last of the people who believe!
>
> (ll. 109–112)

Finally, as the poet, with a wry subtlety, gives the speaker's dramatic lyric epic resonances that implicitly critique it, so he takes a doomsday theme and refuses it an apocalyptic turning. The speaker's vision of a possible future is remarkably placid and secular—of an "age" that "without hardness will be sage,/ And gay without frivolity" (ll. 157, 159–160), references backward to his too-rigorous teachers and to the "eternal trifler" who "breaks [the] spell" of the Romantic poets, suggesting that relatively simple offenses to his cultivated temperament have played a disproportionate part in alienating him from his unfortunate age. Moreover, he turns even that future over to others—"Sons of the world" (l. 161)—and, in a way different from but analogous to that of the Romantic poets and novelists, opts to "slumber in [a] silent grave!" (l. 151). There is a good deal more whimper than bang in his manner of exiting, and all his grand gesturing slides, in the end, very close to nullity.

What, then, was Arnold getting at in *Stanzas from the Grande Chartreuse*? What imaginative intuition does the text of the poem sustain? At the most fundamental level, it is the recognition of how fatal to the spirit of man the spirit of an age can be. A fragmented age fragments its people, and the speaker of this poem embodies, for all his attractive spiritual intensity, the inadequate vision, ambiguous responses, false starts, and gross misdirection of an incoherent moment in time. It is not a one-way movement, of course. The effect of an era having become systemic in its people, they in turn compound the character of the times, closing the circle and making it almost impossible to break out of their reciprocal false enchantments. Context (external cultural metaphors) and subtext (internal personal metaphors) become mutually reinforcing, and the possibilities of cultural renewal are paralyzed by the spiritual depletion of individuals upon whose self-renewal cultural renovation largely depends. Hardness (a tough, circumscribed intellectual rigidity) and frivolity (a trifling disengagement from genuine concerns) invade the age, and many of those to whom its spiritual guidance has been entrusted (its symbolic Byrons, Shelleys, and Senancours) collapse into melancholy, into a self-centered despair that not only does not help but even becomes an irresistible and devastating paradigm of response, especially among younger spirits who might, if they had any inkling of how, search out grounds for reconciliation. But they have no such inkling because they are also victims of their age, perhaps its special victims. They, too, like their failed mentors, despair; but their journey into the self claims a different reference point. They step out of time—current time, future time—and travel into a metaphoric past with which, even if they cannot share it at the crucial center that holds it together and enables it to exist, they can sufficiently identify to make it a source of personal solace during the metaphoric time through which they have yet to live. They can at least be fellow travelers in faith, hope, stability, and brotherhood although they lack the faith and forego the hope. It is a highly Romantic response, of course, but they are, after all, the orphaned "sons" of the Romantics; though we can hardly fail to see the solipsistic ambiguity of a solution that is really another form of capitulation, we may yet acknowledge *Stanzas from the Grande Chartreuse* to be an imaginatively complex and profoundly instructive working out of one of the compelling myths of Romantic Modernism.

Notes

1. See *The Poems of Matthew Arnold*, Miriam Allott, ed., 2nd ed. (London and New York: Longman, 1979), p. 27. All references to Arnold's poems are to this edition and are given in parentheses in the text.
2. The history of the poem can be traced in *The Poetical Works of William Wordsworth*, Helen Darbishire, ed., 2nd ed. (Oxford: At the Clarendon Press, 1952), volume II, pp. 267–272, 518–520.
3. "After Scene," *The Dynasts* (New York: St. Martin's Press, 1965), p. 522.
4. Silenus having been "entrusted with the education of the young Dionysus," the reveller becomes a metaphoric extension of Dionysus. See Philip Mayerson, *Classical Mythology in Literature, Art, and Music* (Waltham, Mass.: Xerox College Publishing, 1971), p. 250.
5. *The Letters of Matthew Arnold to Arthur Hugh Clough*, H.F. Lowry, ed. (London and New York: Oxford University Press, 1932), p. 101.
6. The myth of Eos-Tithonus becomes an inevitable subtext of this story, and Tithonus' pathetic fate would certainly moderate any Romantic enthusiasm one might entertain for the success of the Eos-Orion affair. The Tithonus myth is also a subtext of *Fragment of Chorus of a 'Dejaneira'*, where it lends support to the chorus's advocacy of death when one's powers are in their fullness rather than in decay.

7. Thus Arnold's point, in a note to the poem, that "the Wild Huntsman" "appear[s]" in both earth and sky." See *Poems*, p. 64n.

8. *Letters to Clough*, p. 101.

9. *Letters to Clough*, p. 124.

10. Quoted in *Poems*, pp. 79–80.

11. Preface to the First Edition of *Poems* (1853), *The Complete Prose Works of Matthew Arnold*, R.H. Super, ed. (Ann Arbor: University of Michigan Press, 1960), volume I, p. 7.

12. Preface of 1853, p. 8.

13. Preface of 1853, p. 8.

14. *Last Essays . . . , Complete Prose Works*, volume VIII, pp. 12, 41–42.

15. *Poems*, p. 639.

16. In his lecture-essay on Emerson, Arnold spoke of Emerson's "clear and pure voice," "as new, and moving, and unforgettable, as the strain of Newman, or Carlyle, or Goethe." *Complete Prose Works*, volume X, p. 167.

17. See "Spinoza and the Bible," *Complete Prose Works*, volume III, pp. 176–177.

18. *Letters to Clough*, p. 107.

19. *Letters to Clough*, p. 107.

20. *Letters to Clough*, pp. 105–107.

21. William E. Buckler, *Matthew Arnold's Books: Toward a Publishing Diary* (Geneva and Paris: E. Droz, 1958), p. 97.

22. Unpublished letter, Fales Collection, New York University.

23. Wordsworth, *Tintern Abbey*, ll. 122–123.

24. Kenneth Allott, "Three Early Diaries," *Victorian Studies*, No. 2 (1959), pp. 262–263.

25. See Leon Gottfried, *Matthew Arnold and the Romantics* (Lincoln: University of Nebraska Press, 1963), pp. 213–219, and U.C. Knoepflmacher, "Dover Revisited: The Wordsworthian Matrix in the Poetry of Matthew Arnold," *Victorian Poetry*, No. 1 (1963), pp. 17–26.

26. *Letters to Clough*, p. 146.

27. The suggestion that Arnold referred to Fanny Lu as "F--L" in his 1851 diary "may be glanced at in the title 'Faded Leaves'"would be amusing if it were more playfully intended. See *Poems*, p. 243.

28. The cause of Arnold's own interrupted wooing, insofar as we know it, was that Judge Wightman had forbidden his daughter to see Arnold because he had no visible and adequate means of supporting a wife, a situation that could be, and was, remedied and hence not hopeless. Further, the role played by the woman in *Faded Leaves*—that of an elegant tease—is hardly flattering to either her or her husband's devotion.

29. At the same time, it enables the poet to avoid the ambiguities inherent in Carlyle's revision of the same text to "*Know what thou canst work at,*" Arnold putting greater emphasis on a doctrine of knowledge than on a doctrine of work.

30. *Letters to Clough*, p. 115.

31. In *On Translating Homer: Last Words* (*Complete Prose Works*, vol. I, p. 188), Arnold says, "I think it will be found that the grand style arises in poetry, *when a noble nature, poetically gifted, treats with simplicity or with severity a serious subject.*"

32. Nothing could be further from the truth of Arnold's own childhood and youth, and it confirms in a somewhat lurid way that the speaker is a self-consciously conflicted modern Romantic, a man of feeling magnified into a metaphor of pathos.

33. It looks forward to the Celestial Spirits of Hardy's *The Dynasts*, though Hardy humanizes the children of eternity rather than deifying the children of time.

34. Wordsworth had himself reached a perception of this underlying unity in *Composed upon Westminster Bridge*. See *Lines written in Kensington Gardens*, pp. 91–95, above.

35. *The Letters of Matthew Arnold, 1848–1888*, G.W.E. Russell, ed. (New York: Macmillan, 1895), vol. II, p. 10.

36. Even though it has been shown that the area around the Grande Chartreuse was known as "the desert," that does not remove the ambiguity inherent in the image as used in this poetic context. See Iris Esther Sells, *Matthew Arnold and France: The Poet* (Cambridge: Cambridge University Press, 1970), pp. 295–296.

3.

Tristram and Iseult
and *Empedocles on Etna*

Tristram and Iseult and *Empedocles on Etna*, the two most ambitious poems completed by Arnold in his pre-1853 period, are very different from each other as well as quite distinctive in his canon as a whole. They are obviously the results of his literary search for suitable subjects for poems, and he clearly honed his perspective on the issue of the centrality of the subject—the crucial aesthetic focus of the Preface of 1853—through the process of creating them and the relentless evaluative review to which he subjected them. Both appeared for the first time in the *Empedocles* volume of 1852; though we know so little about the specific calendar of their composition that we must simply call it unknown, we do know that they belong to the most fervid and uneasy period of his poetic creativity, 1851–1852. We know also that though *Tristram and Iseult* was not censured in the ways in which *Empedocles on Etna* was, the two poems were not reprinted in the same collection between 1852 and 1869, though both poems were reprinted twice during that period, suggesting that even after he had made peace with *Empedocles*, Arnold was for some time reluctant to pair them again.

At the external or descriptive level, the two poems are very different. *Tristram and Iseult* is medieval, *Empedocles on Etna* Classical; the one examines the relentless destructiveness of an obsessively tyrannical passion, the other the relentless destructiveness of an obsessively tyrannical mind; the imaginative boldness of the former is centered in narrative, in how to tell a tale, and in a wholly fresh experiment in creative fusion—of narratology with prosody and of poetry with dramatic music (opera) and dramatic art (tapestry painting), while the imaginative boldness of the latter is centered in a truly complex psychological penetration and precision. *Tristram and Iseult* distills a perspective on human life from legend and anchors it poetically in the millennial rhythms of human history; *Empedocles on Etna* distills a perspective on human life from history and reveals how the millennial rhythms of human history, poetically perceived, gradually succumb to the greater imaginative imperatives of myth.

But at the internal or affective level, at the level of imaginative intuition rather than of fanciful association and design, the two poems share a heartbreaking vision of man in his universe that can animate, inspirit, or reconcile only the numb or careless, a view of human life in which, in very truth, "Sorrow is knowledge: they who know the most/Must mourn the deepest o'er the fatal truth—".[1]

Tristram is Sorrow's child; in the first printed version, Iseult of Ireland's terrible farewell to life is the briefest, bitterest rebuke to Sorrow: *"Ah Sorrow—Fool! thou missest—we are both unmov'd!"* (Part II, ll. 99–100), and a bizarrely heroic acceptance of their eternal coupling in the passionless peace of death.[2] Iseult of Brittany, "The sweetest Christian soul alive" (Part I, l. 54), takes from her knowledge of life in this world the appearance of one "dying in the mask of youth" (Part II, l. 75) and a heart-weariness so complete that she identifies, in the oblique way in which poetry tells a truth,[3] with that child of Death on the battlefield of life, Vivian. "For she was passing weary of his love" (Part III, l. 224) applies with equal manifest force to Vivian's and Iseult's judgments of their late love relationships and with even darker latent force to a transformed Iseult's anniversary feelings about Tristram, her emotions recollected in bitter tranquillity.

Empedocles' suicide is, of course, an act of will made absolute by its *ad hoc* irreversibility: it simply alters the rules and writes *finis* to life as we know it. Empedocles justifies it, in a state of intense emotional dilation, on the basis that it is the only available way of avoiding total enslavement to the awful truth of human life (Part II, l. 406); but it is "unforgivable" in the sense that it negates all further consideration, and his last-minute shift to feeling rather than thought as the proper grounds for knowledge (Part II, ll. 404–409) is itself, from the Classical point of view, philosophically suicidal. But the terrifying "truth" of *Empedocles on Etna* is not the self-destruction of the poet-philosopher himself, which can be easily explained psychologically (an unbalanced mind) or religio-philosophically (transmigration believed in and accelerated) or even perceived as an act of self-liberation (the will effecting a birth into life, a resurrection, out of this grave of a world— [Part II, ll. 410–416]). The really terrifying truth is Empedocles' symbolic erasure of human life itself through his erasure of all grounds for human hope, of all expectation of human poise, of all possibility of resistance to that relentless metamorphosizer of our identity that makes futile even the most dedicated of efforts to know ourselves:

> we will once more fall away
> Into some bondage of the flesh or mind,
> Some slough of sense, or some fantastic maze
> Forged by the imperious lonely thinking-power.
> And each succeeding age in which we are born
> Will have more peril for us than the last;
> Will goad our senses with a sharper spur,
> Will fret our minds to an intenser play,
> Will make ourselves harder to be discerned.
> And we shall struggle awhile, gasp and rebel—
> And we shall fly for refuge to past times,
> Their soul of unworn youth, their breath of greatness;

And the reality will pluck us back,
Knead us in its hot hánd, and change our nature.
And we shall feel our powers of effort flag,
And rally then for one last fight—and fail;
And we shall sink in the impossible strife,
And be astray forever.

(Part II, ll. 373–390)

It is an elegant analyst's apocalypse, a man of mind's measured, circumspect cry of doom; its conscientiousness is incontrovertibly validated—its "truth" put beyond question—when, seventeen lines later, *"He plunges into the crater"* (following Part II, l. 416).

Tristram and Iseult and *Empedocles on Etna* belong to that half-decade in the nineteenth century—the period also of *In Memoriam* (1850), *Maud* (1855), and *Men and Women* (1855)—when a genuinely inspired effort to put a new poetry in place was at work, and they are thoroughly substantial, wholly respectable exemplifications of that inspired effort—fascinating and fully competitive examples of the new poetry. Both poems reflect Arnold's growing commitment to the centrality of the action, and together they reveal some of the underlying reasons for Arnold's dependence on and faith in dramatic poetry.

Independent of the issue of one's mature critical judgment of the degree of poetical success Arnold achieved in *Tristram and Iseult*, every aspect of the poem is genuinely interesting, and the poet must be credited with having been very much alive to the new poetical possibilities inherent in his "thousand-year-old" subject. It is England's first modernized version of the legend of Tristram and the two Iseults, and Arnold clearly felt that "a modern expression of a modern outlook," in Hardy's phrase, on this new-old tale invited a manner of treatment very different from the allegorical narrative of its own medieval tradition or the epic narrative of the Classical tradition recently employed by Tennyson in his *Morte d'Arthur*. Indeed, how to tell the tale—what *form* of narrative concentration and release to use—became such an imperious question that it gradually absorbed into itself both aesthetic and substantive considerations and took focus as the primary poetical issue.

Several relevant factors were apparently taken into account in settling the issue of narrative form. One was the general principle of authorial self-effacement. Another was the dramatic principle of enabling the action to subsist as it did in nature—immediate, intense, economical, but fully adequate to the depth and range of the subject's significance. On the other hand, it was a generally unfamiliar subject—new to the poet[4] and new certainly to the great majority of his readers—and this, coupled with the essential strangeness of certain aspects of the story, called for some form of narrative mediation. The choice of an imaginary Breton bard as narrator seemed a happy solution to the problem. It kept the poet wholly effaced; it cast in the narrator role, implanted in the text, a qualified commentator who could be expected to see vividly, tell crisply, ruminate relevantly, speculate on the significance of the total action with appropriate circumspection and depth, interpret worthily but not infallibly; and it brought the poet and the reader into analogous roles—watching a fascinating watcher watch. It was a happy solution in yet other ways. Brittany, Cornwall, and Ireland have an anthropological common denominator (their people are Celts) with fundamental poetical implications: an unusual susceptibility to belief in magic and to the animism of objects; a highly developed sense of ill-starred love, of destiny-cum-doom; a particular relish for the wandering romantic hero, battle-scarred and eternally threatened with existential loneliness; a joy in language so intense that the distinction between music and the spoken word often becomes moot. By adopting a narrator with this ethnic-poetical identity, Arnold gave his poem the authority of an insider and made available to it the rich tradition of the Breton lay that he exploits so penetratingly in Part III.

Such bold, innovative poetic telling can only be had at a price, of course; most readers find their initial contact with *Tristram and Iseult* both confusing and frustrating, and even repeated readings of the poem do not wholly eliminate the need to be perpetually alert to its narrative idiosyncrasies. Moreover, it would be foolish to equate one's authentic aesthetic excitement over what Arnold is doing experimentally in *Tristram and Iseult* with the notion of formal perfection: the poem has some very rough edges and makes some very distressing leaps. But, even so, its poetical accomplishments are real, and it leaves little doubt but that Arnold could have been one of the major poetic craftsmen in the modern tradition.

The overall aesthetic effect that Arnold achieves in *Tristram and Iseult* is a harmony of immediacy with distance, the immediacy of unmediated drama in combination with the distance of mediated narrative. The fusion of forms through which the tale is told is the chief bearer of this effect, but the shifts in tense between past and present contribute to it, and this metaphor of tense—implanted in Part I and enlarged in Parts II and III—is translated into a metaphor of universality when the pastness of the action's presentness is given a millennial rhythm: "Cold, cold as those who lived and loved/A thousand years ago" (Part II, ll. 192–193).[5] Even the superb and varied metrics[6] contribute to this idiosyncratic, neither/both placement of the poem's aesthetic effect. In the wonderfully effective operatic duet (Part II, ll. 1–100), an immediacy that is real is moved to a heightened ritualistic distance that possesses its authentic order of reality too.[7] The tetrameter lines of the narrative passages in Parts I and II,[8] through a generous use of iambs in a predominantly trochaic texture, combine the flexuous vigor of prose (immediacy) with the stylized rhymes and rhythms of verse (distance); in Part III, which is all mediated narrative, the heroic couplet is used with such apparent casualness and ease as to draw very little attention to itself. The character portraits partake of the same quality. We have a painter's vivid sense of peopled scenes (Tristram and his attendants in the feverish opening scene, Iseult and her children in the subdued, indicting closing scene) and of genre portraits (Tristram and Iseult in death, Part II, ll. 101–111, Iseult in frozen, sexless domesticity, Part III, ll. 79–95); but we also have a ghostly sense of the long ago and far away, an almost allegorical sense of a population of symbols rather than of individual persons. This animistic feeling is startlingly corroborated by the "ghostly tapestry" (Part II, ll. 152–193): is it art looking at life or art imitating life or art looking at art? Or is it Tristram of the Woods before his metamorphosis of identity looking blankly at Tristram of the Pleasaunce after, in Empedocles' words, "reality" has kneaded him in "its hot hand"

and changed his nature and set him "astray for ever" (*Empedocles on Etna*, Part II, ll. 385–390)?

Though Arnold obviously drew the public legend of *Tristram and Iseult*—and the inner legend of Merlin and Vivian—from public sources (La Villemarqué, Malory, Southey), the poem's distinguishing dramatic and narrative characteristics, including the interpretive positioning of angles of vision, are all Arnold's own inventions. Each has its own special interest, but the most startling and far-reaching is that of Part III, in which the character of Iseult of Brittany is treated with unprecedented expansiveness and is subjected to a psychological transformation that is terrifying. It is an interesting redress since Iseult of the White Hands, the patient Griselda of the legend, had always been treated as mere grist for the passion mill of Tristram and the Irish Iseult. The legend of Merlin and Vivian is an integral part of that treatment, of course, and Arnold's comment on its presence in the poem is curious: "The story of Merlin, of which I am particularly fond, was brought in on purpose to relieve the poem, which would else I thought have ended too sadly; but perhaps the new element introduced is too much."[9] There is no mention at all of Vivian, though she is obviously at the center of "the new element" referred to, and this may be seen simply as a poet's typical evasiveness; it also may suggest that it was only after he had brought the "story of Merlin" into the poem's compass that Arnold discovered the mirroring analogy between Iseult and Vivian, which relieves the poem's sadness rather through terror than through a species of fabliau comedy.

That Iseult has to some extent identified with Vivian is suggested rather stunningly by the inescapable applicability of the last line of the poem to her situation as well as to Vivian's: "For she was passing weary of his love" (Part III, l. 224). As we begin seriously to examine the degree to which such a startling notion can be true, our minds review the whole poem with some very interesting results.

It is difficult—perhaps impossible—to be quite firm about the exact nature of the love relationship between Tristram and Iseult of Brittany from Iseult's point of view. Arnold does not let any dimension of the poem slip into the oversimplifications of allegory, and the Breton bard of the piece puts the matter beyond simple solution by persistently probing various possibilities. Her external demeanor is clear enough—sweet, gentle, so self-effacing that the burly, simplistically obsessed Tristram takes her for granted, like a childish nonentity. But that this cannot be the whole truth of the matter, the narrator makes abundantly clear. She is undergoing so fundamental a change in her nature that her features are becoming a mask of the inner reality (Part III, ll. 69–75), her days an effigy (Part III, ll. 76–95); it is the narrator's intuition of what is happening to her that provokes his unusual diatribe against "the gradual furnace of the world" or "some tyrannous thought, some fit/ Of passion, which subdues our souls to it . . ." (Part III, ll. 112–150), rejecting the more apparent and superficial explanation that she is dying of grief ("sorrow," "suffering," "pain") in the ordinary sense.

The profounder explanation is comparable to one that Tennyson had already explored in *The Lady of Shalott* and would study again in *Lancelot and Elaine*: the deadly soul distress that certain kinds of persons must suffer when caught in a naive but violent discrepancy between the world of reality and the world of fantasy. Like Tennyson's variations on the "lily maid" psyche, Iseult has been raised in an isolated world, far removed from "the furnace of the world." As a result, she has had to create, like "Elaine, the lily maid of Astolat," a fantastic world of her own, a "fairy-haunted" world (Part III, l. 153) that has become more real to her than that other world people generally call real. She has done this with the help of "the tales/ . . . She gleaned from Breton dames, when a child,/In every hut along this sea-coast wild"; they have always had the power to make her "forget all to hear them . . ." (Part III, ll. 106–111). Their logic has become her logic; in her innocence of the world, they have become her frame of reference, her models of arbitration and valuation. That other world has invaded hers, not in the person of such a scarred nobility as Lancelot's, but in that of one obsessed by a single "tyrannous" thought/ passion, Tristram. Like Elaine, she has fallen in love with this alternative "reality"—has nursed him, guarded him, given his "exiled loneliness" safe haven in her "orphan" heart, married him, borne his children (Part I, ll. 190–210). He has, in turn, been mostly gentle toward her, but his obsession has made his life "but a diseased unrest" (Part III, l. 135), and while he has been furious with himself, he has been impossible to please (Part III, ll. 140–142). In their darkest hour—dark for her as well as for him—he has been both cruel and gentle, but he has turned her away while he has turned to his obsession.

A year has passed since Tristram and his Irish Iseult have died in each others' arms and been laid to rest together in King Marc's chapel in Tintagel; and during that time, Iseult has had time to think over, work over, pray over her experience of that other reality, to judge it, and finally to let her children know what she thinks of it. Being a true, deep-rooted Breton, knowing best the Breton tales, and casting herself for the moment in a role analogous to that of a Breton bard, she chooses an "old-world Breton history" (Part III, l. 37) through which to tell her truth obliquely—a poetic parable that the children (like the reader) can interpret according to their capacity and their sympathy with the teller. She chooses the story of Merlin and Vivian and assumes, in a way that is both unmistakable and evasive, the part of Vivian. In so doing, Iseult reasserts her faith in the structure and content of her created world, indicts the inferior logic and values of that other, so-called real world, and provides at least a tentative basis for believing that her pain, though extreme, has not been wholly wasted since her judgment of Tristram's love, even if severe, is accurate and fully justified. More than that, one can hardly say: there is no promise of any new dispensation of romantic joy; the children, who listen to her with such totally mesmerized intensity, may have to grow toward adulthood on an ever-"darkening heath" (Part III, l. 63); her insight has perhaps been achieved at a truly terrible price—a metamorphosis of identity, a kneading in the "hot hand" of "reality" that has changed her nature and set her, too, "astray for ever."

But our delight in the skill with which Arnold handles his dramatic/narrative innovations and the prophetic modernity with which he probes the psychological issue at the center of Iseult's story must not prevent our asking the ultimate critical question that Arnold directed at Clough: "but what does it *do* for you?"[10] Does it *"animate"* or does it "at best" awaken a "pleasing melancholy"? It is surely critically just to say that, though the formal qualities of *Tristram and Iseult* animate, its final impact is one of strangulated catharsis. Parts I and II are, as Arnold saw, unrelievedly sad: though the imperious inescapability of the effects of the love potion are not recurrently stressed, it is clear that Tristram and Iseult can do nothing but endure their sorrow until death makes them *"both unmov'd."* The more deeply the reader is touched by the *Liebestod* of Part II, the profounder must be his melancholy. Even Arnold's efforts to ease the poem's sadness through the story of Merlin and Vivian in Part III is a failed effort. The comic element of its January-May rooting does not emerge, and the degree of insight Iseult achieves into the true nature of "the furnace of the world" does not offset our terror at her identification with the wily Vivian or promise adequate redress for her thoroughly disquieting metamorphosis of identity. It is at best psychotherapeutic rather than cathartic, and our understanding does not purge our pain. No matter how completely we may agree with the Breton bard that our lives are gradually consumed in the "furnace of the world" or our souls wholly subdued by "some tyrannous single thought, some fit/Of passion," we can hardly opt for Iseult's alternative of an isolated fantasy life in "the deep forest-glades of Broce-liande" (Part III, ll. 153–158). So whatever fragmentary insights into beauty and truth *Tristram and Iseult* may contain, they are not reconciliatory insights, and the poem must be seriously faulted for the penetrating ambiguity of both its pleasure and its pain.

It should hardly be necessary to credit anew the marks of a satisfyingly complex craftsmanship in *Empedocles on Etna*. Its merits have been so emphasized since Robert Browning's advocacy of the poem in the 1860s that its place as Arnold's chief single work has never been seriously challenged from that time that, at Browning's urging, he restored it to his canon, after a fifteen-year hiatus, in 1867. It has been acknowledged, along with *In Memoriam*, as one of the authentic poetic representations of mid-century man's soul-sickness; since no adequate antidote has been found for man's profound discouragement, *Empedocles on Etna* has held its place as one of the most significant poetic testaments in the background to modernism, Empedocles' failure to find an alternative to suicide having had for many modern readers a truer ring than the slow, complex, but finally unequivocal conversion to renewed hope painstakingly traced in *In Memoriam*. This seems entirely coherent with the poem's intention. Arnold was initially attracted to the subject because of its profound relevance to the contemporary human condition: "Into the feelings of a man so situated there entered much that we are accustomed to consider as exclusively modern . . . ."[11] It was one of the major expressions of Arnold's overall effort to represent in his poems "the main line of modern development."[12]

Still, we must consider that, though Arnold restored *Empedocles on Etna* to his regular canon, he never negated his reasons for censuring and withdrawing it. Despite or because of its conspicuous modernism, it contains in itself the metaphors of modern poetic failure and, to the degree that it is an accurate representation, of the failure of modern life itself. In a very real sense, Arnold never recovered from *Empedocles on Etna*— *from the insight into the truth of his imaginative self that the poem's insight into the truth of modern poetry and of modern life enabled him to achieve*. He issued a declaration of faith that, if modern poets would only purify and clarify their notions of what poetry was all about, they could in fact write poems worthy of the name. He himself wrote two long experimental poems-in-evidence (*Balder Dead* and *Merope*) trying to demonstrate that what he had experienced in the making of *Sohrab and Rustum* and had asserted in the 1853 Preface could be the basis for a renaissance in modern poetry. Turning away from poetry, he launched a critical crusade in prose fueled by the dual convictions that modern life was too chaotic and confusing, too intellectually, socially, and spiritually lawless, to produce a truly worthy poetry and that modern man must reconstitute his civilization, must put his moral, intellectual, social, political, and religious life in some reasonable semblance of order, before it would be sensible even to think of a creative—a "poetic"—renaissance.

Even a vague recognition of the watershed locus of *Empedocles on Etna*, both in Arnold's literary life and in the spiritual life of the century, and of the host of nuances which that implies, determines the order of one's critical approach to the poem. Individual felicities, unique fancies, particularly fetching phrases—these can have little critical interest that is competitive with the imaginative intuition at the heart of the poem as a whole. They are so secondary as to seem irrelevant in the context of so taxing an imaginative undertaking, both grandly implicative and subtly graded, as *Empedocles on Etna*—a simultaneous creation and revelation of the practical (that is, the gesturing, speaking, panicking) soul of modernism so true that its maker can see in it something about himself that is so clear and fundamental that it changes his whole life. Those felicitous fancies and phrases are not irrelevant, of course, but the reader can have the critical patience to look at them only after he is at peace with his sense of the poem's grand and simple design.

Surely, too, *Empedocles on Etna* is no place for the serious critic to dawdle (to use a term that Arnold, in a highly exercised state, rather petulantly applied to Tennyson) with such secondary notions as its autobiographical context and the place in it of "orthodox" Arnoldian ideas. No serious critic would fail to acknowledge the legitimacy of such analytical interests legitimately pursued; equally, no serious critic would yield them a *primary* place in the wholly demanding effort to discover a challenging poem's critical hypotheses in the poem itself on the basis of "direct, internal evidence"[13] because doing so immediately dispossesses the poet of his critical hypotheses in favor of our own. This destroys all hope of constructive criticism by distracting us from the creation in our own minds of something roughly equivalent to what the poet had created in his. Until we have done that, we have nothing to criticize.

But suspending, at least until the poem's autonomous dynamics have been perceived and evaluated, any inclination to impose upon it known aspects of Arnold's own life and works is not enough; the critic of *Empedocles on Etna* must also resist succumbing to the singular lure of its objective "ideas." It is "A DRAMATIC POEM" and hence a poem in which form *qua* form gets its "severest and most definite expression . . ."[14]; nowhere in his own discussions of dramatic poetry does Arnold isolate a poem's "ideas" and treat them as things in themselves. He talks about action or subject, character representativeness, motive, unity, probability, tradition, recognition, catharsis, style, surprise, and so forth; he talks about "the most urgent demands of the human spirit," its demands for variety and range, for depth and concentration—*but never about ideas in the twentieth-century sense of that term.* From this we must conclude that, for Arnold, our notion of ideas ("the history of ideas") had very little relevance to essential literary experience, that, for him, imagination had not, as with us, been so shackled by thought that we have become as uncomfortable with the concept of the *imagination* as Pilate was with the concept of *truth.* The "idea" that was "everything" to poetry for Arnold was an overall sense of the truth of things, an apprehension of the reality underlying and conditioning man's place in the universe, a revelation of a fundamental kind "On man, on nature, and on human life."[15] A poet's distinctiveness depended, not even on "ideas" thus holistically characterized, but on the way in which he *treated* those ideas, on the quality of the *form* he brought to them, on the *manner* in which they were released into the literary tradition. This is the most fruitful critical frame of mind in which to approach *Empedocles on Etna.*

A large part of our mature response to a major poem must necessarily be a response of wonder. No matter how profoundly and repeatedly we have studied the text, we are left with numerous bases for saying, "I wonder. . . ." It is true of the poet, it is true of the critic; knowing at what points and in what degree to be tentative is one of the subtlest and most crucial signals that the critic can learn to pick up from his poet. It is a matter of shading, and shading is everything in both creation and criticism. In spite of the heavy-handedness of many of Arnold's critics—their rough-and-ready inclination to take it *all* and put it *all* where it *all* belongs—*Empedocles on Etna* requires more than the usual portion of tentativeness. At whatever level one is considering the poem—as historical fact, as historical metaphor, as timeless myth—there are no grounds for dogmatism. Arnold thought that he had succeeded in delineating "the feelings" of Empedocles in a "particular, precise, and firm" way[16] and that, therefore, the poem was true; but even in that regard Arnold had to depend on a lively and trustworthy fancy for spinning a whole cloth from Empedocles' few surviving fragments and from quasi-historical accounts that did not go much beyond the marvels dealt with in the opening scene. The reconstruction of Empedocles' philosophy and its re-fusion with the living, breathing, haunted man is the result of Arnold's own strong inventive fancy, but that was the easiest part of the poetic task that Arnold had set himself. The conversion of this historically reconstructed Empedocles into a necessarily specialized but representative human type moving through and registering on his psyche the peculiar stresses of a mutating moment in history was another. Though Arnold was reasonably confident that he had also caught the spirit, the "feeling," of this larger dimension of his subject or action, he was much more tentative, subjecting the metaphoric or signifying Empedocles to the contrasting evaluative responses of Pausanias and Callicles and thereby giving witness to the evasiveness inherent in the subject at this level and preparing the reader to make the final ascent, like Empedocles himself, alone. When, after the protagonist's broadside recapitulation of the fundamental hopelessness of human life (Act II, ll. 373–390), he takes a brief but crucial moral-spiritual inventory of himself, concluding

> Yea, I take myself to witness,
> That I have loved no darkness,
> Sophisticated no truth,
> Nursed no delusion,
> Allowed no fear!
>
> (act II, ll. 399–403)

we are forced to wonder if it is true. Even if we credit Empedocles with absolute sincerity of insight and language, we must wonder, not just if *this* man in *this* overall fabric of language can thus "take [himself] to witness," but if any man can do so, and really mean what he would have himself mean. In the case of Arnold's Empedocles, we have 1,121 lines of poetry to bring us to or impede us from reaching a conclusion in this crucial matter, a rare opportunity that life in a state of raw formlessness can hardly offer. But whatever our conclusion, we must hold it tentatively, because as art is life at the remove of form, life's formlessness denies a dogmatic transfer of a world whose very principle is imaginative control to a world characterized by an artless infinity of details.[17]

As a timeless myth, *Empedocles on Etna* is wholly implicit, and the quality of its pleasure for the reader is centered in the quintessentially poetical way in which it connects time-frames while eschewing explicit historical markers—the way in which it is both unmistakable and evasive. We begin with Arnold's crucial revelation of the reason for the subject's initial fascination for him and of his intention in writing the poem:

> I intended to delineate the feelings of one of the last of the Greek religious philosophers, one of the family of Orpheus and Musaeus, having survived his fellows, living on into a time when the habits of Greek thought and feeling had begun fast to change, character to dwindle, the influence of the Sophists to prevail. Into the feelings of a man so situated there entered much that we are accustomed to consider as exclusively modern; how much, the fragments of Empedocles himself which remain to us are sufficient at least to indicate. What those who are familiar only with the great monuments of early Greek genius suppose to be its exclusive characteristics, have disappeared; the calm, the cheerfulness, the disinterested objectivity have disappeared: the dialogue of the mind with itself has commenced; modern problems have presented themselves; we hear already the doubts, we witness the discouragement, of Hamlet and of Faust.[18]

Clearly an idea of modernism is inherent in the very intuition of the poem, and the enthusiasm of the poet for his subject is centered there. But just as clearly a revision of the customary idea of modernism is inherent too: "much that we are accustomed to consider as exclusively modern" is there in full view of the mind's eye in the ancient story of Empedocles, "a Sicilian Greek born between two and three thousand years ago. . . ." So our customary idea of modernism is an anachronism, and it is a particular function of poetry to de-provincialize that kind of anachronism and to show that the elementary plot of man's life is timeless: stripped of its accidents, of its details more or less myopically perceived, man's life is mythic. But poetry does not assert such truths, however incontrovertible they may be or seem to be to the adequately instructed. Poetry *informs*: despite the evasiveness that is a necessary aspect of its non-assertiveness, poetry is the most inductive mode of enlightenment available to civilized man, since the experience of the poem is the meaning of the poem, its total form being both its method of informing and the substance of its information.[19] This connection between the purpose of poetry and its method is developed by Arnold in the third paragraph of his Preface. Drawing for authority upon Aristotle, he associates our love of poetry with our love of knowledge and concludes that any poetic representation that is "particular, precise, and firm" is interesting to "mankind at large," while a representation that is "vaguely conceived and loosely drawn," that is "general, indeterminate, and faint," does not *interest* us because it does not *inform* us. Hence, there is no inconsistency between claiming that a major poem must necessarily be evasive and, at the same time, that it cannot be both "interesting" and "vaguely conceived and loosely drawn."

The relevance of this to our critical view of *Empedocles on Etna* is that, although we know that a revision of our customary idea of modernism was an important dimension of Arnold's imaginative enthusiasm for his subject, *the poem nowhere says so,* and hence it is not the appropriate place to begin our critical consideration. We must begin with Arnold's "particular, precise, and firm" delineation of Empedocles: that is our only possible constant; that is the only action or subject with which the language of the poem actually deals; that is our only way of avoiding the two variables that would make of the poem an insoluble problem that could teach us nothing "particular, precise, and firm." Only if the poem is legitimate at the most matter-of-fact level can it be legitimate at the most imaginative; the historical *fact* makes the timeless *myth* possible. In that sense, *Empedocles on Etna* is a poem about poetry—an exemplification of the relationship between poetry and truth (*Dichtung und Wahrheit*) and a reinforcement of the recognition that unless myth is rooted in the rich soil of real human experience, it can be neither true nor relevant to human experience.

Then how does *Empedocles on Etna* move from a legitimate matter-of-factness to a legitimate imaginativeness, from literalness to a timeless myth whose very subject is timelessness? It does so very tentatively and, to use a word that Arnold often uses to describe the language and method of poetry in *Literature and Dogma,*"approximatively"; it works by analogy and allusion—techniques of illustration, insinuation, and enrichment rather than of argument—toward a real but undogmatic goal. Empedocles is not the anachronism, we are; he is simply dealing with the climactic moment in a long and varied life in which all the traditional supportive structures have collapsed. Through a ritual of laying aside the symbols of faiths that are dead, he detaches himself from the fragile, fatigued hold life has on him, induces an inverted epiphany, and, with a final desperate cry of fellowship with the elements, "*plunges into the crater,*" to join both Nature and that other "self-helping son of earth" oppressed by Zeus, Typho (act II, ll. 103–104). If we see our own faces in that mirror, recognize in the external conditions of Empedocles' life the conditions of our own, identify with his feelings of an erosive self-consciousness and his sense that every decision he can identify as available to him has a paradoxical character to it, conclude that his view of the fundamental hopelessness of human life coincides with our view and, if a few of our circumstances were altered, we would adopt his solution to the problem, it is because the mirror is clear enough and the pattern of insight and behavior impressive enough to thus inform our minds and spirits—because the analogy is "particular, precise, and firm"—not because the poet has suborned his witness. This is what made the selection of an action or subject of a poem so crucial and primary to Arnold: unless the original mirror was clear, the analogy would be impotent or else tempt the poet to falsify it.

Like many poems of large and imaginative resonance, *Empedocles on Etna* functions on one of its levels as an introduction to literary experience itself. At the time of writing it, Arnold's mind was saturated with the works of the ancients and moderns who had attracted him because of their penetrating way of critiquing life. Homer, Sophocles, Epictetus, Empedocles himself, Lucretius, Marcus Aurelius, Shakespeare, Spinoza, Goethe, Wordsworth, Senancour, Byron, Carlyle—ideas, phrases, and images of these and others, ancient and modern in almost equal numbers, occupied his critical and creative consciousness in persistent and formative ways, and through allusion he made their presence felt by qualified readers in such a way as to acknowledge, not just his debt to them, but the indebtedness of any modern critic-poet who traversed ground that they had traveled. The discouragement and doubt of the moderns found representative expression through Hamlet and Faust, that of the ancients through Empedocles and Lucretius; both the protagonist and the structure of Byron's *Manfred* appear to have influenced in a rather tentative way the actual making of Arnold's dramatic poem. But except for the fidelity that he very carefully brought to the representation of Empedocles, Arnold was under the special dominance of no single writer or combination of writers in the creation of *Empedocles on Etna*. The poem does not contain a single idea that is abstruse or esoteric enough to require special explanation or authority. Though the most compacted thoughts are those of Empedocles' "essay on man" (act I, scene ii, ll. 76–426), they do not seem to boggle the rather ordinary mind of Pausanias; the songs of Callicles, which require as much attentive watching as anything Empedocles says, depend only on a knowledge of the myths and familiarity with the young harpist's poetic-musical technique of free association. In short, ideas as such are no impediment to a careful reader of *Empedocles on Etna*. Once we suspend any disbelief we may have about the accuracy of the historical delineation, the movement to the metaphor and then to the myth is simply a matter of repetitive reading and a gradually increasing capacity to recognize the analogies and the allusions.

How we read *Empedocles on Etna*, of course, will determine what, in Arnold's phrase, it "does" to us. That Empedocles enacts a serious man's serious decision is beyond much doubt. The central question then becomes this: is his *subjective* sincerity, which we may cede, matched with a corresponding *objective* sincerity, which we may cede only with rather frightening symbolic implications for our own lives? So Arnold seems to have created a situation in which the poetic protagonist and the poetic reader or co-creator have diametrically opposed

interests that each has sufficient reason to rationalize, a situation
that automatically suspends absoluteness of judgment by making each in a degree interested and therefore suspect.[20] Empedocles' symbolic erasure of human life is unacceptable to
most of us, but can we fault it sufficiently well to make our
defense of human life as imaginatively respectable as his
indictment of it? The issue is not one of sympathy for Empedocles in his devastating plight: the more we accept the
timelessness of his myth, the more fully we can say, "*Empdocles
c'est moi!*" The issue is self-preservation: is our sympathy for
Empedocles to be so complete that it allows him to sweep the
field and destroy us along with himself, or does the text provide
us with a mechanism of detachment that will enable us to be
both sympathetic and critical, feeling his pain while perceiving
his fallibility to a self-saving if remnant degree? We know that
Arnold withdrew the poem from his canon because it left
Empedocles' pain unpurged and hence disqualified his *treatment*
of his subject by Classical standards of tragedy. But that speaks
to a different issue that one may refine but still, on the whole,
accept. Here the issue is not heroism but persuasiveness: *is
Empedocles right?*

Certain broad tendencies of the text have a direct bearing
upon this question. The poem begins with an exuberant sense
of almost universal well-being: for Callicles, the gods are in
their earth-heaven, all's right with the world. There is only one
discordant note—Empedocles "is half mad/With exile, and with
brooding on his wrongs" (act I, scene i, ll. 23–24)—and one
curious subtextual implant—Pan and Apollo are cast in different but complementary roles (act I, scene i, ll. 5–6, 19–20),
suggesting that the seeds of ensuing conflict are inherent in
some variation on the Dionysian-Apollonian tension-in-part-
nership. Secondly, the discrepancy between the views and
motives of Pausanias and Callicles with respect to Empedocles,
though very simply and matter-of-factly represented in the
orthodox tradition of Greek dramatic poetry, has implications
of an infinite kind. Both are satisfied in their own minds that
they simply want to help this monumental, agonized, admirable
old man. But Pausanias, with the ironic inconsistency characteristic of the would-be astute, sees Empedocles as a master of

occult powers sorely put upon by his enemies and hopes to be rewarded in a way that will enable him to hedge the bet of life—

> that when the Gods
> Visit us as they do with sign and plague,
> To know those spells of thine which stay their hand
> Were to live free from terror.
> (act I, scene ii, ll. 23–26)

Callicles, on the other hand, sees Empedocles' "root of suffering in himself" (act I, scene i, l. 151) and wishes to "serve him, soothe him" if he can (act I, scene i, l. 75) because of his mixed admiration for and terror of one whom he has taken as a role model. This simple combination of views and motives is subject to endless variations and, in a metaphoric sense, brings the "viewiness" of the whole world to bear upon the action.[21] Further, it is clear from the beginning of the action of the poem, as we can reconstruct his unspoken thoughts, that Empedocles has already decided that death is for him the only way out of the human dilemma—has even previously rehearsed his act (act I, scene i, ll. 94–95). Therefore, the text that we are scrutinizing, especially in Act II, is not the language of decision, but of rationalization—the "last word" in justification rather than in discovery. It is also clear that Act II is an "anatomy of feeling" rather than an anatomy of thought, though Empedocles' object at the conscious, manipulative level is a thoroughgoing indictment of thought. But when we remember that in Act II, scene ii, Empedocles enunciates a completely orthodox theory of mind—

> Mind is the spell which governs earth and heaven.
> Man has a mind with which to plan his safety;
> Know that, and help thyself!
> (act II, scene ii, ll. 27–29)

—and then, in his elaborate essay on man (act I, scene ii, ll. 77–426), illustrates in detail the mind's mastery over feeling, we recognize that there is a wide chasm between his constructive thought and his destructive feeling and perceive that the source of his erosive agony is centered there. Empedocles' isolation in Act II is also clearly symbolic, and this is deeply ironic. Isolation has been one of the polar points of his life, one of its attractive but ultimately intolerable conditions; yet, knowing this full well, he creates that condition in its severest aspect so that, "the atmosphere he breathes not being modified by the presence of human life,"[22] his determination to die will not be constructively enervated.

Finally, there is the wholly original, complicated, and delightful role of Callicles in the poem's broad, inevitable movement. In the first place, it appears that Arnold has designed a double role for Callicles—one to "serve" and "soothe" Empedocles, which is Callicles' explicit motive, and one to "serve" and "soothe" the reader, which is the poet's implicit motive. While these two roles overlap at the beginning, they gradually, as Empedocles' dissociated sensibility becomes more and more evident, diverge, until Callicles' final paean to Apollo and his celebration of Apollo and the Muses becomes a stern epitaph to the fallen Empedocles and a full reaffirmation for the reader of the very faith that Empedocles has lost. And while its terrifying severity can hardly be winked away, it is a consolation *in extremis*, asserting the purposefulness and justness, albeit the implacability, of the Apollonian way of life.

Callicles' first song (act I, scene i, ll. 36–76) is attuned to the simple, natural world of Pan, whose sacred hour of noon is twice referred to. It was a time when man and Nature existed in productive harmony, with just a side glance, through the image of Etna beyond the tree line and the report of Peleus' account of the life and death of heroes, at the more ambitious struggle that would lead to the exile of man from, and his sense of conflict with, his natural origins. This mythic vignette of the education of the greatest of Classical heroes, Achilles, is then immediately followed by Empedocles' efforts to re-educate an average Romantic man, Pausanias, in the Classical wisdom of Apollo, his educational ode turning upon the two famous precepts of the god inscribed on the walls of his great temple at Delphi: "Know thyself" and "Nothing in excess." Callicles' second song (act I, scene i, ll. 427–460), which Empedocles refers to as "the Theban story" and which he uses as a spur to get on with his own transformation, celebrates the metamorphosis of Cadmus and Harmonia into "two bright and aged snakes" after their woeful experience of the calamities that befell the House of Cadmus, a symbolic instance of man being returned, after a catastrophic experiment in mixed Apollonian-Dionysian heroism, to a "placid and dumb" state at the lowest rung of the Panic world. Empedocles' divergence from the detached tone and intent of Callicles' songs, already implicit in his self-personalization of the metamorphosis of Cadmus and Harmonia, becomes pronounced in his identification with Typho, the sub-subject of the next song (act II, ll. 37–88). The real subject of the song is "the lyre's voice," the power of the musical instrument sacred to Apollo—"The sweet notes whose lulling spell/Gods and the race of mortals love so well" (act II, ll. 64–65). Only Typho—"the rebel o'erthrown"—hates it, and Empedocles, in contradiction to his whole life's experience, identifies with Typho and exposes the degree to which he is exiled, not only from "Gods and the race of mortals," but from himself. His, like that of "the mountain-crushed, tortured, intractable Titan-king" (act II, l. 98), is a case of "plainness oppressed by cunning" (act II, l. 101), of "Great qualities" "trodden down" by "littleness united/[And] become invincible" (act II, ll. 92–94). It is a peevish and disingenuous charge unworthy of Empedocles, but he has become an advocate, not a critic, and is indulging himself in petulant case-making. Callicles' next song (act II, ll. 121–190) builds on the former as the poem's Panic-Apollonian subtext[23] is brought climactically to the surface in the musical contest between Apollo and Marsyas, with its terrifying result. The divergence between Callicles and Empedocles is now complete. Though Callicles has full sympathy with Marsyas' awful pain, he knows that he was the dupe of Pan and that Apollo's victory was not only just but necessary for the sake of the preservation of the awful truth of the highest beauty:

> Oh! that Fate had let me see
> That triumph of the sweet persuasive lyre,

That famous, final victory,
When jealous Pan with Marsyas did conspire. . . .

                                        (act II, ll. 125–128)

Empedocles, on the other hand, uses the song as an excuse for laying aside his Apollonian ensign and for indicting the god as "Though young, intolerably severe!" (act II, l. 206), though "young, implacable" (act II, l. 232), rejecting now the gift of Apollo that he had enjoyed so long—rejecting the severity of Apollonian "thought" and yearning for the simpler, more natural, less demanding pleasures associated with Pan:

> The sports of the country-people,
> A flute-note from the woods,
> Sunset over the sea;
> Seed-time and harvest,
> The reapers in the corn,
> The vinedresser in his vineyard,
> The village-girl at her wheel.

                                        (act II, ll. 251–257)

At this point, of course, we can answer our basic question without the least ambiguity, having been guided there, in large part, by this divergence between Callicles' and Empedocles' uses of myth and by Callicles' firm and unembittered hold on the terrible beauty of the truth. No, Empedocles is not right; he is grossly if sincerely self-deceived. He had wanted to play God, and when this was refused him, he decided not to play the game at all. He is a mightily persuasive man, and he shows himself extremely adept at building a subtle case of injured feeling as if it were a case of injured thought. He has won the laurels of Apollo, but when Apollo has demanded his inevitable price, Empedocles has switched parties and indulged his wit in making a shadowy case for Pan. He is right when he says that he has not been a "Slave of sense," not being a gross and lascivious man;[24] he is right in declining to claim that he has or has not been the "slave of thought"; and he is right in admitting that he has "lived in wrath and gloom/Fierce, disputatious, ever at war with man,/Far from [his] own soul, far from warmth and light" (act II, ll. 390–396). But he is self-deceived when he claims that, though he has "not grown easy in these bonds," he has "not denied what bonds they were" (act II, ll. 397–398). That is precisely what he has done. He is an old man who has come to the end of a celebrated life having succeeded reasonably well with one Apollonian precept— "Nothing in excess"—but having failed subtly but conspicuously with the other—"Know thyself." This is what makes him wretched and, with the relentless inevitability of poetic justice, this is what he cannot see. His insight is, so far as it goes, a true one—he needs to be renewed, but his method is a childish evasion of man's most heroic undertaking, namely, a searching, fearless, and distressingly evasive self-knowledge.

In the final curve of the narrative that follows Empedocles' extremely painful reaction to Callicles' song of the fatal contest between Apollo and Marsyas, despair of "poise" or "balance" brought about by chance and a horror of being "miserably bandied to and fro/Like a sea-wave" (act II, ll. 230–235) drive Empedocles to the severe but pathetic conclusion that, since he "will not change" (act II, l. 266) in the living, growing sense, then he must change in the dying, extinctual sense—that mechanical metamorphosis must take the place of vital metamorphosis. He admits, moreover, that his failure has been a failure of spirit, that he has not "Maintained courage and force, and in [himself]/Nursed an immortal vigour . . ." (act II, ll. 318–320). But what he refuses to recognize is that a dichotomous view of life is, in its very sternness and rigidity, a simplistic view of life; that the victory of Apollo over Marsyas does not wholly erase the uses of Pan; and that the decision to live in the face of seemingly overwhelming odds brought about by change is nobler than the decision, made in despair of change and on the basis of altered premises, to die.

It is fair, then, to see Arnold's *Tristram and Iseult* and *Empedocles on Etna* as two of English poetry's most profound critiques of Romanticism. In view of their respective themes of timelessness—the millennial rhythms of the medieval *Tristram and Iseult*, the myth of modernism under more than millennial revision in the Classical *Empedocles on Etna*—there can be little question about the archetypal character of Arnold's conception, in 1852, of Romanticism. That in itself reflects a rapidity of growth in Arnold's thought and craft between 1849 and 1852 with few precedents other than the legendary growth of Keats: if we take his title poem of 1849, *The Strayed Reveller*, and compare it with his title poem of 1852, *Empedocles on Etna*, the intellectual perspective has expanded almost immeasurably, and the craft has become competitive with the best of the century. This is highly significant because it means that Arnold redacted his poetic performance not only when he was at the top of his poetic form, but also when he had every reason to believe that he was becoming rapidly and conspicuously better at his craft. Arnold's insight and Arnold's conscientiousness demanded more. Though *Tristram and Iseult* and *Empedocles on Etna* were strong and crafty indictments of an archetypal Romanticism—the former of Romanticism's enervating love affair with sadness, the latter of the fatal self-deception inherent in Romanticism's sophisticated confusion of thought and feeling—*Tristram and Iseult* and *Empedocles on Etna* were themselves archetypally Romantic, unable to rise even to the level of their own critical consciousnesses and cleanse their own souls of a heavy portion of the Romantic malaise that confronted sadness with bitterness and self-deception with suicide. Its crippled poetry was the symptom of a crippled age, and Arnold finally concluded that the best he could do for poetry was to work at restoring to health the crippled spirit of the age. In the meantime, the world did not need to do without the edifying joys of poetry: the best that had been thought and said from Homer to Wordsworth had only to be made available in authentic translations and trustworthy editions introduced by competent scholar-critics. Moreover, an acquaintance with the world's best poetry was, Arnold thought, just what his countrymen needed to get themselves out of themselves and something else into them. So after a brilliant start—the Preface of 1853—and a well-intentioned stumble or two—*Balder Dead, Merope*—Arnold hit his stride and did more than any other Englishman of his age to open the national windows and let in the international air.

Notes

1. Byron's *Manfred*, Act I, scene i, ll. 10–11.
2. Professor Kenneth Allott (*Poems*, p. 224n), having misread the passage completely, carps at the poet rather pointlessly. Arnold's demotion of this crucial passage after 1852 is consistent with his condemnation of joylessness in the 1853 Preface. His omission from the first and second editions of *Poems* (1853 and 1854) of his bardic narrator's efforts to pinpoint the difference between a sentimental "sorrow" or melancholy and a fundamental and fixed joylessness that shrivels our lives and "leaves the fierce necessity to feel,/But takes away the power" (Part III, ll. 112–150) may have been based on a sense that this impassioned "essay" or "sermonette" disturbed the narrative texture—the oblique "telling"—of the poem, and that would seem a legitimate motive. But it is also likely that he had a more substantive reason—namely, the recognition that "sorrow" in the sense that Byron has Manfred use the word fully qualifies as a cause of that metamorphosis of identity that the narrator of the passage has in mind and that is exemplified in the life of Iseult of Brittany. As he got further removed in time from the poem, the possibility of a quibble between the thrust of the passage and the intent of the poem as a whole probably seemed less significant to him. Professor Allott's assertion that ll. 133–150 of this passage "are clearly autobiographical" is rather more clearly an instance of the argumentative circularity into which blind devotion to the autobiographical matrix frequently leads its exponents.
3. In Part III of the poem ("Iseult of Brittany"), Iseult plays the role of bard to her innocent children—"their blue eyes/Fixed on their mother's in wide surprise" (ll. 46–47)—who fall so completely under the spell of her narration that all their childlike habits and distractions are suspended and their innocence is initiated into the awful truth—the "tyrannous" reality (l. 127) of the life they have not yet experienced. Part III is, in some ways, the most disquieting sequence in the poem, much of our discomfort being rooted in the terrifyingly inconclusive suggestion of the pollution of innocence that converts Merlin and the children into refractive metaphors of each other and, in turn, makes sister souls of Vivian and Iseult. Tennyson does not exploit this theme in *The Last Tournament*; and Swinburne's portrait, in *Tristram of Lyonesse*, of Iseult of Brittany as a demonic-psychotic religious fanatic, though it may owe some of its intuition to Swinburne's creatively sensitive reading of Arnold's poem, and though its bold primary coloration may be aesthetically justified by the thunderous lyrical intensity of Swinburne's poem as a whole, has none of the subtlety—the near-pornographic subtlety—of Arnold's treatment.
4. Arnold said, "I had never met with it before, and it fastened upon me. . . ." See letter of November 5, 1852, to Herbert Hill (*TLS*, May 19, 1932), quoted in *Poems*, p. 206.

5. Professor Allott says that "we are forced [thereby] to realize that Tristram and Iseult 'lived and loved/A thousand years ago'" (*Poems*, p. 228n). It seems more to Arnold's purpose not to literalize it one way or the other, the story being an eternal one. Their immortality is a poetic immortality, partaking of the perpetuation myth at the heart of poetry, a myth that undoes itself unless the actions the poet selects appeal to "those elementary feelings which subsist permanently in the race." Nor is it helpful to insist that the Breton bard is a "medieval bard": he partakes of both the medieval and the modern.

6. Surely one is justified in preferring J.D. Coleridge's characterization of the metrics as "exquisitely managed" (in a review in *The Christian Remembrancer*, reprinted in *Matthew Arnold: The Critical Heritage: The Poetry*, Carl Dawson, ed., 1973) to Professor Allott's partial judgment that they are "perhaps . . . unsuccessful" (*Poems*, p. 220n).

7. W.S. Johnson's conclusion that "the narrative and descriptive lines" are "closer to the rhythm of speech" than are those of the duet is true but off the critical mark, and his judgment that those lines "reveal them more objectively and more movingly" has itself no objective validity. See *The Voices of Matthew Arnold* (New Haven: Yale University Press, 1961), p. 100.

8. George Saintsbury called them "the equivalenced octosyllable of the Coleridge stamp" in his book *Matthew Arnold* (New York: Dodd, Mead, 1899), p. 24.

9. Letter to Herbert Hill cited in note 4, above.

10. *Letters of Matthew Arnold to Arthur Hugh Clough*, H.F. Lowry, ed. (London and New York: Oxford University Press, 1932), p. 146.

11. Preface to First Edition of *Poems* (1853), *The Complete Prose Works of Matthew Arnold*, R.H. Super, ed. (Ann Arbor: University of Michigan Press, 1960), volume I, p. 1.

12. *The Letters of Matthew Arnold, 1848–1888*, G.W.E. Russell, ed. (London: Macmillan, 1895), volume II, p. 10.

13. Throughout *Literature and Dogma*, Arnold stresses the indispensability to the critic of "direct, internal evidence." See, especially, Chapter VI, "The New Testament Record."

14. Preface to *Merope*. See below, pp. 158–163.

15. The line is from Wordsworth's *The Recluse*, quoted by Arnold in *On Translating Homer: Last Words, Complete Prose Works*, volume I, p. 210.

16. Preface of 1853. *Complete Prose Works*, volume I, p. 2.

17. Thus R.C. Trench's reputed warning to Tennyson, "Tennyson, you can not live in art," has its natural retort, "Trench, you cannot live in life"— that is, a wholly unexamined and disordered, an artless, infinity of details.

18. Preface of 1853. *Complete Prose Works*, volume I, p. 1. This statement was written long after *Empedocles on Etna* had been published, of course, and therefore it is a comment on what he had meant to do and what he thought he had accomplished.

19. Archibald MacLeish's *Ars Poetica* fails in trying to make the principle simpler than possible.
20. This brings the procedure of the poem very close to that of Browning in *The Ring and the Book*. Since Browning urged Arnold to restore *Empedocles* while he himself was deeply engrossed in writing *The Ring and the Book*, perhaps his enthusiasm for Arnold's poem was engendered by his burgeoning enthusiasm for his own.
21. The standard assertion that Callicles represents youth, Pausanias middle age, completely ignores their marks as individuals and seems far too mechanical and simplistically allegorical. Also, the more interesting suggestion that Callicles is embarked on the road that eventually leads to Empedocles' situation ignores the many choices available to him along the way and is implicitly contradicted by the argument of this essay.
22. Yale manuscript, as quoted in *Poems*, p. 155.
23. Pan and Dionysus were closely associated in Classical religious rites, and, depending on the context, "Panic" and "Dionysian" have so much overlap as to be interchangeable terms. Dionysus had been admitted into partnership at Delphi by Apollo, and Cadmus had introduced the worship of Dionysus at Thebes.
24. Arnold is reaching back, in a major way, to the central awareness of *The New Sirens*, Empedocles attempting to substitute the subtle for the gross fault.

4.

The Main Tendency
of Arnold's Poetry after 1853

The critic of Arnold, like the critic of Hardy, gradually learns that a dogmatic approach to his poetry is the least serviceable of all possible approaches. Arnold is accused of being a shallow dogmatist by such virulent anti-Arnoldians as Harold Bloom and Donald Davie; in different ways, Arnold is a curious source of uneasiness to them both. Davie is an Arnold-like anti-Arnoldian, his quick literary perceptiveness, his boldness as a literary historian and profiler, and his lithe, flexible command of language having their nearest analogue in Arnold, and perhaps seeing his face in the Arnold mirror contributes to Davie's petulant sting. Harold Bloom resents Arnold's massive critical presence—vulnerable, of course, but unwithdrawing—and creates occasions to say overheated things about him, like one suffering acutely from one's own belatedness. But neither Bloom nor Davie can deal with an Arnold text objectively and constructively, and hence they cannot reasonably be called Arnold critics.

The idea content of Arnold's poetry, like that of Hardy, is very high. After his career as a competitive poet was several years in the historical background, Arnold claimed that his poems as a whole had insistently attended to "the main movement of mind of the last quarter of a century," "the main line of modern development."[1] But Arnold insisted, too, that the primary poetic obligation of the poet was the selection of a suitable "action" or "subject"[2]; although a secondary purpose of his famous Preface was the admission that he had himself often failed, poetically, in the *treatment* of his selected actions, most particularly in *Empedocles on Etna*, he casts no doubt on the poetic primacy of action, even suggesting that, to a much more implicit degree, lyric poetry is also dependent on action.[3] Thus, as Arnold diminished history as an imaginative imperative—"The date of an action ... signifies nothing"[4]—he subordinated thought to myth, mind to a more all-embracing *persona* phenomenon, philosophy to poetry. Thought, for Arnold, presumed a thinker, and poetry humanized ideas, which are vitally important, by subjecting them to the crucible of "human actions," which are even more vitally important. Hardy, too, subordinated the high idea content of his poetry to phenomenology by his oft-repeated insistence that his poems were "in a large degree dramatic or personative in conception"[5] and that their thoughts were merely "fugitive impressions."[6] For both Arnold and Hardy, the crucial significance of this imaginative positioning of ideas is that, without questioning the importance of ideas to man's efforts to cope with life, it establishes a non-dogmatic relationship between the poet and his reader by dismantling the poet's obligation to be ideologically convincing—ideologically adequate, but not ideologically convincing. It also greatly increases the poet's responsibility for observational acuteness in one of the subtlest areas of civilized human experience—the interconnections between ideas and actions, between how one thinks and what one does, or, to put the matter in terms of poetic procedure, between the curve of the narrative and the curve of the *persona* consciousness. It democratizes the mutually supportive poet-reader roles through an assumption by the poet of a position vis-à-vis the action analogous to that of the reader, the latter witnessing the former witnessing.

In his Preface of 1853, Arnold clarified, organized, and

impressively stated ideas, insights, and musings that had been on his mind for some time[7]—ideas derived from the most constructive and circumspect critic of all times, Aristotle, insights into the character, limitations, and misdirections of the Romantic poets, and musings about the ruinous state of contemporary poetry. But two of the most self-referential aspects of the Preface were Arnold's oblique but climactic declaration that, if he could not become a better poet than he had been, he would cease being a poet[8] and his open declaration of the test by which his success or failure could be measured: "to afford to the men who live in [his age] the highest pleasure which they are capable of feeling."[9] He knew, he thought, the poetic procedures by which serious poetry could be made; he recognized that his poetry up to that time had not been sufficiently "dedicated to Joy"; but he did not know for sure if, under the impetus of clarified procedures and purposes and in light of a quite honest self-appraisal, he could write a poetry worthy of a criterion endorsed from Schiller, "The right art is that alone, which creates the highest enjoyment."[10]

Arnold was undoubtedly encouraged in the possibility of writing truly worthy poetry by the success of *Sohrab and Rustum*, the Homeric episode that he had written during the winter of 1852 and the spring of 1853. We do not know the exact interrelationship between the composition of this poem and the Preface, though a connection is established by a letter of May 1853 from Arnold to his mother in which he speaks of the "story" of *Sohrab and Rustum* as "a very noble and excellent one" and of the poem as "by far the best thing I have yet done" and says that he has made arrangements for its publication "and one or two more new ones, with the most popular of the old ones . . . with a preface, and my name."[11] Allowing for the happy accident of Arnold's timely recollection and recovery of the subject in the essays of Sainte-Beuve and the apt analogy he drew between Firdousi and Homer, one may reasonably construct the following tentative scenario. After the publication of *Empedocles on Etna and Other Poems* in October 1852, Arnold had a pervasive and troublesome sense that something was radically wrong with his poems. By December, he thought he knew what was wrong with them,[12] but he expressed the "doubt whether I shall ever have heat and radiance enough to pierce the clouds that are massed around me." But Arnold did not easily yield to crippling discouragement. There was about him a muted sanguinity that led him to experiment with redemptive possibilities, and his personal need led him to the imaginatively redressive potential inherent in the Homericism of Firdousi's *The Book of Kings.* Here at last was "an excellent action," one of those that "most powerfully appeal to the great primary human affections: to those elementary feelings which subsist permanently in the race, and which are independent of time."[13] Moreover, it was an action that enabled him to make literature out of literature out of literature—something English out of something Persian via something Greek—and at the same time to efface authorial imposition at almost an ideal level. It was the perfect subject inviting the application of Aristotelian principles validated, for both Aristotle and Arnold, by the example of Homer. It succeeded far better than anything he had ever tried, and Arnold had a paradigm by which to set right what he had recognized as wrong with his poetry. As he wrote to Clough, "Homer *animates*—Shakespeare *animates*—in its poor way I think Sohrab and Rustum animates. . . ."[14] Arnold's "nature" had found a way to integrate itself with his "poetics," and *Sohrab and Rustum*, which took the place vacated by *Empedocles on Etna* in the *Poems* of 1853, became, in a metaphoric sense, the text to which both Arnold and his Preface went to school: he had himself "pierce[d] the clouds" by the *created* "heat and radiance" of imaginative joy, and so he knew first-hand both the contagion and the cure of the current malaise in poetry and he knew, besides, that the ancients (the old masters) had known it all along.

The critical history of *Sohrab and Rustum* has been a long and essentially futile catalogue of impressions and counter-impressions, of facile and subjective likes and dislikes. Its relentless anti-Romanticism has been offensive to a systemically Romantic age. Adherents to the widespread cult of tortured bardic mystery, of poetry as an incantatory magic surpassing human understanding and inducive of reverential awe rather than reconciliatory insight, have read in it and in the prose documents surrounding it a textbook theory of poetry—of creation by paradigm or rule—and have assumed that no self-respecting critic could take it seriously. Like Trilling, they have sometimes borrowed for the poem a piquant psychological interest,[15] but they have hardly ever considered the possibility that it was in truth "by far the best thing [Arnold had] yet done. . . ." Its literary indebtedness is, at one level at least, too transparent to be teasing; though few have questioned simplicity, directness, rapidity, and nobility as defining qualities of Homer's literary grandeur, they have not thought to allow these identical characteristics to sustain their critical estimates of *Sohrab and Rustum*. Having assumed that the poem rests on false critical premises, they have disdained to take it quite as seriously as, independent of theory, it deserves.

And yet, *Sohrab and Rustum* is one of the most accomplished narrative poems of a century in which how to tell a tale poetically was one of the chief focuses of reflection and experimental endeavor. The eye that watches and the voice that tells are an embodiment of Classical empathy, of a mainline way of looking at life antiphonal to the self-torturing Romanticism that loses the thing seen in the self-reflective distresses of the seer. Whether it is a better or worse way of looking at life is a question that it inevitably provokes and that will be answered according to the personality of the critic, but it is a thoroughly representative way having an enormously large human constituency, and as a metaphor of perception it is masterfully managed by the poet—as masterfully, for example, as Wordsworth's *Michael* and Tennyson's *The Passing of Arthur*, two of the few nineteenth-century poems in its mode that are worthy of comparison with it. It is the wholly legitimate counter-voice to that implicit in *Empedocles on Etna*. It is omniscient in its penetration of the drama enacted before it, sophisticated in the ways and needs of men, generous in its sympathy yet detached in its judgment, fully cognizant of the catastrophic character of men's deeds while wholly reconciled to man's destiny, a reconciliation that is deepened and reconfirmed by the tragic episode it relates. *Sohrab and Rustum* thus makes a serious and successful statement about the profound moral implications of narrative style.

The more we expand the metaphor of action at the center of *Sohrab and Rustum*, the less inclined we will be to read it in Professor Trilling's much too literal "psychical sense." Any reasonable extension of the significance of the action that monitors the architecture of a narrative poem, whether that significance points inward to the "anatomy of sentiment" or outward to the situation's universal recurrence as a typical human action, must be at least tentatively allowed. On the principle of a self-effacement that is as complete as possible, the author has interdicted his own intrusion as explicit mediator of meaning and has imposed upon himself the co-creative obligation of stationing his metaphors in such a way as to enable them, through the patterns they assume and the language texture by which they are both individually pointed and connected as a whole, to tell their truth obliquely, as Browning said, "do the thing shall breed the thought,/Nor wrong the thought, missing the mediate word."[16] Just as we allow analogues in the *Iliad* for Sohrab's sleeplessness on the night before his confrontation with Rustum takes place,[17] we must allow analogues in Arnold's life and in our own. It is unthinkable that an action that, like the action of *Sohrab and Rustum*, "most powerfully appeal[s] to the great primary human affections" would not release in our memories a whole cluster of analogous metaphors or that we would refuse to an author what we easily acknowledge of ourselves. Indeed, an author, like a reader, could hardly recognize an action as one that appeals "to those elementary feelings which subsist permanently in the race, and which are independent of time" unless it appealed to his own "elementary feelings" and subsisted permanently in himself. But there is a very great difference between "those elementary feelings ... which are independent of time"—imaginative consciousnesses or semi-consciousnesses that authors and readers alike share and probe perpetually—and poetic incidents that we literalize and then impose upon the author's life as matter-of-fact if "shadowy" equivalents. That is a diminution of imaginative insight into a species of literary gossip, however seemingly astute and urbane, and a rather gross depletion of constructive imaginative experience, moving us in the direction of mental tackiness rather than toward the Classical ideal of a globally detached and charitable understanding of the utmost possibilities of the imaginative consciousness.

The action of *Sohrab and Rustum* is much larger than a knightly youth's disastrous efforts to find and touch his father, although that is the central image upon which the human understanding is concentrated and from which the poem's more cosmic implications radiate outwards; that is the focus of the poem as human drama or plot, but the plot is not coterminous with the poem as existential parable.

Sohrab and Rustum occupy very different places on the spectrum of human existence, but in one existential respect they refract each other. Sohrab is young, noble, brave, tender, battle-tried and battle-proven, universally applauded by a rugged and relentlessly demanding people; however, he suffers from "'an unquiet heart'" (l. 65), travels restlessly in the Tartarean darkness of anonymity, and cannot claim a full and distinct identity, a mature individual separateness, until he has been anointed as worthy by a father of suprahuman, mythic proportions. He has taken the myth for the reality and modeled his life on the pattern most likely, he thinks, to command the recognition and approval of a father of mythic and imperious proportions. Sohrab is love striving in love's name for the omnipotence that an omnipotent father will applaud and by which the father will be induced to return the son's love. Rustum is old, noble, brave, recognized on all sides as the most powerful of men. But he too suffers from an unquiet heart. Though he is tender toward his ancient father, he is blind to the existence of his son, and his love flows only to the past, not to the future. He is congestive in his omnipotence, peevish with his peers, enviously self-protective of his fame, dyspeptically *(indigestion)* irreverent toward the gods, recalcitrant in his self-enclosing *hubris*.

This is not to say that *Sohrab and Rustum* represents a veiled parable by which a variation on the Judeo-Christian myth of God the Father and God the Son is examined and critiqued, but it does seem to draw an oblique analogue of that myth into its imaginative orbit and thereby both to enlarge to a cosmic level the implications of its action and to suggest that "elementary feelings" like those at the foundation of the story of

Sohrab and Rustum perhaps led, at some primitive stage in man's imaginative thought, to speculations that eventually emerged as the sophisticated and humanly satisfying myth of a son who allayed his father's wrath by dying of a totally self-immolating love of him and thereby reconciled the father's omnipotent imperiousness to the catastrophic errors to which even the best of men are prone. And at that enveloping level of significance—the limitless level of a truly good poem—there is less difficulty in seeing the organic integrity of such elements of the poem as Sohrab's slightly distorted Christ imagery, the cumulative consciousness of the harsh rigors of man's life in this world reflected by the network of epic similes, the near-apocalyptic character of Nature's response to the poem's catastrophe, and the coda's recapitulation of human life ending in luminous cosmic repose after many impediments and much inevitable self-distortion in the struggle to gain and to maintain one's identity in the contest with one's identity.

Moreover, Arnold handles the details of narrative procedure with utmost deftness. He quietly implants metaphors that expand the poem's frame of reference while he steadily builds its narrative curve; irony counterpoints pathos as both rise together toward a terrifying crescendo, enabling us to sustain a grand climax of pity and fear without moral devastation and collapse; Sohrab's sudden paralysis at the unexpected roar of *"Rustum!"* is wholly consistent with his deeply vulnerable naiveté, and Rustum's resistance to a recognition of the awful truth is managed with masterly gradualness and inevitability. The delicate exchange of protagonists, from Sohrab to Rustum, by which an insufferable pathos is avoided and a tragic austerity secured, is precariously but successfully achieved. For the first time in his poetry, Arnold does, metaphorically speaking, "afford the men who live in [his or any age] the highest pleasure which they are capable of feeling"—the profoundly cathartic enjoyment that, ironically, can be afforded only by a terrifying situation elevated by a fine poet into a genuine tragic vision.

Balder Dead is also a poem fed by two foreign literary sources: it is an English poem based on Norse materials monitored stylistically by a Roman model. Virgil, of course, is frequently supplemented by a literary memory saturated with Homer, but the overall tone is Virgilian rather than Homeric, and the moral implications of the narrative style are Roman rather than Greek. Arnold himself spoke of the poem's "natural *propriety* of diction and rhythm which is what we all prize so much in Virgil,"[18] and this keen sense of literary decorum on Arnold's part is explosively fascinating when seen as integral to the subject or action of the poem. The primitive but highly sophisticated myth of the dark and rugged North is already infected with the malaise of the sun-drenched, epicurean South. History has become imperious, a sense of belatedness infectious, world-weariness all-pervasive. The Homeric tale of the epic hero—solitary, self-reliant, vulnerable but indomitable even in the face of catastrophic circumstances—has been replaced by the Virgilian tale of the tribe—socialized, circumscribed, dwarfed by prudence and responsibility, paralyzed by its own cumulative and irreversible acts, dependent on the duplicity of sorcery and the fantastic expectations of magic, caught in a Manichaean dualism in which apocalypse is inherent, compensated by visions of a "New Jerusalem-New Asgard" but perpetually embattled and fatigued unto death by the endless corrosions of conflict. The twilight of the gods and the twilight of man meet in a frank anthropomorphism, and though man still clings to intuitions of a benign immortality, a place of universal well-being, the inevitability of death in a world without surcease from sorrow induces a racial death-wish and an ambient sadness which that death-wish in turn induces. Thus the Virgilianism of *Balder Dead* is integral rather than cosmetic, and its transfer to Norse materials is a stroke of perceptual genius.

The situations, characters, and outlooks that give imaginative body to the action of *Balder Dead* project a misshapen world of which gentle men like Balder inevitably become heart-weary. Evil like that of Lok is known but tolerated, easily making an instrument of hate out of such sorely afflicted innocence as that of blind Hoder; the landscape and climate are throughout either positively hostile or so difficult to master, so threatening, that the very process of survival tends to brutalize the souls of men, reducing them to such an animal level that they hack and

tear each other in a sort of devil's fun; the women are weird
in the ancient sense, moving about like stately somnambulists
and speaking with the solemnity of oracles. The sport in which
Balder is slain, though presumed innocent, reflects a deeply
torn racial psyche: having secured, they think, his invulnerable
innocence, their favorite pastime is a ritual of symbolically
wreaking his destruction. This has its counterpart in the effort
to redeem Balder from Hell: it is clear that so long as Lok
lives, the lament over Balder's death cannot be universal, yet
the gods undergo the elaborate charade of attempting to
achieve what is transparently futile. The twilight of Hell more
darkly mirrors the twilight of Heaven, and the "Journey to the
Dead" reflects in a more concentrated and climactic way the
daily journey of the living. These are the qualities that the
poet's "rhythm and diction," by analogy with Virgil, capture:
solemnity, relentless inevitability, vigor with the edges softened
by darkness, a universal doleful lament, ruggedness dissolving
toward futility. The blank verse is always good, sometimes
exemplary (e.g., part II, ll. 47–69, part III, ll. 160–205), and
the magnification of the dirge to epic proportions is measured
and authentic, climaxing in the universal ritual of weeping to
release the dead, which has its vegetal analogue in the spring
thaw by which a dormant Nature comes to life again.

Then how and how well does *Balder Dead* meet Arnold's
criterion of "afford[ing] to men who live in [his age] the highest
pleasure which they are capable of feeling"? He attempts to do
it, at any rate, by broadening the base of the reader's literary
experience, connecting a mythology largely foreign to him with
a stylistic manner that had been made a part of the mainstream
of the European poetic consciousness; by appealing to the
universal taste for elegiac poetry; and by so treating his action
as to connect a pervasive worldly melancholy, which is one of
man's "elementary feelings," with the hope that the future
holds a "happier day," which is one of his elementary feelings
too. As Balder says in expressing his disinclination to return to
Asgard as it now is:

> "I attend the course
> Of ages, and my late return to light,

> In times less alien to a spirit mild,
> In new-recovered seats, the happier day."
> (part III, ll. 510–513)

How well he does it is a question that can never be settled with anything like general satisfaction and certainly not in complete textual isolation. Arnold's motive for writing *Balder Dead* was not such as to make it popular. Without diminishing his serious and sustained intent, one may even reasonably find in a comparison between *Balder Dead* and *Sohrab and Rustum*, not only alternative poetic styles, but also an implicit recognition on Arnold's part that Homer was a more crucial model for the modern poet than was Virgil or, through Virgil, Dante: a return to Homer's heroic individual seemed to be one feasible way for poetry to help to exorcise the Romantic melancholy that was one modern inheritance from Virgil's tale of the tribe.

But most importantly these two poems, together with *Merope*, project two of Arnold's fundamental critical recognitions — that the ultimate power of poetry is in style and that the indispensable European exemplars of poetic style are Homer, Virgil, and Sophocles. Thus Arnold's motive for writing the three long experimental poems associated with the Preface of 1853 was larger than just the creation of three substantial poetic experiences, though he knew that his degree of failure in that regard would be the inevitable result of his real but limited poetic talent. His very last word on the subject is the self-characterization with which he concludes the Preface to *Merope*: ". . . one with inadequate time, inadequate knowledge, and a talent, alas! still more inadequate: one who brings to the task none of the requisite qualifications of genius or learning. . . ."[19] Nor was he in any sense competing with his great poetic models or simply suggesting to young contemporary writers what a treasure trove of poetic subjects could be found in the works of Homer, Virgil, and Sophocles. He was trying to alert young writers to the recognition that the ruinous state of contemporary poetry was, in a large degree, the result of false counsel compounded by misleading models and to direct them to sound principles reinforced by excellent models so that they might renew their experience of Homer, Virgil, and

Sophocles and discover empirically from the very best secular examples that poetry is above all a matter of style, because style is one unequivocal revelation of how a poet views the world and of the values he has to offer.

Critics are nearly unanimous in the condemnation implicit in their neglect of *Merope*. This is entirely understandable since it is the last and least interesting of the sequence of long exemplary experiments. The subject is relatively inaccessible to a modern reader, and persons who habitually neglect Sophocles' *Electra* are not likely to be attentive to Arnold's *Merope*. The general statement that Arnold was trying to make about style was already clear to those who had been induced to follow it, and if they were more inclined to spend time on Sophocles than on Arnold, his purpose had been admirably served. That Arnold, independent of his aesthetic theories, had set himself a near-impossible task with an English audience is suggested by the fact that only one Greek dramatic emulation had ever truly succeeded in England—Milton's *Samson Agonistes*. There is simply no comparison between the degree of genius that the two poets brought to their respective efforts or between the appeal of Milton's subject to a Bible-reading public and the essential strangeness of Arnold's. *Merope* is a thoroughly respectable poetic imitation, and its action is not only interesting in itself and well suited to Arnold's illustrative purposes but also reasonably provocative as an exemplum of the stresses and strategies indigenous to any heightened effort to deal with life in this world. But admittedly only a reader totally susceptible to the charms of poetry's way of critiquing life could ever burn with a hard gem-like flame over *Merope*, and even he would have to concede that it is not competitive with the best poetic experience. *Merope* is not first-class Arnold, and Arnold is not a poet of the very first class.

But the Preface to *Merope* is indispensable to a full understanding of Arnold the first-class critic. Despite its somewhat misshapen architecture as a prose essay, it gets down to some very important cases and clarifies some bedrock issues. It is the chief source available to us for an understanding of much that Arnold meant by the term *style* and why the term had such a crucial significance for him in what, as the event shows, were his years of transit from poetry to prose.

Arnold uses a historical-comparative method in the Preface both as a way of rooting his concerns in a distinguished critical-creative European tradition and as a way of separating his arguments from the Neoclassicism of Italy and France, particularly as represented in Maffei and Voltaire. But the source of his authority is not there. Although the continental Neoclassicists had attempted, like Arnold, to correct the literary debasement of their times by turning contemporary writers back to Classical models, Arnold takes his guidance strictly from Aristotle and from the works of the literary practitioners upon which Aristotle had built his *Poetics*. So just as *Sohrab and Rustum* represents a simultaneous return to both Homer and Aristotle, *Merope* represents a simultaneous return to Aristotle and Sophocles. Implicit in this rather obvious fact is a principle of great importance: in the most successful period of Greek Classicism—which Arnold sees as, on the whole, the most successful period of literary endeavor in the history of man—there was complete coherence between art and aesthetics. Though Homer, Sophocles, and Aeschylus wrote their poems without any help from Aristotle, there was complete harmony between their performances and his codifications: he gave orderly exposition to their orderly practice. Thus Aristotle's *Poetics* is prescriptive in only a very relative sense: if you want to do what the Greek masters did, this is the way you must do it.

Arnold clearly recognized this relativism of Greek art and Greek rubric; "The laws of Greek tragic art, therefore, are not exclusive; they are for Greek dramatic art itself, but they do not pronounce other modes of dramatic art unlawful; they are, at most, *prophecies of the improbability of dramatic success under other conditions*" (I, 58, Arnold's emphasis). In Arnold's judgment, the "forms" of Greek tragedy satisfied "some of the most urgent demands of the human spirit" (I, 58), and this was certainly ample justification for his insistent efforts to bring those "forms" to the attention of the young critics and writers of his day, but his controlling premise was considerably larger than that. Arnold believed that unless poetry's motive has little or nothing to do with the ego-satisfaction of the poet or the self-satisfaction of the age, then it can never serve a truly serious autonomous purpose—or, put in the positive way it demands, only that poetry which serves mankind as a whole at the most needful and vulnerable points of his existence is worthy of poetry's high and incomparable calling. Unless a poet knows this, he can have little more than a trivial notion of what his craft is all about, little or no knowledge of what it is that mankind at large wants in the way of poetry. Thus the connection between a constructive art and a constructive aesthetics is axiomatic; while a modern age may conscientiously reject "the laws of Greek tragic art," they cannot, if they are serious about poetry, conscientiously reject the luminously self-evident need for something at least analogous to them. It is simply fanciful and irresponsible to think that "the power of true beauty, *of consummate form*" (I, 39, emphasis added) works without laws; while the laws of a genius like Homer or Dante or Shakespeare may be implicit in their poetic structures rather than in some formal external codification, it is quite clear that law rather than lawlessness was their operative principle and that a large part of their labor was devoted to the transformation, according to some more compelling law, of the work of their predecessors. Further, the more poetry withdraws from such peaks of genius as Homer, Dante, and Shakespeare, the more explicit those laws need to become if their example of greatness is to be even approximately maintained.

The morality of art, which in the best art is the *"profound moral impression"* (I, 60) it has upon the serious reader, is a matter of poetic practice, not of preachment, of the overall idea of life that the artist projects rather than of some apothegm that he might attempt to promote. Thus the "morality" of art is assumed into art's "style," which is the most enveloping term to which our thoughts about art are susceptible. This is what makes "dramatic poetry" so crucial a term of reference for Arnold because in dramatic poetry "form" gets its "severest and most definite expression" (I, 39). In dramatic poetry, any but the most recalcitrant and capricious author is wholly self-effaced, and nothing anyone in the drama says has any importance unless the total form, including the complete action, makes it stylistically affective, unless its importance emerges organically and inevitably from the form. The "subject" is the "action" in the sense that the truth a great dramatic poem embodies is inseparable from the emblematic action that embodies it. Arnold had spoken in the Preface of 1853 of men's "elementary feelings" and their "highest pleasure"; in the Preface to *Merope* he combines these in a vivid description of poetic style in a state of all-encompassing action. He is speaking of "some of the most urgent demands of the human spirit":

> If, on the one hand, the human spirit demands variety and the widest possible range, it equally demands, on the other hand, depth and concentration in its impressions. Powerful thought and emotion, flowing in strongly marked channels, make a stronger impression: this is the main reason why a metrical form is a more effective vehicle for them than prose: in prose there is more freedom, but, in the metrical form, the very limit gives a sense [of] precision and emphasis. This sense of emphatic distinctness in our impressions rises, as the thought and emotion swell higher and higher without overflowing their boundaries, to a lofty sense of the mastery of the human spirit over its own strongest agitations; and this, again, conducts us to a state of feeling which it is the highest aim of tragedy to produce, to *a sentiment of sublime acquiescence in the course of fate, and in the dispensations of human life.*
>
> (I, 58–59, Arnold's emphasis)

Everything about a piece of poetic art has its ultimate significance in style. *Simplicity* is a poet's way of not making excuses for himself. *Probability* is an expression of faith in the subject or action that he has selected. *"Poetical feeling"* is a reflection of the work of art as a whole emblem of life, and dependence on the "shocks of surprise" is an indication of authorial caprice, an assertion of a disproportionate concern with authorial ingenuity. *Reliance on tradition* is an indirect statement that one's faith in truth is greater than one's faith in mere inventiveness: it does not preclude new forms, new angles of vision, new idioms, but it does place one's work in a comparative context that invites measurement against the achievements of one's predecessors and one's peers. The *unities*, the *scale of the rhetoric*, the *reversal* and the *recognition* are all organic elements of style, of the formal design through which a profoundly serious and gifted student of human nature—of how men feel and think, of how they use and understand language, of their structured patterns of perceptual response—seeks to dispose other serious students of human nature to an expectation of self-revelation and to provide the symbolic action in which they will see their generic humanness at a deeply penetrating level.

The Preface to *Merope* was the final preamble to Arnold's long career as a prose critic. He was now Professor of Poetry at Oxford, and he would be reading and re-reading the best that had been thought and known in the Indo-European tradition to new purposes. He had searched the masters of Western literature as a practicing poet seeking poetic guidance; though they had served him well in that respect, they had gradually taught him that he had another work to do in England for which, comparatively speaking, he was better qualified. The critical consciousness that had been so conspicuous in all of his poetry and that had taken a graver and more constructive turn in the long experimental poems of the 1850s needed the freedom that he recognized as a defining characteristic of prose. As he perceived the prevailing situation, a great deal of critical work needed to be done before there could be any hope of a new creative renaissance. It was true of him, and it was true of his countrymen. Arnold did not immediately admit that his days as a practicing poet were virtually over—nor need they have been had circumstances altered. But the new role, which his professorship greatly facilitated, took on the all-absorbing character of conspicuous success: his criticism had a distinctive and unprecedented quality, and though there was some gnashing of teeth, there was also an undeniable and substantial chorus of acclaim. Arnold was a very busy man; his daily inspection of schools and his special educational assignments, while they contributed significantly to his expertise in one of his main areas of interest, were heavy drains on his energy and time. But as his enthusiasm for the critical role he had created for himself gradually magnified, he deployed the new energy that it generated with exemplary economy and effectiveness. Things were working for him, and he took great care that they should work as well as they possibly could. He continued to write poetry as a second avocation—all of it interesting, some of it inherently significant—but the broad-gauged critic gradually overwhelmed the poet of narrower gauge, and Arnold took hold of the cultivated consciousness in search of further cultivation as England's most flexible and trustworthy guide to the very idea of purposeful cultivation.

Only three poems from Arnold's last period require comment in the context established by this essay—*Rugby Chapel, Thyrsis,* and *Obermann Once More.*[20]

Rugby Chapel is a model of constructive steadiness in a low creative key. It is not an emotionally electrifying elegiac lament, nor is it ambitious of being one. Though it lacks the emotional turbulence of a comparable poem like Dylan Thomas's *Go Not Gentle into That Dark Night,* it also does not play Thomas's inauthentic game of employing an elegiac occasion for rhetorical self-inflation. It rises to its muted emotional affirmation by a process of disciplined thought that gradually, very gradually, releases feelings probated by a speaker who is disposed to repay with generosity and affection a recognized debt of gratitude toward the deceased and to voice genuine admiration, but who also is determined that the grounds for gratitude, affection, and admiration be scrupulously true. Thus the poem's procedure is monitored by the poem's subject and is a verse celebration whose tone, metaphors, and statements are scaled to the speaker's honest estimate of what the deceased himself would demand in the way of literary decorum. The poem is Classically restrained rather than Romantically effusive and is minutely precise on both the factual and the metaphoric levels.

Rugby Chapel was published a quarter of a century after Thomas Arnold's death, though the time metaphor of the text specifies fifteen years and the "November 1857" following the title suggests that Arnold had initially conceptualized the poem (that is, "written" it, in the Classical sense) then. But he also tells us that Fitzjames Stephen's "thesis," in a review of *Tom Brown's Schooldays* (January 1858), that the elder Arnold had been "a narrow bustling fanatic" "moved [him] first to the poem"[21]; it may be that the poem's stress on the tireless efforts of the subject to be "Cheerful, and helpful, and firm" (1. 139), *ever* beckoning and *ever* extending a helpful hand (ll. 131–133), is meant to give a friendlier interpretation to rather than ignore characteristics that had irked Stephen.

Though positive, the poem's estimate is carefully measured and seems to leave room for other interpretations. It was, after all, written under very real constraints, and it is remarkable that Arnold did not abandon it altogether or at least withhold it from publication. It is not only a real father/real son poem, which the paucity of the record shows is difficult enough; it is a poem about a very public father by a very public son, tempting a failure in taste even in the best. Further, the more symbolic, psychological father-son literature of the generation gap had begun to appear all over Europe, and we have abundant proof that readers have been only too eager to deconstruct the historical record and to substitute a psychoanalytic, novelistic record of their own invention. Arnold, we may be sure, would have been sensitive to this possible outcome and would have considered it both personally and poetically regrettable. This suggests another reason for the poem's matter-of-factness, its explicitly rational linkages and measurings, and the generic—almost formulaic—character of its metaphors and parabolic analogues.

The opening landscape is detailed and funereal like those of such earlier "elegies" as *Stanzas in Memory of the Author of 'Oberman'* and *Stanzas from the Grande Chartreuse*, but there is a remarkable difference. In the earlier poems, there had been such complete reciprocation between the outer landscape and the landscape of the mind of the protagonist that they seemed to feed upon each other and to cast a shadow over the question as to whether the landscapes were wholly real or largely perceptual. *Rugby Chapel* is stripped of this equivocation of the pathetic fallacy, and the speaker is not only not victimized by such natural allurements, but uses them to draw a sharp contrast between outer darkness and inner light, between formulaic *"gloom"* (l. 16) and the mind's "radiant vigour" (l. 18). This is the Classical key to the poem's—that is, to the subject's—essential revelation: any white sunny light, any "white radiance of eternity," that man's world can hope to have must come from the mind and spirit of man himself. He may find helpful analogies in nature, but they will serve him only if he internalizes them and converts them to his individual wisdom and strength. That is the austerity—both the glory and the precariousness—of his role.

Light and strength—"radiant vigour"—are the indestructible qualities of heroic men. Since, by analogy with matter, it is unthinkable that light and strength can ever be destroyed, the mind has a basis sufficiently empirical for an imaginative affirmation of "some far-shining sphere" (l. 44) in which those who possess it continue their labor, not lost, like "most men" (l. 60), in the Faust-like anonymity of a watery grave (ll. 67–72). Such a reasonable intimation of immortality is one gift of heroes to other men who have some degree of availability to the idea. Another is mythic affirmation: to the generation that comes into contact with them, they give full-bodied personal experience of what otherwise would seem to be "but a dream of the heart/ . . . but a cry of desire" (ll. 151–152)—namely, that the heroes of the past are true, including especially the hero who called himself the Good Shepherd (ll. 143–144) and, variously, the Son of God (ll. 162–167). And if that is credible— if, through personal experience, we can accept the reality at the center of that image, can know that in very truth there are these miraculous persons "Radiant with ardour divine!" (l. 191)—then it is possible, again with a strong sense of empirical rooting, to take the next step and believe that "the City of God" exists beyond the wasteland of life for those who, guided by their faith in heroic endeavor, do not panic and despair (ll. 197, 207–208). There is nothing dogmatic about these affir- mations, but they do show how a well-disposed consciousness can, with a little imagination, confirm a strong faith through a rational use of privileged human experience. *Rugby Chapel* deploys, in its quite distinctive way, the basic formula of *In*

Memoriam for verification of the compelling, wholly usable truth at the heart of myth. Again, as in the case of its stylistic decorum and propriety, the poem is monitored by its subject: Thomas Arnold's liberal theology and his imaginative historicism, well known in his time, are mirrored in the speaker's substantive thought.[22]

But perhaps the most teasing textual sequence in *Rugby Chapel* is that in which the speaker characterizes himself (ll. 73–123), and the fascination is twofold—one metaphoric or poetic, the other historical or personal.

The metaphoric or poetic speaker of *Rugby Chapel* is a generic *persona* typed as an individual. He represents his group as unlike the great generality of men, who live as purposelessly as a grain of sand caught in a whirlwind, improvident persons whose name is legion and who have thousands of literary analogues, from the Biblical squanderer to the Wordsworthian trafficker in an all-consuming worldliness. The shared imagery of a mountainous struggle with life's impediments draws him and his group to a real but limited degree into the orbit of the heroic spirits that the poem ultimately celebrates. Explicitly, the differences between the speaker's group and the group represented by the subject of the poem are triviality of goal ("the lonely inn 'mid the rocks" [l. 109] versus "the City of God" [l. 208]) and a self-centeredness that limits one's energy to one's own salvation ("Hardly ourselves we fought through" [l. 120.]). At this level of more or less explicit statement, therefore, that special middle group for which the speaker is a generic stand-in, though not wholly powerless and purposeless like the great generality of men, has inadequate light and inadequate strength for anything like truly heroic action.

But in a poem that depends, to a significant degree, on rational linkages for its substantive movement, this characterization of the speaker-group raises the question *why*. What infected them at such an extra-rational level that they could not see then what is so clear to them now? This teasingly evasive question brings us to the poem's implicit level—to its tone and imagery and to a subtle distinction between what the *poet* knows and what the *speaker* knows. The *speaker* in this textual self-characterization shows himself to be a man of his

time in the imagery he uses and the parable of life he narrates—
a precarious journey over threatening mountainous terrain
("A long, steep journey, through sunk/Gorges, o'er mountains
in snow" [ll. 87–88]) that begins with lighthearted friends (l.
89) and ends in conscience-stricken loneliness (ll. 110–123).
The *poet* shows him as a representative Romantic or post-
Romantic with a vivid perceptual and moral consciousness of
Nature's impingements on the curve of a man's life and an
unexamined tendency to blame Nature (the "storm," the "av-
alanche") for his own physical and moral failures. This is what
the *speaker* actually does in the strategic use he makes of the
imagery. And, as the *poet* shows, the implications of what he
says are greatly magnified by the tone in which it is said. He
converts parable into the most heightened gothic melodrama
by the way in which he choreographs it:

> Then, on the height, comes the storm.
> Thunder crashes from rock
> To rock, the cataracts reply,
> Lightnings dazzle our eyes.
> Roaring torrents have breached
> The track, the stream-bed descends
> In the place where the wayfarer once
> Planted his footstep—the spray
> Boils o'er its borders! aloft
> The unseen snow-beds dislodge
> Their hanging ruins; alas,
> Havoc is made in our train!
>
> (ll. 90–101)

Thus the *speaker* makes himself the center of some cosmic
cataclysm that, with its literary echoes of *Manfred* and *Faust*,
implies that he is a solitary Promethean heroically enduring
universal violence and hostility, while the *poet*, operating
through the experience of the poem as a whole, represents
him as a hero *manqué*. Thus *Rugby Chapel*, in which both
Arnolds are moved to a metaphoric, generic level, measures
the volcanic, emotional, self-centered heroism of Romanticism
against the austere, rational, socially serviceable heroism of

Classicism and finds the former sterile, self-deceived, morally dwarfing—theatrically impressive but hardly edifying.

The "historical or personal" fascination of the speaker's self-characterization is extra-poetical, and the following speculations about it should in no way be thought of as literary criticism. It is not so-called "biographical criticism" if "literary" is to be understood as standing before "criticism," in that ambiguous, hermaphroditic phrase. It is pure biographical speculation, and any usefulness it has must derive from its character as that and that only.

The chief reasons for wondering if this passage projects a personal sense of self on Arnold's part are the date "November 1857" and the great dearth of hard evidence as to just how Arnold felt about himself during these crucial years of transit from poetry to prose criticism, say, from 1852–1853 to 1857. Except for the Preface to *Merope* (dated "London: December 1857"), the record of these years was complete, and Arnold gave his inaugural lecture as Professor of Poetry at Oxford on November 14, 1857. So it would not be surprising if, in a poem so dated and with a real father/real son relationship in its historical background, a poet who was almost thirty-six years old was led to consider how his light was spent.

It would be dramatic to consider the violent imagery of the passage under review as a projection of the *Sturm und Drang* of this period in Arnold's life which does not get expression elsewhere, but that would be tantamount to transferring imagery got up for the characterization of a generic Romantic speaker to a literal personal level, and one knows from experience what a common novelistic biographical technique that is. Nor can one quite justify seeing the poem's contrast between Romantic and Classical conceptions of the hero as having *prima facie* personal relevance to Arnold; though this is a bit more plausible since Arnold had recognized his imaginative infection by Romantic *Weltschmerz* in the mirror of *Empedocles on Etna*, there is no evidence that he ever thought of himself in heroic terms. Finally, we can hardly assign to Arnold personally the muddled attitude toward Nature inherent in the speaker's tendency to blame cosmic forces for personal failure, since that fine point is authored by Arnold and had long been an aspect of his dissatisfaction with the Romantics. So what we are essentially left with is the poet's reflective sense of the vast difference between his early gregarious enthusiasm for the challenge of life and the naively narrow goal with which he had confronted it, on the one hand, and, on the other, the sobering realization, learned from harsh experience, that the world's needs would not have been largely served even had that narrow goal been fully realized and that the world's work must often be done in solitude, without the psychological and emotional reinforcements of sympathetic comradeship. There is no hint of boyish enthusiasm for new-found goals, only a mature outlook on the need to avoid narrowness and to accept the inevitability of personal separateness. Though this is not very titillating as literary gossip, it is more Miltonic than Byronic and has that quality of detached honesty that makes Arnold so profoundly trustworthy.

A quality of detached imaginative honesty, severe but gracious, is at the heart of the Classicism of *Thyrsis* and distinguishes it from *The Scholar-Gipsy*, which is, initially, a more ingratiating Romantic lament. The more one sees the ultimate strength and seriousness of poetry in the relentlessly truthful inevitability with which it discloses its reconciliatory insights rather than in heartwarming, spirit-relaxing incantations over the might-have-been, the more one is inclined critically to prefer *Thyrsis* to *The Scholar-Gipsy*. Arnold was quite right in saying of *The Scholar-Gipsy* that it "at best awakens a pleasing melancholy" and, by implication, that it "merely" adds "zest to [our] melancholy or grace to [our] dreams."[23]

The Scholar-Gipsy, Arnold told his brother Tom, "was meant to fix the remembrance of those delightful wanderings of ours in the Cumner hills"—"the spring of life and that unforgotten Oxfordshire and Berkshire country."[24] Thus poetically anchored in a particular time and place, it is a miracle of imaginative device, a mid-century quintessence of some of the most constructive currents of the new age in poetry launched by the Romantics. Wordsworthian remembrance of things past, with its qualities of moral and psychological rehabilitation, blends with Wordsworthian emotion recollected in tranquility as the essence of poetic constitution; the particularity and authority of the bodily eye, which we associate with both Wordsworth and Keats, combine with Wordsworth's and Keats's mutual revitalization and refinement of the topographical poetic tradition of the seventeenth and eighteenth centuries; Wordsworth's escalation of sight into insight, of object into spirit, fuses with Keats's wholly secular but equally intense aestheticism; the Romantic redirection of myth comes to such perfect poise that the dream-vision is converted from poetic strategy to organic poetic metaphor. The poem's prosody and stanzaic structure are directly indebted to Keats's odes, and its climactic anxiety lest the last remnant of imaginative integrity be fatally infected by "this strange disease of modern life" (l. 203) is a latter-day projection of a fundamental source of Romantic imaginative tension.

In order to see why Arnold was justifiably distressed over the poem, why he found a delightful conception so beautifully worked out in its first hundred and fifty lines essentially crippled, it is important to see the speaker as the protagonist of the poem, not the scholar-gipsy, who is its provocateur. The "plot" of the poem turns on the speaker's "action," not the scholar-gipsy's, and that action, like the poem's bifurcated structure, has two main movements—the imaginative creation of the fully textured myth of the scholar-gipsy (ll. 32–150), at which he is superbly successful, and the effort to correlate that creation in a positive way with the demands of life in the modern world (ll. 151–231), at which he fails. His *delineation* of modern life is full and firm, as full and firm *and mythic* as his delineation of the life of the scholar-gipsy. Indeed, if one wants to pare the two mythic constructs down to essentials, the speaker gives approximately the same number of lines to each, and the very delight of the image of the created world of the scholar-gipsy motivates him, in the second half of the poem, to create the image of the modern world, not exactly as it is, but as a coherent counter-image. Thus he traps himself in his own imaginative architecture, and his two created worlds are brought to an impasse. Finally, the coda (ll. 232–250), which is fairly seen as a recasting of the poem in new symbols, is so full of dark, indignant imagery that the impasse is broken only by the implication that, though the Tyrian trader/scholar-gipsy may hold out a while longer, he is ultimately doomed to defeat by the "intruders on his ancient home" (l. 240). So even if we credit *The Scholar-Gipsy* with a degree of poetic magnificence, it is hard to fault Arnold's judgment that it "at best awakens a pleasing melancholy"; and if one sees it as an attempt on Arnold's part both to reconstitute and to critique Keats, it must be judged a failed attempt. Arnold had become a Romantic critic of Romanticism, setting out to show, critically, both the mesmeric beauty of Romantic vision and its fundamental inadequacy but finding himself so imaginatively co-opted by the beauty—so mesmerized—that his own work faltered as a corrective to the perceived inadequacy of Keatsian Romanticism.

If the failure of the speaker's efforts to establish an adequate and credible basis for imaginative permanence in a world of half-believers, half-feelers, half-willers, a world of hesitators and falterers, was the affective import of *The Scholar-Gipsy* (see particularly ll. 171–180), then a more resolute Arnold, an Arnold who felt that he had clarified both his "nature" and his "poetics," would presumably not return to approximately the same subject unless he felt that he had now discovered such an adequate and credible basis. Thus, despite all the conspicuous likenesses between it and *The Scholar-Gipsy*, *Thyrsis* invites the reader to measure the difference between it and the earlier poem on this specific issue. Put more positively, *Thyrsis* implicitly asserts that it has corrected the fatal flaw of *The Scholar-Gipsy*. Moreover, since Arnold was a wholly adequate poet who sometimes got himself entangled in inadequate perspectives, the poetic statement that *Thyrsis* makes is infinitely larger than a narrow, if fascinating, thematic deposition: it is an experiential exemplification of how *poetically* different two poems that "look" very much alike can be.[25]

Like *The Scholar-Gipsy*, *Thyrsis* is centered in the action of the speaker-protagonist. Having fulfilled his myth of the return to the topography of the scholar-gipsy's countryside, his primary concern is to sort out the various omens of permanence and change that register themselves on his consciousness so that when, in due realistic course, he returns to "the great town's harsh, heart-wearying roar" (l. 234), he will take with him something of permanent value. Since he will return to the city with only himself, that something of permanent value must be internal, the permanent result of some alteration in his way of seeing things.

The "plot" of *Thyrsis* is considerably more complex and intellectually sophisticated than that of *The Scholar-Gipsy*. Its retrospection covers a much longer period of time and derives from a much older man of the world; the death of a spiritually complicated companion who shared the speaker's youthful enthusiasm for and faith in the scholar-gipsy has been added, and the elegiac need to commemorate the deceased companion demands that some scrupulously honest basis be found for an ongoing internalized relationship with the dead. The immediate goal is not the sensuous recreation of the scholar-gipsy and his world, but the discovery of a symbol on which the speaker and his dead friend pledged *their faith in their faith* in the truth and imaginative significance of the scholar-gipsy, making their fidelity to each other inseparable from their faith in his continued existence.

All of this results in a wholly different imaginative focus from that of *The Scholar-Gipsy*. *Thyrsis* is not a poem of sensation, of total sensuous immersion; its "poetical feeling" is deliberative, reflective, exploratory. And so is its tone. Its imagery is intensely visual, just as particular in that respect as is *The Scholar-Gipsy*'s, but its sights are put to meditative uses: the tone by which the temperamental identity of the speaker is immediately revealed spontaneously translates sight into insight, object into the speaker's sense of the object's significance. In fact, there is so marked a difference between the temperamental identities of the speakers of *The Scholar-Gipsy* and *Thyrsis* that, by comparison, the difference between the speaker himself and Thyrsis seems sharply narrowed and the distance created by death, geography, and lapse of time partially erased.

As *Thyrsis* is not a poem of simple sensuous immersion, so it is not a poem of simplistic, black-and-white dichotomies, as *The Scholar-Gipsy*, in which a bridge cannot be established between the imaginative world and that of endless wordly trafficking, tends to be. The speaker of *Thyrsis* is a thoughtful pluralist who perceives many shades and grades of meaning, many variations among the fluid metaphors of permanence and change. His heightened sense of urgency is counterbalanced by a conspicuous degree of patience; external metaphors of change have, he sees, their internal counterparts in himself; he does not despair in the face of disappointment, and he assumes personal responsibility within the recognized limits of his capacity. He displays a high degree of resolution and independence reminiscent of Wordsworth's Old Leech-Gatherer: though things are not what they once were, they are sufficient unto his fundamental needs.

It is this mood of sober maturity, keenly responsive but unyielding to sentimental self-indulgence, that enables the speaker of *Thyrsis* to achieve the reconciliatory insight that he seeks. By gradually becoming available to the happiness and power of this sacred place, by recognizing that his thoughts have been troublesome in part because his "visits here" have grown "Too rare, too rare" (ll. 31, 231) and physical distance has led to a degree of spiritual separation and alienation, he gains perspective on an irreducible minimum of self-restorative truth and becomes reconciled both to Thyrsis and to the necessity of living at the world's active center despite its concomitant "fatigue and fear" (l. 236). He becomes reconciled to Thyrsis through a recognition that, despite the latter's willful defection from this hallowed countryside, a defection that led to his death, he never abandoned "visions of our light" (l. 227). Having reconfirmed his faith in the scholar-gipsy's continued existence through his rediscovery of the symbolic tree and having refreshed in his mind the authentic image of the scholar-gipsy seeking "A fugitive and gracious light" (l. 201), pursuing his heart's desire without personal following and without a soul-mate (ll. 209–210), the speaker sees a reflection of both Thyrsis and himself in that mirroring image and is reconciled. Then, having restored Thyrsis to his rightful place in his spiritual affections, he contentedly looks to him for needful reminders to keep the faith that they as renewed and clarified soul-mates continue to share. In short, he reenacts their earlier pledge of faith by making a new and more delicately spiritual contract with the deceased that will be renewed on every occasion on which despondency needs faith's corrective because Thyrsis will be the bearer of the spirit's good news:

> —Then through the great town's harsh, heart-
>   wearying roar,
>   Let in thy voice a whisper often come,
>   To chase fatigue and fear:
> *Why faintest thou? I wandered till I died.*
> *Roam on! The light we sought is shining still.*
> *Dost thou ask proof? Our tree yet crowns the hill,*
> *Our Scholar travels yet the loved hill-side.*
>
> (ll. 234–240)

Thus *Thyrsis* is a far less Keatsian poem than *The Scholar-Gipsy*; indeed, although it is, so to speak, an exact overlay of *The Scholar-Gipsy*, *Thyrsis*, in the larger sense, is not Keatsian at all. As Carlyle had reached a point at which he had to close his Byron and open his Goethe, Arnold had reached a point at which he had to close his Keats and open his Moschus, Theocritus, Sophocles, and Homer, while keeping free an avenue of access to the most spiritually Classical of all the Romantic poets, Wordsworth.

One gradually learns not to underestimate Arnold's intuitive poetic cunning, as one learns not to underestimate Hardy's. It is possible that Arnold intended *Obermann Once More* as a kind of gloss on *Thyrsis*, a "statement" that what he was explicitly doing in *Obermann Once More*, he was implicitly doing in *Thyrsis*—redacting his life as a poet, making peace with particular metaphors of his past. His creative work on the two poems apparently overlapped at least occasionally; his difficulties in establishing an appropriate relationship with Clough were a vivid part of his memory of the period of *Stanzas in Memory of the Author of 'Obermann'*; as in *Thyrsis* he was finally able to make honest and immortal[26] peace with himself in his recollected relationship with Clough, so he was enabled, in a subtly interconnected way, to make honest and immortal peace with his memory of that period in his life when Senancour had become ambivalently crucial.[27] Being a redaction through the all-encompassing metaphor of style, *Thyrsis* functions implicitly, does "the thing shall breed the thought"; being a redaction of and through thought, *Obermann Once More* had to be more explicit, and its discursive quality is the source of real critical discomfort. But the poem is not quite as explicit as it appears, at first flush, to be, and to that degree it is critically stimulating.

In the first place, it reverts to a species of poetic primitivism— the simple lines of the ballad of consciousness that Arnold had used in the earlier "Obermann" poem and in *Stanzas from the Grande Chartreuse*. Compared to the intricate artistry of the *Thyrsis* stanza, which Arnold had mastered under the tutelage of Keats, the quatrains of *Obermann Once More* have a quality of directness that seems to strip the poem of the dangers of rhetorical diversion and to declare implicitly that its poetic experience is of a primary, elemental kind, revelatory in a simple Biblical way. But, like *Thyrsis* vis-à-vis *The Scholar-Gipsy*, it shows that identical prosodic techniques are responsive to very different kinds of "poetical feeling," the involuted, recalcitrant, self-harrowing psyche of *Stanzas in Memory of the Author of 'Obermann'* being very different from the direct, accessible, self-redemptive psyche of *Obermann Once More*. As the earlier "Obermann" poem had been strangulated by a self-binding Romanticism, *Obermann Once More* is suffused with a self-releasing Classicism, and this is a second implicit resonance of the poem. In his long oration, which is cast in the oratorical tradition of Greek Classicism and embodies the chief substance of the poem, Obermann experiences the Second Coming which, physically, he cannot have: as Orpheus experienced a second death, Obermann experiences a second birth, resurrectional or *redivivus* in the speaker's imaginative consciousness, so that he may enjoy the repose of a second and final death, having confessed, despite the unquestioned authenticity of his symbolic enactment of Hell on earth, that he had simply misinterpreted its significance. Although his life had been a firm delineation, a true representation, of the way things in fact were, at that historical moment, his self-fixation had frozen time, like his heart, into an agonizing present that denied to the future the fluidity of the past. So despite his authenticity, his "firm delineation," he had lost the power to think clearly, and his nobility had been a shrunken nobility. In short, he had been a Romantic and had suffered inevitable Romantic flaws.

Implicit in Obermann's redemption are the Classical virtues of self-awareness without self-fixation, reason, an outward-looking rather than an inward-looking eye, a view of man in his social relations that looks deep into historical time, a recognition that despair is an intolerable defect of character because it paralyzes the very energy for creativity that makes man capable of survival. Obermann's bold and splendid myth of history is especially Classical in that, while it creates a crisp and credible view of the Christian era—its roots in the all-pervasive *Weltschmerz* of a hard, materialistic Roman civilization, its long tenure in an entirely new kind of *contemptus mundi* leavened by a childlike faith in the soul's renewal through gentleness and an august act of sacrificial love, the death of its unifying spirit in man's act of disbelief, the prolonged, drawn-out post-mortem over its corpse—it recognizes that the death of one grand mythic dispensation does not spell the doom of the myth-making imperative process itself. Rather, it looks forward to the new sustaining myth that, after much suffocating dormancy and under the guidance of his indispensable bards, man's informed thoughtfulness and his innate determination to make joy the true basis of his creative life will inevitably enable him to build. What the shape of that myth will be, Obermann does not say, though he does suggest that the French Revolution was the dividing point between man's lamentation over his dead past and the prospective vision out of which the new myth will ultimately emerge. The "I" of the Romantic has become the "we," complicit but detached, of the Classic.

The speaker in *Obermann Once More*, therefore, is cast essentially in the role of listener, the introductory stanzas setting up the fiction and revealing his deep spiritual susceptibility to the experience that he undergoes, the concluding stanzas rounding out the fiction and quietly suggesting its profound affectiveness. The whole matter is deftly rather than complexly handled. There is an initial tension between metaphors of permanence and change, but symbols of a fundamental permanence very quickly become predominant. Having become attuned to this permanence of physical aspect, the speaker then enables his myth of the return to assume a deep spiritual character as his memory travels back in time so wholly that it induces a mystical experience, a sort of waking dream-vision, in which the permanence-change motif is orchestrated through the "genius" of the place, a *Zeitgeist* figure who occupied a huge spiritual space in his "wandering youth" (l. 39). After the vision is ended, there is no comment about the experience itself, only an all-enveloping atmosphere of solemnity in which the speaker, drawn by some unknown force to shift slightly his *angle of vision*, sees the world in its sublimest aspect as, "glorious there,/without a sound,/Across the glimmering lake,/High in the Valais-depth profound," he sees "the morning break" (ll. 345–348).

Arnold made *Obermann Once More* the epilogue to his poetic life, and the mood of Classical serenity, thoughtful but joyous, that it projects should not perhaps be critically disturbed. It was a repose that had been hard-won, the precious result of a relentless effort to be intellectually and imaginatively honest. It would be an overstatement to say that, despite even the best poetic intentions, Arnold had wallowed in Romanticism and washed in Classicism, but it would not be indefensibly false to say so. Arnold's judgment may be faulted, but it is hard to see how his integrity can be. He had a realistic view of himself as a poet, and he knew that, despite his very considerable if limited talent, he had some individual awarenesses that people should know about. But he was not, finally, self-indulgent in his determination to make his mark as a modern poet. He continued until his death to be an urbane and accomplished verse-maker, but he knew when the central core of his significant poetry was complete, and he wasted little energy deceiving himself. His poetic canon has been ill-treated by commentators who have confused criticism with biographical speculation, by critics who have sought to formulate his "ideas" as if they had a legitimacy quite independent of the emotional and imaginative textures that enable them to hold together and exist, by dogmatists and theorists who code his work hastily and superficially and then deny his relevance to the doctrines they so singlemindedly advocate. But Arnold persists. There are signs abroad at the present time of a new readership willing to listen to his unique voice in the expectation that, if they are accessible enough and creative enough and flexible enough, he will add something of inestimable value to their lives.

Notes

1. *Letters of Matthew Arnold, 1848–1888*, G.W.E. Russell, ed. (New York: Macmillan, 1895), volume II, p. 10.
2. Preface to the First Edition of *Poems* (1853), *The Complete Prose Works of Matthew Arnold*, R.H. Super, ed. (Ann Arbor: University of Michigan Press, 1960), volume I, pp. 3–7. Subsequent references to this edition are given as "Super, I" with appropriate pagination.
3. Preface to the Second Edition of *Poems* (1854), Super, I, 16–17.
4. Super, I, 5. One wonders about the aesthetic legitimacy of the commonly used phrase "the historical imagination." It represents a use of the term *imagination* that is derivative and popular rather than philosophical and precise; while it may lend to history a rare and desirable quality, it may actually deplete poetry and her sister arts by dissipating into vague descriptiveness the one concept indispensable to their unity and wholeness.
5. E.g., Preface to *Wessex Poems and Other Verses, The Complete Poems of Thomas Hardy*, James Gibson, ed. (New York: Macmillan, 1976), p. [6].
6. E.g., "Apology" prefixed to *Late Lyrics and Earlier, Complete Poems*, p. 558.
7. See Alba H. Warren, Jr., *English Poetic Theory, 1825–1865* (Princeton: Princeton University Press, 1950), chapter 9, and S.M.B. Coulling, "Matthew Arnold's 1853 Preface: Its Origin and Aftermath," *Victorian Studies*, volume VII (1964), pp. 233–263.
8. Super, I, 15, sentence beginning "If we must be *dilettanti*. . . ."
9. Super, I, 13.
10. Super, I, 2.
11. *Letters*, I, 30.
12. *Letters of Matthew Arnold to Arthur Hugh Clough*, H.F. Lowry, ed. (New York: Oxford University Press, 1932), p. 126.
13. Super, I, 4.
14. *Letters to Clough*, p. 146.
15. Lionel Trilling, *Matthew Arnold* (New York: Columbia University Press, 1939), pp. 134–135: ". . . it is almost impossible not to find . . . at least a shadowy personal significance. The strong son slain by the mightier father, and in the end Sohrab draws his father's spear from his own side to let out his life. . . . We watch Arnold in his later youth and we must wonder if he is not, in a psychological sense, doing the same thing." This is a misreading of the poem (Sohrab is clearly the mightier warrior and by far the greater man), but it is too novelistically appealing ever to be refuted.

16. *The Ring and the Book*, Book XII, concluding argument.

17. Allott cites the sleeplessness of Agamemnon and Menelaus at the beginning of Book X and of Achilles at the beginning of Book XXIV. See *The Poems of Matthew Arnold*, p. 322n.

18. G.W.E. Russell, *Matthew Arnold* (London: Macmillan, 1904), p. 42.

19. Super, I, 64. All further references are given in parentheses in the text.

20. Though not published until 1855 and 1867, respectively, *Stanzas from the Grande Chartreuse* and *Dover Beach* reflect the spiritual and poetic climate of 1851–1852 and were probably "composed" (conceptualized and/or written) then.

21. *Letters to Clough*, p. 164. Clough had been one of Dr. Arnold's most brilliant pupils.

22. With Dr. Arnold so insistent in the background of the speaker's thinking, there may be less pressing reason to see Carlyle as the source of the poem's use of the hero metaphor than commentators on the poem usually assert.

23. *Letters to Clough*, p. 146. Professor M. Allott (*Poems*, p. 356) attitudinizes very strangely indeed over this poem, the Preface of 1853, and Arnold's poetry generally. Having cited a reminiscent letter from Arnold to his brother Tom, she says: "This letter and A.'s classification of the poem as an elegy show that it should be read as a lament for youth and its wholeheartedness and energy, which are sapped by life in the world, i.e. the scholar-gipsy is a Callicles miraculously preserved from turning into an Empedocles. A. knows that such 'miracles do not happen,' but to oppose the ideal and the actual is the method adopted here for a criticism of Victorian civilization (which is also a Romantic criticism of life for its failure to match expectation)." Thus she would deprive Arnold of such maturity as he did have in 1852–1853 and would seem to cherish his not attaining any more.

24. Mrs. Humphry Ward, *A Writer's Recollections*, quoted in *Poems*, p. 356.

25. That the fundamental poetical difference between the two poems was crucial to Arnold's imaginative conception is reinforced not only by their deceptive stylistic identity but also by Arnold's note in the 1867 edition of his poems, in which *The Scholar-Gipsy* did not appear, that "Throughout this Poem there is reference to another piece, *The Scholar-Gipsy* . . ."(*Poems*, p. 538).

26. In *Rugby Chapel*, he had given "immortality" to both his *personae* and to his poetic sense of his father—had frozen them into public, unerasable language.

27. We may some day understand better the curiously haunting overlap of Clough and Senancour in Arnold's earlier life, including possibly a connection between Arnold's poetic abandonment of "Obermann" and his dramatic temptation to throw Clough over.

5.

Arnold and the Crisis of Classicism

That Matthew Arnold was a persistent critic of Romanticism is well recognized by students of his poetry,[1] though there has been no comprehensive review of the way in which Arnold drew the English Romantics into the poetics of his prose by using them as metaphoric reference points throughout his critical writings, and there has been no consensus among the critics as to the exact character and justness of Arnold's evaluation of the Romantic experiment—its failures and, especially, its successes. Moreover, various broad results of Arnold's critical attentiveness to the Romantics have not been adequately examined and defined. For example, although his perception of Romanticism never lost its literary rootedness, it gradually underwent a process of expansion that enlarged it from a more or less specialized literary concern to an archetypal metaphor as large as one dominant aspect of life itself. In the Preface to *Merope* (1858), for example, he speaks of England as the "stronghold" of Romanticism[2] and suggests thereby that the metaphor has assumed an encompassing psycho-cultural significance that, in the ensuing decade, must reconcile itself to that other dominant strain in the spirit of contemporary England, Philistinism. The idea of Romanticism gradually coalesces in Arnold's mind with the idea of Modernism; and because the archetypal contention between it and Classicism as an antiphonal metaphor necessarily persists, Arnold is gradually drawn into the larger arena where his critical consciousness can do battle with those general excesses of Romantic Modernism that have overwhelmed Classical correctives and induced a cultural crisis.

For further example, Arnold's relentless criticism of Romanticism was not just a matter of intellectual insight but gradually took control of his constructive imagination, of the way his whole mind worked—of how he thought poetically, how he adopted or created poetic subjects or actions, how he used language. This total integration of the critical consciousness with the creative imagination has not been adequately noted. There is also a corollary to this that requires more attention, or at least a different kind of attention, than it has received so far. Arnold carried his critical response to Romanticism beyond a poetry of statement to a poetry of experience. But being so thoroughgoing a critic, he apparently did not realize the degree to which he was himself susceptible to infiltration by the most massive spiritual tendency of his time. Especially during the period between his first and third volumes—say, from the end of 1849 to mid-1853—he underwent a subtle, unconscious, but profound absorption of Romantic influence. Then, like the Newman who had unconsciously drifted in the direction of Liberalism or who saw his own face in the Monophysite mirror,[3] Arnold suddenly awakened to the climactic recognition that he, too, was a Romantic Modernist.

So the phrase "crisis of Classicism" has a double thrust, one personal, of the kind just described, and one psycho-cultural. On the psycho-cultural side, it points to the failures of imaginative insight, of wholeness and steadiness of view, that result from inadequately rooted enthusiasms or disproportionate glooms, even among supremely talented and impeccably intentioned persons, and, especially during periods of rapid shifts in power and allegiance, contribute to and compound the chaos of life in ignorance or neglect of or conscious contempt for such principles of an authentic renewal as are implicit in Goethe's statement, "From Homer and Polygnotus I every day learn more clearly . . . that in our life here above ground we have, properly speaking, to enact Hell. . . ."[4] This is the kind of corrective insight that Classicism, rightly understood, offers to a Romantic Modernism that, despite the "great . . . sum of force . . . expended" upon it,[5] has been so conspicuously inadequate to the needs of its times. It is to these defects and failures of imaginative insight, visible even in a Romanticism at the moment of its greatest glory but become systemic in a Romantic Modernism that, like Jude Fawley, is "in a chaos of principles,"[6] that the body of Arnold's poetry attends; it is the function of Arnold's criticism in both prose and verse.

It is Arnold's critical verse that provides his most penetrating sense of the psycho-cultural crisis of his times; it was in the critical verse, because of the literary tradition of which that verse became an extension and of the narrower audience implicit in verse, that he could deploy such a seemingly specialized metaphor as Classicism as a wholly appropriate corrective to the malaise of Romantic Modernism. Habitual readers of poetry were the ones most likely to see Classicism as a real frame of mind and a functional approach to spiritual problem-solving; though the fury of contemporaneous topicality that had swept through poetry and criticism in the 1840s and 1850s had created a climate sceptical of, and often positively hostile to, the relevance of antiquity to the new, radical, and increasingly impious order of things, it was the only audience he had even if, for the most part, it did not understand him well or abide with him long.

Our contemporaries have not understood Arnold well either. They have mostly brought to his canon critical hypotheses developed elsewhere, or, if they are historians rather than critics, they have read his rhetoric in an untroubled sort of way and used the less interesting part of him to create a literary portrait of his age that is less than true. Thus the post-textual Arnold, like the post-textual Tennyson and Browning, is simply too frustrating a place to begin to look at him afresh, even if the rubrics of traditional scholarship demand it. The post-textual Arnold—that is, the Arnold that means what the commentators on his literary texts say he means—is, with very few exceptions, too dull a critical product to make the careful stepping that conscientious fairness to the work of others requires seem worthwhile. Unless one is cut from the same cloth as Browning's grammarian, such labor could hardly be expected to merit more than the praise of folly. Know it one must; arbitrate it in detail one need not.

The pre-textual Arnold, on the other hand—the Arnold who looked searchingly at "these bad days" or "these . . . damned times" and saw both the subtle and the gross evil thereof before ever making the decisions about subject, architecture, and language that resulted in individual poetic texts that are specific metaphors, *among many possible metaphors*, of that searching look and that peculiar insight—is essentially unmapped terrain. The a-textual Arnold is familiar enough: the Arnold who wrote to Clough saying that "these are damned times—everything is against one—the height to which knowledge is come, the spread of luxury, our physical enervation, the absence of great *natures*, the unavoidable contact with millions of small ones, newspapers, cities, light profligate friends, moral desperadoes like Carlyle, our own selves, and the sickening consciousness of our difficulties. . . ."[7] Some of the metaphors catalogued here do find their way into poetic texts, but the term *pre-textual* is meant to designate those broad characteristics of the age that can be deduced from individual canonical poems and groups of poems and, in an extrapolated form, seen as broad fields of concern that Arnold chose to create a specific poetic metaphor (action, structure, language) to reflect. This is obviously not the Arnold upon whom the textual critic brings his skills to bear (that is the Arnold of the poetic metaphors themselves), but it is the Arnold who made the decisions that made the texts possible.

The pre-textual Arnold—the Arnold observing critically the multiple gesturing of his age—saw many characteristic movements, none of which was strictly peculiar to the idiomatic nature of those times, but all of which were present and significant. When the poetic record was essentially complete, it was his attention to these—"the main movement of mind of the last quarter of a century," "the main line of modern development"[8]—that he saw as one of the two chief bases for a lasting readership for his poetry, the other being stylistic—his distinctive fusion of "poetical sentiment" and "intellectual vigor and abundance." On the basis of that poetic record, it is wholly reasonable to yield to Arnold's self-criticism and to see his conversion of the physiognomy of Romantic Modernism into style as the defining mark of his career as a poet and the paradigm of modern poetry that he, more than any other English poet of his century, put into place. As the drama was Arnold's central literary metaphor, as the isolated individual, cut off from both tradition and community and attempting to fabricate out of his peculiar temperament and his individual life experience a myth to live or to die by, was his chief existential metaphor, and as his pervasive metaphor of the spiritual ambience in which both poet and *persona* had to function was a Romanticism in ruins, Arnold's poetry is the dramatic transformation of the exacerbated and unredeemed modern psyche into a network of fictions or, as Emerson said of Carlyle's *Past and Present*, the conversion of an era into a style,[9] a style that is both simple and severe, sympathetic and relentlessly critical.

Despite the distinctiveness of Arnold's individual poetic fictions, they are, on the whole, remarkably coherent. The eye of the *persona* is characteristically inward-sinking, and he labors under the presumption that he must work out his destiny alone: that is the enveloping myth of his existence. And it is not the supportive solitude of Newman's "Never less alone than when alone"; it is that stark uprooted loneliness that throws one back upon one's own nerve ends.

Like the dramatic poets who became his aesthetic models and like Homer, Arnold saw life as a network of symbolic human actions. People were representative role-players, and ideas became functional as dimensions of personality—motives for action, assertions of identity. The *dramatis personae* of Romantic Modernism have, therefore, a perennial aspect common to men and women in all ages. What seems to give them a particular historical reality, to make the power of the man reciprocate with the power of the moment, is, besides their existential loneliness, the undertone of futility by which even their most exultant acclamations are disqualified, as if the object of their spiritual quest is sure to dissolve in the very act of discovery, the disbelief that is an implicit dimension of their belief inducing into even their finest recognitions a degree of frenzy rather than full serenity. They are like witnesses of the Heraclitean flux who have no fixed or stable vantage point from which to view, philosophically, a perpetual process of formation and dissolution—no anchoring identity, no satisfactory knowledge of the universe and their place in it, no sufficient religious dogma, no art to stand against time and give the illusion at least of having conquered it. Even the most privileged and favored of Arnold's *personae*—Empedocles—is, in the end, as incompetent as the rest. He is elegant, conscientious, supremely accomplished, and he enacts one of the most fascinating rituals of heroic self-reliance in literature. But his psyche is just as torn as that of the turbulent, ill-starred, near-psychotic speaker protagonist of the *Switzerland* poems; he rationalizes his death wish just as deliberately, if with greater rhetorical control and plausibility, as the speaker protagonist of *Stanzas from the Grande Chartreuse*. His erasure of human life, especially in the face of his magnificently gifted "essay on man" in Act I, scene ii, makes an even greater mockery of human heroism than if he were obviously a weak and distasteful man. The profound pathos that Empedocles embodies cuts deeper by virtue of the solemn literary form out of which he emerges—with its analogy in Classical tragedy—and the nearness of an alternative human response to life in "this meadow of calamity" (act II, l. 365)—Oedipus watching from the wings. His situation is a climactic example of Romantic Modernism. He cannot discover a metaphor by which to define himself in any but a negative way or a myth to live by even though he examines Callicles' myths with varying degrees of eagerness and identification. His view of nature and of man's place in nature is a welter of Romantic confusion, oscillating between the indifference of the universe ("unallied unopening earth," "unrecognizing sea" [act II, ll. 360–361]) and its warm, embracing, womb-like character (act II, ll. 404ff.). When he inflates his will for his final act, his exaltation is half anxiety lest he be tricked out of what is at best a remnant salvation.

The "poise" to which Empedocles persistently aspires verbally but which is contradicted by a brutal physical metaphor when "*He plunges into 'the crater*" (following act II, l. 416) is fragilely attained in *The Scholar-Gipsy*; however, the wonderfully delicate and credible process by which its idyllic pastoral world is made momentarily both psychologically therapeutic and imaginatively stabilizing is deeply rooted in anxiety, in a virulently infectious mortality that suggests that the speaker's "fly our greetings, fly our speech and smiles!" (l. 231) has an analogy in the blighted leper's "Unclean! Unclean!" Even while the illusion of a recovered paradise that has long been lost is being so sensuously, so tactilely, so visually and melodiously created— a sudden and spontaneous growth, rooted in the fertile soil of a desperately felt human need and nurtured by one of those luminously favored moments when waking and sleeping dreams become one with faith and epiphanies are born—even while this illusion is being firmly created, an ominous groundtone becomes increasingly audible (ll. 141–150, 164–170, 171–180, 181–190, 190–196, 203–210) until it rises to a "feverish" counter-crescendo in lines 221–231. The fascinatingly troublesome coda, with its dark and indignant imagery, implies that "the intruders on his ancient home" will eventually leave the gipsy-cum-Tyrian trader no avenue of escape, as indeed the speaker has none beyond the enchantment of this beautiful and evanescent poetic moment.

Arnold's pre-textual world—"the main movement of mind of the last quarter of a century"—was a world of many gestures, of course: self-conscious poseurs facing with theatrical weariness a highly complex state of civilization; escapists from a cumulative modernism turning their backs upon it and going in search of some metaphor of timeless, protective stability, however anachronistic, in which to find solace or to entomb themselves; a growing number of literalists deflating man's imaginative capacity to perceive a mysterious reality in the sights and sounds of Nature and to respond to her crisp yet haunting images at a deep, subliminal level; sentimentalists, stoics, dilettantes, cynics, impassioned rebels, ironists, and misanthropes inculcating their various readings of human destiny. But the two subjects that have a recurrent and pervasive presence in the spiritual climate that his poems implant, examine, and critique are man's search for identity and the role of literature as a *magister vitae humanae*.* It is on these crucial subjects particularly that he proposes Classical correctives to Romantic Modernist misdirection.

Arnold perceived the widespread Romantic efforts to adapt the Classical precept "Know thyself" to the modern milieu as frequently leading to various species of self-deception—an almost prurient seductiveness, an inducement to a subtly inauthentic self-dramatization that has about it marks of melodramatic posturing, a tendency to heighten the emotional rather than the rational content of language and to trap the victim in sophistical arguments that become compounded in fancifulness. Arnold recognized, of course, that self-identification is the most microcosmic of spiritual quests (*what* am *I?*) requiring the most macrocosmic of correlational contexts (*I* and the *universe*) and that, in terms of the wholly secular imagination, it is the quest that promises at its extremes either complete existential defeat (hopeless and unbearable loneliness) or the most magnificent of spiritual epiphanies (the discovery of one's distinctive place and purpose in the infinite correspondences of the universe). Moreover, since it must be undertaken *in medias res*, when one's life is in the very process of fading away and an acute sense of urgency combined with an intense moral conscientiousness and emotional self-consciousness can lead to the endless self-harrowing of a man seeking illumination only in himself by himself for himself, its very high-mindedness can lead to disastrous results. To this dangerous Romantic imbalance of emotional self-consciousness, Arnold applied Classical correctives: a motive that is centered in thought rather than in feeling, in rational understanding rather than in emotional force; a steady persistence based on a clear recognition that self-knowledge is both a process and the cumulative result of a process rather than a sudden,

* A third subject of very large proportions—man's efforts to find a satisfactory relationship to nature—can be traced in many of the poems analyzed in Chapter II. See *In Utrumque Paratus* (pp. 52–54), *In Harmony with Nature* (pp. 40–41), *The Youth of Nature, The Youth of Man, The Future* (pp. 95–102), *Self-Dependence* (pp. 72–74), and *passim.*

apocalyptic, revolutionary conversion; an openness to metaphors of the not-self (the outward-looking eye), including
images of vastness, motion, and serenity like "the intense, clear,
star-sown vault of heaven," "the lit sea's unquiet ways," "the
rustling night-air"; and a willingness to make the leap from
one mode of search (say, the rational) to another mode of
search (say, the imaginative) when the former outruns its
usefulness. But a pre-condition to this imaginative openness to
the natural magic of the universe is a strictly Classical view of
Nature—namely, that as Nature fulfills the law of *her* being,
man may be encouraged to fulfill the law of *his*, not vainly
expecting Nature to serve him as something more personally
penetrative than as a magnificent analogical mirror in whose
reflection he can see an imaginatively serviceable model of his
own very human possibilities.

Every student of Arnold is aware not only of his profound
veneration of and faith in the best literature but also of his
general dissatisfaction with contemporary literature as an
expression of a "deeply *unpoetical*"[10] age and his oft-repeated
unfavorable comparison of the greatest Romantic writers,
despite full acknowledgment of their extraordinary achievement, with the greatest writers of Classical Greece. His was a
failed age creatively, Arnold thought,[11] and the second part of
his career was largely devoted to an explicit effort to establish
the bases for a sound criticism that would enable the literature
of the future to live fully up to such creative potential as it
might have. But England had no exemplary creative writers
(that is, no poets) during the 1840s, 1850s, and 1860s to whom
the young writer of his generation could turn for guidance.
There was more to be learned from Newman than from anyone
else—habits of thought, style—but Newman was, by Arnold's
terms, a supremely critical rather than a supremely creative
writer.

In his prose criticism, Arnold would fault even the great
Romantics for the inadequacy of their ideas (they did not know
enough); for the negligent way in which they selected their
poetic "actions" (their subjects or myths); and for their failure
to give the action primary consideration in a poem's internal
evolution, their disproportionate emphasis on phrase-making

for its own sake, and their woeful inattention to the construc-
tional or architectural aspect of poems. In his poetry, on the
other hand, he sketched general patterns in the disheveled
psychology of an age of Romantic Modernism to whose inadequacy an inadequate literature was contributive. Being an
unheroic age, it had little capacity to recognize either human
protagonists of truly heroic proportions or its own desperate
need of them. Being blind to its own true character and yet
fixated on itself, it lacked an understanding of the austere
beauty and genuine poetic relationship between the Classical
ideals of full self-knowledge and complete self-effacement;
thus writers became its mentors in ignorance of the fact that
they themselves were transparent products of the age and bore
in their own persons its disqualifying faults. The growing
tendency of contemporary writers to emphasize "psychology
and the anatomy of sentiment" contradicted the Classical
recognition that the "grand[est] moral effects" of literature are
"produced by *style*"[12]; thus literature's Classical capacity to treat
the most complex moral themes was dissipated in formless
ingenuity and capricious inflations of a poetic language whose
salutary effects depend on simplicity, directness, and rapidity
of movement. Moreover, its psychology of imaginative and
moral development was grossly oversimplified, resulting in too
great a dependence on "wonders," "rapture," and "Fancy's
dispossession of reality" rather than on "stern resolve," "sterner
will," sorrow, and terror, and a disposition to allow a "super-
fluity of joy," a "nectarous poppy," or stoical disdain to blind
one to the deep revelation inherent in "Glooms that enhance
and glorify the earth" and in the stark "majesty of grief." An
age of Romantic Modernism needed, above all else, a strong
current of critical thought, but instead there was a predominant
allegiance to feeling, to sensuous delight in its most refined
manifestations or to extremely volatile swings of passion,
drawing man away from the austerer implications of thought
and closer and closer to spiritual atrophy. As the craving for
a life of sensation, whether of the gross or delicate sort, became
systemic, as the age's demand for melodramatic fictions and
apocalyptic themes became obsessive, its finer literary spirits
almost despaired of establishing a co-creative relationship with

their readers in which truly original and finely tuned aspects of poetry could continue to function processively. The therapeutic Classical process of myth-making, of creating effective fictions that enable a person to project outward the primary images of his own inner life and to discover satisfactory patterns of resolution to life's disappointments, ran the danger of being lost.

Arnold surveyed the field of letters in this era of Romantic Modernism and identified three barometric voices as representative of literature's position in relation to man's contemporary problems: the apocalyptic voice of an intense social conscientiousness, urgent, melodramatic; the aesthetic, pastoral voice piping reassurances about "breathless glades, cheered by shy Dian's horn,/Cold-babbling springs,—or caves"; and the grim, blunt, necessitarian voice dogmatically dismissing idealistic expectations of human redemption and renewal. Implicit in this literary construct was a thoroughly distressed attitude toward man's social situation insofar as it related to literature: when brought face to face through literature with a truly horrifying human evil, neither the most poetical voice of the age nor the least poetical touched the problem in any adequate way, each being enclosed in its own intellectual and literary system and in that sense imprisoned in irrelevance. Arnold certainly knew such conspicuous exceptions to this profile as Carlyle and Tennyson, but he was somewhat alienated from them both, and he was evaluating the literary situation in representative rather than exceptional terms.

He also judged as inadequate such archetypal attitudes toward poetry as that which makes the poet suffer the agonies of those whose actions he represents (sometimes called the Romantic or, after Schiller, the Sympathetic attitude) and that which invites the poet to emulate the gods, seeing and knowing all but remaining impervious, in their untroubled happiness, to the pain which they witness (sometimes called the Olympian attitude). As Arnold saw it, such essentially pre-Classical or primitive views, though ingratiatingly naive, ignored the moral imperative at the center of the age of the heroes, of *homo agonistes*, which simultaneously ·defines both literature and the human role in an entirely new way, lodging literature's function and man's identity, not in a sensual and riotous nature, but in moral values in which the gods themselves are complicit and in which empathetic understanding replaces the raw force of a soul-devouring identification through feeling.

Finally, there is the troublesome but indispensable question of literary models: to what predecessors could a young writer in such an age turn for guidance, what poets could he emulate? The question must be answered with a high degree of circumspection because, as some critics have failed to notice, nowhere in his poetry does Arnold answer it directly. Each speaker in his poetic canon is himself reacting to the pressures of Romantic Modernism, and it is not safe to assume that any two of them are the same except in poems designated by the poet as sequential, and even there the mood of the speaker and his assumption of a particular role in different but sequential poems can make a significant difference. Even the sonnet *Shakespeare* and the triple epicede *Memorial Verses* reflect very different moods of character that are explicitly generic ("We," "us") and therefore metaphoric rather than literally authorial. The result is that, however explicit the speaker's critical judgment may be, there is no firm implication of a crisp authorial judgment. Rather, criticism is angled into life, so to speak: what would a certain kind of temperament struggling with a personal, if representative, crisis of consciousness *feel* about Goethe or Wordsworth or Byron or Shelley or Senancour, for example? While the resultant evaluation is impressively implanted in the reader's awareness, the relative poetic circumstances are implanted too, and the reader-critic is invited to set aside for the moment so-called objective criticism and to judge, for example, the aptness of such critical metaphors as Shelley's "lovely wail," "The pageant of [Byron's] bleeding heart," and Senancour/ Obermann's ostrich-like hidden head from inside the sensibility stresses of the speaker-protagonist of *Stanzas from the Grande Chartreuse*.[13]

In the prismatic view provided by Arnold's poetry as a whole, no nineteenth-century writer escapes qualification, and only Wordsworth emerges as a model, though a profoundly challenging model, for the young writer. Coleridge never attains a poetic presence; Shelley, though treated with a fair degree of tenderness, is indicted for an ineffectual eloquence rooted in doubtful motives and for a mournful birdsong having little or no significance; despite his formalistic usefulness to Arnold himself, Keats is associated with the "nectarous poppy" of *To a Gipsy Child by the Sea-Shore* and the withdrawn, inconsequential pastoral piper of *To George Cruikshank* . . . ; Senancour, even for the speaker-protagonist of *Stanzas in Memory of the Author of 'Obermann'*, gradually yields place to Wordsworth in the curve of the poem's narrative consciousness. Byron's Titanism and Goethe's Olympianism place them in very different positions on the spectrum of modern poetry, neither of which is in any sense negligible. But we watch their epic-like performances—Byron's "fiery . . . strife," Goethe's uncompromising seeing eye, looking undaunted upon the apocalyptic end of a dispensation—as we might watch quintessentially different heroes at the center of any cataclysmic world-rendering, affected even beyond our capacity to understand but unable to emulate either one. Wordsworth, on the other hand, performed the magical task, essential to all ages, of returning poetry to its earliest symbol, the lyre, to its earliest practitioner, Orpheus, and to its earliest purpose, the redemption of Nature in the hearts of men—that is, the reconciliation of man to a universe that he can actually see, hear, touch, smell, taste, and love. Even in an age of Romantic Modernism, there will be embodiments of sagacity and force, if not quite Goethean sagacity or Byronic force, but these "dark days" make least likely the most essential functions of poetry—the centering of experience in the benign human emotions, the dissolution of the barriers between the harsh external appearance of things and their restorative inner reality, the attuning of the human ear to the eternal music of Nature's voice—and it is this that makes Wordsworth so incomparably important in this time of passionate grossness, myopic literalness, and spiritual deafness.

Titanism, Olympianism, Orpheanism—thus even Byron, Goethe, and Wordsworth have their analogues in Classical myth and poetry. But more explicitly, Homer, Sophocles, and Epictetus are offered as Classical correctives to Romantic Modernism. Homer is there because of the clarity of his spiritual insight, a clarity that, working through inherited myth or human "history," enabled him, though blind, to see the physiognomy of the world with such wholly dependable imaginative truth that even his physical blindness did not lead him into fancifulness and caprice. The authority of the spiritual eye is also Sophocles' chief credential: his sight/insight was so "whole" and "steady" and "even-balanced" that he never fell into the inadequacies of dullness or the misleading volatilities of passion; despite the penetration of his tragic vision, he remained "mellow" and "sweet," never falling into the de-animating, eclipsing mournfulness of a Byronic Manfred. Between these two stands Epictetus, and such company justifies our seeing his insight into the truth of the human prospect as his singular merit too. He was the philosophical spokesman for the detached, self-effacing attitude toward human experience and conduct that, in their individual fashions, Homer and Sophocles absorbed into their epics and tragedies. He was the great corrector of disproportionate human expectation, not a de-spiritualizer of man but his great equalizer, postulating a philosophy of human attitudes that would enable man, at the most dependable level, to be reconciled to the truth of his situation in his universe. Seeing "things as they in fact are," then, seeing the truth without attitudinal extravagance or rebellion, is what the mind "in these bad days" most needs, and one has to overleap, not just the greater part of Romanticism, but much of the Christian tradition in literature, to find firm foundations upon which to build mental attitudes adequate to the present and the future.

Arnold's subtle, unconscious, but profound absorption of the influence of Romantic Modernism and the close correlation between his recognition and rejection of that influence and the virtual end of his career as a poet at the age, say, of thirty-five is a tantalizing subject that defies conclusive resolution. Even if one had full and relevant external data on Arnold's thoughts and motives, a detailed account in his own hand of his recognitions and resolutions in this matter, it would still generate enough theoretical questions to keep the issue forever in solution. As it is, we have very little specific guidance for dealing with a literary event that is not only the chief critical turning in Arnold's own literary life but also the prototype of one of the major critical dilemmas of modern poetry, the difference between Arnold and his successors being that he faced it first and with incomparable *éclat*. The two fundamental questions at the heart of the event are these: what is the purpose of poetry, especially though not exclusively poetry in a modern context, and how imperative for my own poetic practice, indeed for my very continuation as a poet, is a deep and conscientious sense of poetry's purpose? Inherent therein is one of the most relentless of moral questions—*am* I what I *believe?*—and an understanding of the true dimensions of Arnold's essentially aesthetic "action" requires a moral context.

The two documents that Arnold himself placed at the center of the issue are *Empedocles on Etna* and the critical Preface of 1853, the one "A DRAMATIC POEM" Classically monitored and Romantically faulted, the other a poetic manifesto subscribing unequivocally to the dramatic principles of Classical theory and practice and faulting Romanticism for its deviations from those principles. Such central placement is perfectly apt— these are the crucial exemplary documents—but something more than a literal view of them, in fact a metaphoric or symbolic view, must be taken in order to appreciate fully their subtle, oblique significance. *Empedocles on Etna* was Arnold's Iphigenia, the symbolic sacrifice that he made to appease the wrath of the goddess of pure poetry for an offense that, though innocently committed, had become systemic in his practice of her art. The Preface of 1853, besides being an explicit declaration of full faith in the simple, austere, unimpeachable poetic rules of the Classical goddess, is an implicit confession of personal culpability, a plea of "guilty, with an explanation."

The issue is not whether or not Arnold was right in thus indicting the major tendency of his poetic art: that is a legitimate but different issue upon which much critical impressionism has been expended. Here our concern is simply with how he saw the matter, and since the Preface is the chief summary of evidence external to the poetry,[14] the Preface is the place to begin.

Throughout Arnold's Preface, aesthetics is rooted in ethics: that is good poetry which increases the world's pleasure, that is bad poetry which increases the world's pain is how the Preface begins. It ends with a fingering of culture's amoralists, poetry's *dilettanti*, and a solemn moral charge to its writer-audience: "Let us not bewilder our successors: let us transmit to them the practice of poetry, with its boundaries and wholesome regulative laws, under which excellent works may again, perhaps, at some future time, be produced, not yet fallen into oblivion through our neglect, not yet condemned and cancelled by the influence of their eternal enemy, caprice."[15] Thus it is an action Preface, a call to self-recognition and self-renewal or self-restraint, in the light of a refreshed view of the highest kind of moral seriousness involved in the practice of poetry, and a challenge even to accept what for the writer is the ultimate self-sacrificial insight, namely, that an age of no poetry is better than an age of bad poetry.[16] That "human actions" are the "eternal objects" (I, 3) of poetry makes it axiomatic that aesthetic considerations, however indispensable, are secondary to the moral imperative; even the selection of "an excellent action"—one which "belong[s] to the domain of our permanent passions" (I, 4)—invokes, in the first place, a high degree of moral sophistication, though it is at this point that ethics and aesthetics merge and become inseparable as poetic functions, moral affect being thereafter dependent on style. But even such stylistic matters as construction and diction are dealt with in the language of morality, the rhetoric of conscience: the "severe and scrupulous self-restraint of the ancients" (I, 11) in these matters has, for those who have commerce with them, "a steadying and composing effect upon their judgment, not of literary works only, but of men and events in general" (I, 13).

So pervasive in the Preface that it determines its structure is the contrast between the ancients and the moderns, between the Classical Greeks and Romantic Modernist Englishmen. Against the illusion exuded by "the great monuments of early Greek genius"—"the calm, the cheerfulness, the disinterested objectivity" (I, 1)—is set the frenzied chaos of contemporary English poetic practice, with its fragmentariness of view and of performance, its preference for the rhetorical over the genuinely poetical, for the novel and curious part over the impressive and salutary whole, its subjectivity, its inflated contemporaneity, its overabundance of critical counselors, its spiritual confusion, incoherence, and discomfort inducing feelings of contradiction, irritation, and impatience, its lack of moral grandeur, its excessive self-congratulation, its "bewildering confusion" and uncertainty in all respects, the imperious demands it makes for devotion to such provincially topical subjects as theories of progress, industrial development, and social amelioration, its blind expectation that a poetry can be true to the best poetic principles and at the same time faithfully represent so fundamentally unpoetical an age.

And here is where we identify the implicit confession of personal culpability: although Arnold acknowledged at the time of writing the Preface that a poetry that took as its essential object the representation of such an age as that described above could hardly be anything but poetically inadequate because its subject was woefully inadequate and no craftsmanship, however expert, could make adequate poetry out of an inadequate subject, he had largely done just that. It is true that he had consistently represented the age in order to subject it and the Romantic writers who had fathered it to relentless criticism; one may easily yield him credit for having done something far more poetically imaginative than simply creating verse structures through which his persistent critical consciousness could function at a subtle and highly stimulating level. But on the whole and despite notable exceptions, the dominant impression that Arnold's poetry gives to one who knows something of his age is of a representation of that age.

Arnold rooted the feeling of his poems and the rhetoric expressive of that feeling in the Classical tradition of mimetic, representational art, his lyrical as well as his dramatic and narrative poems having, despite their confessional mode, the essential objectivity of action-centered poetry that is "in a large degree dramatic or personative in conception." That he lacked the "discipline" to do it plainly and simply and thoroughly, he confesses, and he admits that therefore his poems do not "breathe its spirit" (I, 1);[17] but he still claims, even in the face of confessed failure, that throughout his career as a young poet he had, in an immature, undisciplined, unsuccessful way, aspired to the goal of the ancients—"not to praise their age, but to afford to the men who live in it the highest pleasure which they are capable of feeling" (I, 13). Judged by the severe standards of the Preface, he had been prone to three basic types of error: of allowing too many relatively inconsequential pieces a place among his published works; not only of critically interpreting his age, but of interpreting it in such a way as to make too many of his poems time-dependent; of grossly miscalculating what gives readers of poetry "the highest plea- sure which they are capable of feeling." He had succeeded in catching "the main movement of mind of the last quarter of a century," "the main line of modern development"; he had been more attentive than any of his contemporaries before Swinburne to the relevance of Classical style to a modern outlook, to the wholesome persistence in an unpoetical age of a supremely poetical tradition. He had put in place, however unsatisfactorily from his own point of view, a canon of poetry that, though it is the least revolutionary in appearance, has had a profound relevance for modern poetry. As Arnold was both the most Wordsworthian and Classical of Victorian poets, so Hardy and Eliot have been the most Arnoldian and Classical of twentieth-century poets.

Clearly, then, Arnold did not need to go on simply doing more of the same, especially in the face of the firmest possible declaration of the purpose and guiding principles of poetry that was at the same time an implicit confession of the inade- quacy of his own poetic practice. He was not a dilettante according to Goethe's strict definitions cited in the final para- graph of the Preface (I, 15), but it would have been dilettantish to go on producing confessedly inadequate poems. There is an unmistakable and decisive self-reference in the following per- orative sentence: "If we must be *dilettanti*: if it is impossible for us, under the circumstances amidst which we live, to think clearly, to feel nobly, and to delineate firmly: if we cannot attain to the mastery of the great artists—let us, at least, have so much respect for our art to prefer it to ourselves" (I, 15). It is a moral principle leading, for a thoroughly honest man, to a moral decision: better no poetry at all than more of the same inadequate poetry.

Arnold had specifically claimed for *Empedocles on Etna* the literary virtue of firm delineation, and it is perhaps easiest to credit Arnold's poems generally with that quality, including the poems or conceptions of poems[18] that Arnold would have had to fault by other standards. So it seems most profitable to look elsewhere for *the reason for the fault* of *Empedocles on Etna* and the other poems for which it was a symbolic sacrificial stand-in, such poems, for example, as *Stanzas in Memory of the Author of 'Obermann', Tristram and Iseult, The Scholar-Gipsy,* and *Stanzas from the Grande Chartreuse.* Arnold designates the fault quite explicitly—a spiritually devastating pathos rather than a tragedy that becomes spiritually restorative through the credible conversion of human catastrophe into human admiration and delight (I, 2–3).[19] But the really teasing question is how a poet so Classically oriented as Arnold and so persistently critical of Romantic Modernism as we have seen him to be could have fallen or drifted into a position so untenable for one like him—in short, *the reason for the fault.*

In the first place, we should note that the fault was not poetically inherent in the "historical" account of Empedocles—historically inherent, perhaps, but not poetically inherent. Arnold specifically says that the error was a literary one—"as I have endeavoured to represent him" (I, 3). This points to one reason for an error in judgment: Arnold was so fascinated by the historical Empedocles that he very carefully portrayed the historical Empedocles, unmindful for the moment of something that he knew very well, namely, Aristotle's distinction between historical responsibility and a higher poetic responsibility: "The true difference is that one relates what has happened, the other what may happen. Poetry, therefore, is more philosophical and a higher thing than history: for poetry tends to express the universal, history the particular" (quoted I, 210n). Further, Arnold describes his discovery of Empedocles in terms that suggest why he was led into a disproportionate emphasis on history: "Into the feelings of a man so situated there entered much that we are accustomed to consider as exclusively modern . . ." (I, 1). That was itself a lesson that might be well taught to his chauvinistic contemporaries; and, along with certain other tendencies of his overtly pedagogical temperament, this led Arnold to teach a truth somewhat lower than the highest poetical truth to which his subject was susceptible.

This failure of the poet to interfere with history in the name of poetry's higher purpose is also characteristic of the other poems cited above: relentless fidelity to character and imagined circumstance brings them to the end of a linear progression for which there is no compensatory reversal and recognition, no establishment of a sternly reassuring alternative possibility (the "what may happen" of poetry versus the "what has happened" of history). No imaginative salvation is made available to any of the protagonists. The chilling last line of *Tristram and Iseult* suffuses the whole literary experience with a hint of spiritual bitterness; the coda of *The Scholar-Gipsy* darkens the future prospect into a suggestion of futility and ultimate failure; the speaker-protagonists of *Stanzas in Memory of the Author of 'Obermann'* and *Stanzas from the Grande Chartreuse* are victims of a temperamental malaise, the one engaged in an endless search for the very "dreams" that his sceptical nature rejects, the other in a myth of no return.

Why? Because Arnold the poet, despite his persistent critical insights, had become to a significant degree the victim of the very modern history, the Romantic Modernism, that he delineated so firmly and so well. That there should be this discrepancy between his principles and his practice shows that, "under the circumstances in which [he] live[d]" (I, 15), he could not "think clearly" at that imaginative level of thinking that holds poetry true to the poet's principles. Though he could articulate a resounding defense of the modern hero—an Odysseus-like figure who accepts the "general law" of the universe as it in fact is, sees "one clue to life, and follow[s] it," and, "Laborious, persevering, serious, firm," pursues his "track, across the fretful foam/Of vehement actions without scope or term,/Called history . . ."—he so suffered from his era's despair of modern heroism that he devoted his poetic talent and energy to the creation of human types who had ceased to "feel nobly" except in vastly diminished remnant terms and declined the responsibility of the poet-in-charge to give their myths an ennobling turn. Thus the critic of Romantic Modernism had himself become a Romantic Modernist. When Arnold recognized this, he made the most critical decision a poet who venerates his art can make—to correct it even at the cost of ceasing to be a poet altogether.

Despite an essentially detached and good-humored record, it is difficult to imagine that Arnold underwent this crisis in his literary life without some degree of *Sturm und Drang*. It may not have been an event as traumatizing as Carlyle's detection and defiance of the Devil or Mill's irrepressible "No!" to happiness or Newman's discovery of the face of a heretic in his Monophysite mirror or Tennyson's sudden loss of the chief support of his imaginative and emotional life, but it is reminiscent of them all. It was certainly more severe an act of moral/aesthetic self-measuring than most gifted young poets ever subject themselves to, and the results were about as far-reaching as possible, altering the whole course of Arnold's literary life. But Arnold kept his own counsel with Classical aplomb. He was not himself subject to the demonic self-consciousness that possessed some of his contemporaries and some of his own imaginary characters, and even his most confessional moments show an admirable restraint. Modern life was a most serious business, and modern poetry was modern man's chief instrument of articulation and reconciliation. He had, for a substantial period of time, offered it his dedicated service, but as the task became more and more demanding, the need more and more urgent, he recognized with exemplary honesty and without the least suggestion of false modesty his own poetic limitations. His contribution had been substantial, and though he had a genuine if limited faith in its ultimate serviceability, he saw no need to go on replicating it. Instead, he undertook the difficult and delicate task of writing a brief but full-bodied declaration of poetic faith and an oblique confession of poetic inadequacy. It was a very courageous and forthright action for a young man who had thus far appeared before the reading public only as "A." As literary history would have it, both the difficulty and the delicacy were richly rewarded: in the whole century, Arnold's Preface of 1853 is surpassed in importance only by Wordsworth's Preface to the Second Edition of *Lyrical Ballads*. With it, Arnold launched the most spectacular critical career in the history of English letters.

Notes

1. See particularly William A. Jamieson, *Arnold and the Romantics* (Copenhagen: Rosenkilde and Bagger, 1958); D.J. James, *Matthew Arnold and the Decline of English Romanticism* (Oxford: The Clarendon Press, 1961); Leon Gottfried, *Matthew Arnold and the Romantics* (Lincoln: University of Nebraska Press, [1963]).

2. See *Complete Prose Works*, volume I, p. 38. Arnold's exact phrase is "this stronghold of the romantic school," but the extrapolation seems justified by Arnold's conviction that the literature of a nation is the most trustworthy expression of its spiritual condition.

3. John Henry Newman, *Apologia pro vita sua*, A. Dwight Culler, ed. (Boston: Houghton Mifflin, 1956), pp. 34 and 121, respectively.

4. "*Briefwechsel zwischen Schiller und Goethe*, vi, 230," as noted in *On Translating Homer, Complete Prose Works*, volume I, p. 102.

5. *On Translating Homer, Complete Prose Works*, volume I, p. 140.

6. Thomas Hardy, *Jude the Obscure*, Norman Page, ed. (New York: W.W. Norton, 1978), p. 258 (Sixth Part, First Section).

7. *The Letters of Matthew Arnold to Arthur Hugh Clough*, H.F. Lowry, ed. (New York: Oxford University Press, 1932), pp. 111–112.

8. *Letters of Matthew Arnold, 1848–1888*, G.W.E. Russell, ed. (London: Macmillan, 1895), volume II, p. 10.

9. "*Past and Present*," in *Emerson's Complete Works* (London: The Waverley Book Co. Ltd., 1893), volume XII, pp. 247–248.

10. *Letters to Clough*, p. 99.

11. "The Function of Criticism at the Present Time," in *Essays in Criticism, First Series, Complete Prose Works*, volume III, *passim*.

12. *Letters to Clough*, p. 101.

13. Arnold uses an analogous strategy in his prose criticism. For example, he carefully and elaborately creates the Joubert *persona* as a way of angling into life critical evaluations of Voltaire and Rousseau. See "Joubert" in *Essays in Criticism, First Series*.

14. For studies of the background to the Preface, see Alba H. Warren, Jr., *English Poetic Theory, 1825–1865* (Princeton: Princeton University Press, 1950), chapter 9, and S.M.B. Coulling, "Matthew Arnold's 1853 Preface: Its Origin and Aftermath," *Victorian Studies*, volume VII (1964), pp. 233–263.

15. *Complete Prose Works*, volume I, p. 15. All further references to the Preface are given in parentheses in the text.

16. Thus the Preface reaches levels a good deal more profound than can be dealt with in the debate as to whether it is "descriptive" or "prescriptive."

17. All that can be said here of Arnold's poems that were clearly designed

according to the principles of the Preface—e.g., *Sohrab and Rustum* and *Merope*—is that in composing them Arnold assumed the "discipline" and in a plain, simple, and thorough fashion attempted to infuse into them its *stylistic* spirit. Many commentators have been neglectful or dismissive of the Preface to *Merope*, visiting their disregard of the poem upon its apology. But it contains expansions and clarifications of crucial ideas nowhere else to be found in Arnold's prose and by that test must be called indispensable. For example, it is the fullest statement Arnold ever wrote on the moral implications of style, makes clear the organic rather than the mechanical function of tradition, distinguishes between the kind of Classicism he is advocating and that of eighteenth-century France, and so forth. *Sohrab and Rustum*, of course, was completed five months before the Preface (I, 217n), but it seems to have been an experiment in poetic validation, Arnold trying out his critical theories in the composition of the poem, which took the place vacated by *Empedocles on Etna*.

18. Our knowledge of the dates of Arnold's composition of his poems, including initiation, continuation, and completion, is extremely uncertain, especially of poems conceived before the 1853 Preface. A vague situation becomes even vaguer if Arnold meant to apply to himself the story of Menander's considering his comedy finished, its action having been constructed in his mind, even though he had not yet written a single line (I, 7). Except for the order Arnold gave them as published texts, it is virtually impossible to establish even workable criteria for fitting Arnold's poems into a calendar of composition. Usually, the only firm date is that of publication, and that means little more than that the poem could not have been written later than that date. Hence, one does not have the external evidence for dividing the canon by a pre-1853/post-1853 criterion except in such a broad way that it fails to hold where most critically needed, and dependence on internal evidence has customarily led to endless controversy.

19. It is easier to comprehend Arnold's intense concern over this literary issue as well as the reluctance of many modern critics to accept his point of view in the matter if one recognizes two implications of it—that the tragic sense of *Empedocles on Etna* is an early example of the modern tragedy of circumstance in opposition to the ancient tragedy of character and that the modern tragedy of circumstance is a dramatic metaphor of an all-enveloping *Weltanschauung*.

Primary Names and Literary Titles